Domestic Adjustments to Globalization

edited by
Charles E. Morrison *and* Hadi Soesastro

Tokyo • Japan Center for International Exchange • *New York*

The surnames of the authors and other persons mentioned in this book are positioned according to country practice.

Copyediting by Michael D. Evans and Pamela J. Noda.
Cover and typographic design by Becky Davis, EDS Inc.,
Editorial & Design Services. Typesetting and production by EDS Inc.

Printed in Japan.
ISBN 4-88907-012-5

Distributed worldwide outside Japan by Brookings Institution Press,
1775 Massachusetts Avenue, N.W., Washington, D.C. 20036-2188 U.S.A.

Japan Center for International Exchange
9-17 Minami Azabu 4-chome, Minato-ku, Tokyo 106-0047 Japan

URL: http://www.jcie.or.jp

Japan Center for International Exchange, Inc. (JCIE/USA)
1251 Avenue of the Americas, New York, N.Y. 10020 U.S.A.

Contents

Foreword

Domestic Adjustments to Globalization is the product of nearly two years of research by a multinational team of scholars participating in the Global ThinkNet, a multipronged cluster of policy research and dialogue activities launched by the Japan Center for International Exchange (JCIE) in 1996. The Global ThinkNet activities are designed to contribute to strengthening the Asia Pacific as well as the global intellectual networks among research institutions.

The multinational research team organized under the umbrella of the Global ThinkNet for the project "Domestic Adjustments in the Face of Globalization" was guided by Charles E. Morrison, president of the East-West Center in Hawaii, and Hadi Soesastro, senior fellow at the Centre for Strategic and International Studies in Jakarta. The team members sought to identify policy issues created or substantially affected by the integrative forces of the international economy and to identify relevant research priorities by reviewing the current debate in their countries or regions, including Canada, China, Indonesia, Japan, New Zealand, the Philippines, South Korea, Thailand, and the United States.

The surveys collected in this volume were completed on the eve of the mid-1997 Asian financial crisis and focus on important economic and social dimensions of the process of globalization and the policy issues they raise. Although the rapidly evolving international environment and the stunning events in Asia in particular since the financial crisis began make it difficult for analysis to keep pace with the change, it is our conviction that the findings presented here are timely and provide a foundation for further understanding of the process of globalization in our world today.

7

On behalf of JCIE, I wish to thank Charles Morrison and Hadi Soe-sastro for directing the research team and for the close personal attention they gave to the preparation of the participants' papers. JCIE is grateful to the members of the research team as well for the invaluable contribution of their expertise. I would also like to express our profound gratitude to the Nippon Foundation, whose generosity made launching the Global ThinkNet possible, for its continuous support.

YAMAMOTO TADASHI
President
Japan Center for International Exchange

Domestic Adjustments to Globalization

1 · Overview

Charles E. Morrison

D URING 1996 and 1997, Hadi Soesastro, senior fellow at the Centre for Strategic and International Studies in Jakarta, and I participated in a survey of domestic adjustments to globalization in selected countries for a Global ThinkNet project sponsored by the Japan Center for International Exchange. The project put heavy emphasis on developing Asian countries but also included surveys from Canada, Japan, New Zealand, and the United States, as well as inputs from Europe. The result is a snapshot of globalization pressures and domestic policy debate on the eve of the Asian financial crisis, which, by exposing the dark side of globalization in all too great relief, has intensified debate on many of these issues.

WHAT IS GLOBALIZATION?

Globalization is a relatively new buzzword in the media and think tank world, and it is often not well defined. In business school literature, it appears to refer mainly to company-specific strategies to overcome the constraints of national political boundaries through globalized production and marketing. In other contexts, it has been treated almost akin to economic interdependence, covering increased trade and capital flows. In the political debate, however, the term seems to be used for virtually all kinds of integrative forces drawing national societies into a global community, including speculative capital

11

flows, direct foreign investment, technology transfer, increased trade in goods and services, the movement of legal and illegal labor, tourism flows, and even the spread of ideas, norms, and values. Because the purpose of the project was to survey issues and debates, authors were allowed to define globalization as best fit national debate, and most focused on phenomena having economic, social, and political consequences.

Soesastro distinguishes between two kinds of adjustments. First-order adjustments involve the process of opening up the society to forces of globalization, whereas second-order adjustments entail coping with domestic changes that come as a consequence of opening up. Both kinds of adjustments can take place simultaneously, but the surveys for our project from Northeast Asia focused primarily on first-order adjustments. These dealt with such issues as Japan's financial "big bang" and the deregulation debate, South Korea's trade and capital liberalization policies, and China's concerns about the future of its large state-owned and subsidized enterprises. A survey of New Zealand also gave considerable emphasis to that country's experience in making first-order adjustments. The other surveys in Southeast Asia and North America tended to focus on social and economic issues resulting from opening up or maintaining already open societies.

OPEN AND CLOSED SOCIETIES

The differences among countries seem to reflect the current degree of globalization, itself a reflection of historical legacy. All societies, of course, have been subject to foreign influences, but China, Japan, and South Korea have gone through long periods of isolation in their relatively recent histories as they attempted to shut out foreign influences and foreigners, especially the Europeans and the Americans. China has oscillated between outward-looking and inward-looking policies; currently, it is finishing a second decade of an outward-looking approach against some significant opposition. Although the postwar economic development of Japan and South Korea depended heavily on exports, resistance to globalization is reflected in low rates of inward foreign investment in both countries and negative attitudes and sometimes policies toward foreign products.

In recent years, the governments of these three countries have pushed first-order globalization under rubrics such as "open door," "internationalization," and "big bang." Opposition comes from affected industries as well as publics and elements of the bureaucracies that remain skeptical of foreign influences. Chinese survey author Ding Jingping notes, for example, the grass-roots opposition to foreign brand names, and in Japan and South Korea globalization projects have had an idealistic quality that failed to fully come to grips with the nature of adjustments required of true globalization.

In contrast to the countries of Northeast Asia, parts of Southeast Asia have long been globalized. Located along transportation routes between the Indian Ocean and the South China Sea, the island and peninsular parts of Southeast Asia have always depended on the sea both for food and trade. With trade came infusions of foreign commercial communities and new religions, leading to pluralistic societies with substantial overseas connections. With their poorly developed interiors, these Southeast Asian countries lacked depth and succumbed relatively easily to European colonialism, which further oriented their economies and cultures toward the global economy of the days of Western imperialism. While there is, of course, resistance to many aspects of globalization and some of these countries adopted import substitution policies in the 1950s and 1960s, their historical orientations, geopolitical positions, and high levels of dependency on international markets force them in the opposite direction. The continental Southeast Asian countries of Vietnam, Cambodia, Myanmar, and even Thailand have been less open.

The North American countries remain quite ambivalent about globalization. Canadian survey author Paul Bowles notes several waves of economic nationalism in Canadian history, mostly directed toward its southern neighbor. As for the United States, despite its heritage as an ethnic melting pot and its dependence on European capital and technology in the 19th century, it was one of the least globally integrated national economies a half century ago, with imports and exports each amounting to less than 4 percent of gross national product (GNP). The shocks of a new wave of globalization came in the late 1960s and early 1970s when American companies expanded their investments abroad to reduce labor costs: The share of imports in GNP doubled (but increased much faster for labor-intensive manufactured goods); the Nixon administration was forced to delink the dollar and gold, in effect devaluing the dollar; and the Organization of Petroleum Exporting Countries forced a dramatic increase in petroleum costs. This period of globalization was associated with the hollowing out of certain manufacturing industries and a growth in protectionist sentiment, which took its most virulent form in the labor-supported Vance-Hartke legislation to restrict imports and investment outflows.

GLOBALIZATION ISSUES

If a central fault line exists in the globalization debate, whether in East Asia or elsewhere, it comes between those who emphasize the macroeconomic benefits of globalization and those who focus on its social adjustment costs. The former stress the need to strengthen competitiveness, consumer benefits, and macroeconomic statistics such as increasing overall employment and income levels. The latter worry about growing income disparities, influxes of foreign workers, the impact of new values on traditional society, and problems of microeconomic adjustments for smaller companies and the less advantaged groups in society. Let us look at several of these aspects.

Trade and Investment Liberalization

All of the East Asian economies have been engaged in substantial trade and investment liberalization. This is seen as inevitable because of the need for companies and countries to take advantage of the most cost-effective supplies of goods, capital, and labor. In theory, it should still be possible for central authorities to wall off their economies, as North Korea has done, but the costs of so doing are high. As Japan's experience in the financial sphere has demonstrated, it is difficult for even the strongest national industries and companies to remain competitive if the economy is overregulated and protected from the forces of foreign competition.

While much of the trade liberalization in the region is unilateral and even private-sector driven, global and regional organizations such as the World Trade Organization (WTO), the Asia-Pacific Economic Cooperation (APEC) forum, and the Association of Southeast Asian Nations (ASEAN) play a continuing role in justifying policy changes. Domestic forces opposed to globalization might even target these organizations. The November 1996 APEC Leaders' Meeting in the

Philippines, for example, attracted protest demonstrations from several domestic nongovernmental organizations (NGOs) which argued that APEC was a conspiracy of the advantaged and thus not sufficiently attentive to the plight of the poor. Similar protests occurred at the 1997 APEC Vancouver meeting.

The WTO is the key institution because countries undertake legally binding liberalization efforts through its periodic negotiating rounds. Its importance is illustrated by the lengthy process of admitting China into the WTO. China's trading partners insist that a requirement for membership be a satisfactory program to bring China's trading system into conformity with long-established international standards. While China is engaged in liberalization, it is also wary that WTO obligations might undercut national sovereignty and force a pace of liberalization that will be difficult or impossible to sustain politically. Some observers are concerned that if the standards are set too high, China will be unwilling to pay the price of WTO membership. The 1997–1998 Asian economic crisis has increased Chinese misgivings about WTO membership and further trade and investment liberalization.

APEC is a new player in the trade and investment liberalization game, but it may also become a critical factor simply because its member economies have agreed to a program of free trade and investment in the region by 2010 for developed countries and 2020 for all other members. Although commitments made through APEC are not legally binding, the members have a political commitment to achieve this goal. Each economy is obliged to come up with individual action plans for liberalization. This process keeps pressure on the governments to continue opening their societies to globalizing forces. APEC liberalization is still quite abstract, but if and when the liberalization of Northeast Asian agricultural markets must be undertaken because of APEC commitments, APEC could suddenly become quite controversial.

ASEAN has a program for a free trade area to be achieved as early as 2003. Because ASEAN countries do not trade with each other that much, except for border trade between Singapore and its two neighbors, the ASEAN program in and of itself is unlikely to generate significant controversy. However, because some ASEAN members may globalize their trade reductions made for ASEAN, the tariff and nontariff reductions in ASEAN may become more significant than it now appears. But the economic crisis and political uncertainties, especially in Indonesia, are jeopardizing the whole program.

Foreign Labor

Aside from the movement of goods, services, and capital, the movement of labor has become a significant element in the globalization debate. In terms of the size of their economies, Malaysia and Singapore have the greatest numbers of foreign workers; it is estimated that 15 percent of the Malaysian work force is foreign and one in every seven Singaporean households has a foreign maid (mostly Filipina). In contrast, the foreign proportion of the work force remains minuscule in Japan, South Korea, and Taiwan, although the numbers of foreign workers are sharply higher in cities and thus highly visible to the urban citizens of these relatively homogeneous societies.

No government in the region allows for the free international movement of labor. But migrant workers, seeking higher wages and in collusion with domestic groups looking for cheap labor, have often found ingenious methods to escape detection. Because foreign labor is often illegal or of marginal legality, foreign workers can easily become prey to exploitation. The movement of labor thus raises many difficult questions. What level of foreign employment should be allowed? How should it be regulated? What rights and protections should foreign workers be given? Today, in the wake of the Asian financial crisis, foreign workers are becoming targets for deportation. Thailand plans to deport mostly Myanmarese labor. Malaysia could send as many as one million workers packing, most of these Indonesians.

Domestic Income Disparities

It is widely believed that globalization increases the gaps among individual regions within national economies, as well as between workers most able to take advantage of globalization and those less able. For example, employment generation associated with foreign investment in manufacturing has usually been in major cities with established transportation routes. This has favored such cities as Bangkok, Jakarta, Manila, Saigon, and Shanghai, whereas it has disadvantaged northeast Thailand, Mindanao, eastern Indonesia, and the interior provinces of China. The result has been both domestic labor movements toward the cities and increased income disparities between globalized enclaves and their hinterlands. Although even the hinterlands may be experiencing absolute gains in income, the growing size of the relative gap may create social unrest.

In theory, countries should be able to compensate for these disparities through programs of social adjustment and income transfer. In practice, such programs are often difficult to establish and implement. Moreover, competitive economic forces have discouraged taxation or large social adjustment programs. On the whole, those disadvantaged by globalization have lower educational levels and limited political participation and access, and thus they have not been effective in slowing globalization. However, it is difficult to imagine that globalization policies can be effectively pursued indefinitely without addressing this important set of second-order consequences.

The Growth of Civil Society

Although not always perceived as such, the growth of civil society throughout East Asia is also in part a consequence of globalizing forces. Globalization has increased pluralization, enhanced international educational opportunities, and strengthened awareness of the global issues of importance to civil society, including the environment, social justice, and political representation. The international mass media and the telecommunications revolution have encouraged the rise of NGOs and promoted the international transmission of independent perspectives.

Whether civil society in turn promotes or inhibits globalization is a complex issue, because it does both. On one hand, the emergence of vibrant civil societies enhances activities that depend on global contact and collaboration. On the other hand, many of the newly emerging independent organizations are concerned about the impact of globalization on social stability and well-being. Internal debates in more democratic societies allow expression for those opposed to globalization as well as those in support of it.

IMPLICATIONS OF THE ASIAN FINANCIAL CRISIS

The Asian financial crisis has dramatically intensified debate on globalization issues since the Global ThinkNet project was initiated and has resulted in a significant backlash against globalizing forces in the most affected countries. Although it is difficult to put fast-moving, contemporary developments into perspective, the crisis is clearly testing many ideas and institutions associated with globalization. We focus on three dimensions of these tests: economic strategies, governance, and leadership.

Economic Strategies

Where concerns already existed in many countries about the impact of globalization, the financial crisis has certainly heightened these. Some in the West have been quick to argue that the crisis has fully discredited the notion of a special Asian (or Japanese) road to development. Proponents of Asian values and models have been notably less voluble since the economic turmoil began. But the crisis has hardly vindicated any other model. Today, it can be argued that what is being tested is less Asian values than Western notions of globalization and economic liberalization. These strategies are associated with the flood of mobile capital, which for a period brought untold wealth but which basically could not be absorbed by Asia's underdeveloped financial markets and supervisory systems.

Of course, those countries that have received bailouts from the International Monetary Fund (IMF) are already so economically dependent on the global economy that they had little real choice of direction. In the area of financial access, the IMF agreements are forcing liberalization that would have taken years to negotiate through the WTO. But for those countries with policy choices still to be made, it is unclear what lessons will be drawn from the financial crisis. China is patting itself on the back for its slower pace of capital liberalization. The privatization of state-owned enterprises, reaffirmed at the 15th Party Congress in September 1997, now seems sure to be delayed and with it China's admission to the WTO. Vietnam appears to be moving away from liberalization policies, although it is unclear how much this is tied to current regional economic turmoil. Among the noncommunist societies, Malaysia has taken the most dramatic step in erecting new barriers by imposing capital controls, but throughout Asia there is strong sympathy for some forms of control over short-term capital movements. Depending on whether and how these are administered, they could considerably slow or reverse the pace of liberalization.

Governance

At the domestic level, governments of the hardest-hit countries—Thailand, Indonesia, and South Korea—face excruciating economic and social adjustments as their IMF austerity programs bite more deeply. The closure of weak or insolvent financial firms is but the tip of the iceberg. Construction projects that employed thousands are halting and companies are going bankrupt under the burden of dollar-denominated debts, whose repayment costs have massively escalated with the dramatic drop in local currency values. By mid-1998, a year after the crisis had begun, unemployment in Indonesia, South Korea, Thailand, and even Hong Kong had reached levels unprecedented in recent years.

With unemployment and social tensions rising, and particularly as economic difficulties affect the middle and professional classes, the pressures on government increase exponentially. Four of the five most affected countries (Indonesia, Malaysia, the Philippines, South Korea, and Thailand) have had new governments since the crisis began. Those in South Korea and the Philippines involved scheduled presidential elections where the incumbents could not replace themselves, and the governmental change in Thailand also occurred constitutionally within the current political parliamentary system. In Indonesia, the economic crisis brought simmering political tensions to a head, resulting in the downfall of long-time leader Suharto. In Malaysia, Prime Minister Mahathir bin Mohamad is also facing his most serious political challenge. Here, economic policy differences between Mahathir and Deputy Prime Minister Anwar Ibrahim helped precipitate a rupture between them. Anwar's arrest on sodomy charges closely coincided with Mahathir's decision to impose wide-ranging capital controls.

The point is frequently made that political legitimacy has rested on economic progress in much of East Asia. This is not uniformly true—in some cases, as just cited for Thailand and South Korea, regime legitimacy also rests upon democratic election. But democracies are typically new and fragile in developing East Asia, and none has faced a challenge of the current magnitude. In both the Thai and

South Korean cases, for example, recent developments have generated nostalgia for former strongmen Sarit Thanarat and Park Chung-hee. Indeed, if the crisis is prolonged and effective responses are not forthcoming, people may fasten onto the democratic systems themselves as the problem.

The crisis has underscored not just the weakness of national supervisory mechanisms in the face of huge inflows, and now outflows, of capital, but also the inadequacies of global governance in the finance/banking/foreign exchange arenas. Until they get into trouble, national governments basically go their own regulatory way. The IMF acts after the fact and only when governments are so desperate that they have no alternative.

The IMF is now being seriously challenged. Some reject the very notion of assistance, arguing that it rewards irresponsible risk-taking. Why should taxpayers bail out irresponsible lenders and borrowers, they ask. Others accept that the IMF loans are critical to stopping the crisis and protecting the world economy, but they question the specific efficacy for Asia. They maintain that the IMF's austerity measures address a past Latin American/African syndrome (government budget deficits, high inflation, and poor macroeconomic policy making) rather than the contemporary Asian one (government budget surpluses, low inflation, and strong macroeconomic policy, but with private-sector debt and a lack of confidence in the banking system). Many argue that the IMF aggravated the crisis by insisting on racheting up interest rates in credit-starved economies.

Much of this criticism ignores the fact that given the crisis psychology and the lack of a single country to provide policy leadership, as the United States did for Mexico, the IMF played an indispensable role in coping with the crisis. Because the governments of the affected countries themselves lacked legitimacy with investors, their ability to reach agreements with the IMF provided a necessary symbol of their will to reform. The IMF also provided essential bridging capital until debts could be restructured or new capital sources tapped. Without the IMF agreements, defaults would surely have occurred in Thailand, South Korea, and Indonesia, with cascading repercussions for the regional and global economies. This is not to whitewash IMF policies, but surely the IMF is also breaking new ground and needs to learn and adapt from its Asian experiences.

Regional institutions are also being tested. APEC, whose annual ministerial and leaders' meetings came in November 1997, seemed ill-prepared for the crisis and was slow to react. The organization has focused on trade and investment liberalization and facilitation, and senior officials are preoccupied with action plans in these areas. These officials are based in foreign and trade ministries and generally have weak relationships with their finance ministry counterparts. Finance ministers meet separately in APEC rather than in conjunction with the leaders' meetings, and no APEC finance ministers' meetings were scheduled in the second part of 1997.

Nevertheless, APEC showed its worth as well as its limitations. The November 1997 APEC Leaders' Meeting was an action-enforcing event with actions taken in South Korea and Japan in advance of the Vancouver summit, which would have been delayed otherwise. Also, the deputy finance ministers held a special meeting in Manila just before the summit to develop a common position on the crisis, and agreed that the IMF must take the lead and that any special Asian currency fund should be a subordinate and compatible mechanism. But APEC itself has proved no venue for sustained regional action on the crisis.

Leadership

Leadership is critical where confidence is lacking. By economic size, Japan and the United States are the natural leaders. The crisis, however, brings into question both countries' individual leadership capabilities and seriously tests their relationship. With its heavier investments in Southeast Asia, Japan was quicker to make an initial response, proposing an Asian currency stabilization scheme. It was unclear how seriously the proposal was thought out in Japan itself. Certainly, it was not coordinated with the United States, which feared that it could undermine the IMF disciplines. Moreover, some analysts in Asia and the West interpreted the Japanese proposal as a cynical means of bailing out the heavily exposed Japanese financial institutions. The idea of an Asian currency stabilization scheme has survived as an adjunct to the IMF and indeed Japan has contributed generously and substantially to every bailout, but its international policy role was weakened to almost the point of disappearance.

The biggest failure, however, has been Japan's inability to get its own economy back into a growth mode. Although then–Prime

Minister Hashimoto Ryūtarō took a surprise step in December 1997 following the ASEAN-sponsored East Asian summit to provide about US$15 billion in income tax relief, this was widely regarded as too little, too late. Japan is only gradually coming to grips with its problems because policy leadership remained hostage to bureaucratic rigidities and domestic political squabbling. Actions to stimulate the economy, provide tax relief, and spend public money to help bring the banking crisis to a soft landing were all delayed by intense political debate and maneuvering. By mid-1998, it appeared that any significant Japanese recovery from the deepening recession would be delayed until the year 2000.

The United States was initially slower to react and did not contribute to the Thai IMF package, to the continuing bitter resentment of the Thai. Dismissing the very great dangers to the United States and its economic interests in the Asian meltdown, many Asians seem to believe the Americans secretly welcomed the crisis and its result of cutting upstart Asian economies back down to size. Others believe the United States and its firms will seize on the crisis to promote a narrow set of economic interests, using the IMF to shoehorn concessions that would have taken U.S. negotiators years to achieve and taking advantage of the devalued Asian currencies to gobble up competitors at bargain prices.

Through the first year of the crisis, Washington experienced repeated cycles of deep concern and relief as individual problems in South Korea in December 1997 and Indonesia in the earlier part of 1998 surfaced and then appeared to be resolved. Growing pessimism about Japan, the sharp fall of Wall Street stock prices after July 1998, the spreading of the crisis to Russia and Brazil, and growing evidence of negative effects on the U.S. economy resulted in more consistent Washington attention after mid-1998. Despite initiatives on new financial architecture, however, the American ability to provide consistent leadership remained seriously weakened by the presidential scandal and Congress's skeptical treatment of internationalist actions. A US$18 billion commitment to replenish the IMF and provide for a new borrowing agreement remained caught in Congressional politics until October 1998, and the president's request for "fast track" trade negotiating authority was sidetracked. Clearly, ambivalent U.S. leadership, weak Japanese leadership, uncertainty about China's future direction, and many other questions about the international financial system remain major shadows on the market.

Given that most Americans believe the crisis to be a substantial political and economic burden in the form of financial support (despite how limited this has been compared with Japan's efforts) and the likelihood of massively increased trade deficits, there will surely be more pressure directed at Japan to increase its share of the burden. Japan will receive the lion's share of the U.S. attention, because it has the largest trade surplus, its companies are the strongest U.S. competitors (and will be significantly strengthened by the lower yen), and Japanese banks are the biggest foreign creditors in the region.

CONCLUSION

Globalization, taking on a virulent form in the Asian financial crisis, has created domestic pressures as well as challenges to international governance that were not envisioned at the initiation of the Global ThinkNet domestic adjustments project. The challenges associated with globalization now have taken on a new urgency in light of the profound effect of the crisis on regional well-being and order. The region and the entire world need to carefully think through whether globalization has proceeded at too fast a pace for national societies, particularly developing ones, to make needed adjustments without undue dislocation and economic pain.

2 · Domestic Adjustments in Four ASEAN Economies

Hadi Soesastro

S INCE the 1980s, Association of Southeast Asian Nations
(ASEAN) members have been among the developing countries
that have integrated most rapidly into the world economy.* The
World Bank's (1996) index of integration shows that in the early 1980s,
Indonesia, the Philippines, and Thailand had a much lower level of
integration than two of their ASEAN neighbors, Malaysia and Singapore. The index of integration consists of four components: the ratio
of trade to gross domestic product (GDP); a creditworthiness rating,
as determined by *Institutional Investor* magazine; the ratio of foreign
direct investment (FDI) to GDP; and the share of manufactured goods
in total exports. Using this measure, Thailand was the fastest of the
late entrants to ASEAN to catch Malaysia and Singapore. However,
each of these five countries has seen much improvement in all four
components of the index. Most remarkable, however, have been the

*This chapter discusses the surveys of four ASEAN economies—Indonesia, the
Philippines, Thailand, and Vietnam—undertaken for the Global ThinkNet project
on domestic adjustments in the face of globalization. The information on Vietnam
and Indonesia is based on papers presented at the workshop in Bali on January 10,
1997. Regrettably, the survey on Vietnam could not be published.

continuing increases in the ratio of trade to GDP and the share of manufactured goods in total exports. A later ASEAN entrant, Vietnam, which opened its economy only in the mid-1980s, has followed closely the pattern of its ASEAN neighbors.

These ASEAN members have developed open economies. From 1985 to 1996, the ratio of trade to GDP increased substantially for most of them (table 1). In 1996, the ratio of trade to GDP was 281 percent and 150 percent for Singapore and Malaysia, respectively, whereas it was almost 70 percent for both Thailand and the Philippines and 82 percent for Vietnam. Indonesia lagged the others at only 42 percent.

In Indonesia, there was a significant shift during the period from oil-dominated exports to manufacturing exports. As a result, changes in the ratio of trade to GDP do not capture the extent to which Indonesia's economy has opened. Since the mid-1980s, Indonesia's trade and investment regimes have been substantially liberalized in response to the government perception of a trend toward globalization. The country will likely gain significant net benefits from its participation in this process. This policy of globalization has necessitated a series of structural adjustments in the domestic economy through liberalization, marketization, deregulation, and privatization.

All of the ASEAN members have made these adjustments, which can be regarded as first-order adjustments in the globalization process. Such adjustments enhance international competitiveness, which the ASEAN members believe is a prerequisite to take part in and fully benefit from globalization. Thus, these first-order adjustments aim to increase the attractiveness of the ASEAN economies as a production base for the global market. Such reforms are a continuing process for ASEAN members because they have chosen to implement reforms gradually rather than with a "big bang." This gradual approach allows the process to demonstrate the positive outcomes of globalization and thus creates ever-larger constituencies for reform.

The first-order adjustments by the ASEAN members have been successful thus far. In the first half of the 1990s, GDP growth rates were 8 percent or above, except in the Philippines, which has achieved sustained high rates of growth only since 1994. Merchandise exports grew at double-digit rates for the ASEAN economies from 1985 to 1996 (table 2).

The challenge facing the ASEAN economies is to maintain high and

Table 1. Ratio of Trade* to GDP in the ASEAN Economies, 1985 and 1996 (%)

	1985	1996
Indonesia	36.3	41.9
Malaysia	83.7	149.8
Philippines	31.4	65.3
Singapore	269.0	281.1
Thailand	39.5	67.2
Vietnam	48.9	82.0

Source: Asia Pacific Economics Group (1997).
*Exports plus imports.
GDP: Gross domestic product.

Table 2. Growth of GDP and Exports in the ASEAN Economies, 1990–1996 (average percent per annum)

	GDP	Merchandise Exports
Indonesia	8.0	11.7
Malaysia	8.7	17.3
Philippines	2.0*	14.8
Singapore	8.3	16.1
Thailand	8.6	16.3
Vietnam	7.9	26.9

Source: Asia Pacific Economics Group (1997).
*About 5 percent per annum (average) in 1994–1996.
GDP: Gross domestic product.

sustainable rates of economic growth and exports. This requires them to continue economic reform. Although they have come a long way in liberalizing their economies, their tasks are far from complete. Globalization provided governments with a strong justification for initiating reform. Although somewhat paradoxical, participation in and efforts to promote regional cooperation are an important element of ASEAN members' globalization policies. Regional cooperation helps participants take part in global economic integration more effectively—as a group of regional economies. In Southeast Asia, the ASEAN Free Trade Area (AFTA) and the Asia-Pacific Economic Cooperation (APEC) forum are widely seen as representing the globalization phenomenon, because of their emphasis on trade and investment liberalization. Effective participation in AFTA and APEC necessitates a series of domestic adjustments that are parallel with, or even identical to, those that are undertaken in response to globalization.

It is precisely because globalization is used to justify economic reform—albeit successfully to date—that the sustainability of reform programs will depend to a large extent on the ability of the government and the society at large to address the negative impacts of globalization as perceived by the public. In many ASEAN members, a widely shared view holds that governments have successfully undertaken first-order domestic adjustments, when measured in terms of enhancing their economies' international competitiveness. The current concern is whether government, in particular, and society, in general, can make the adjustments necessary to alleviate, overcome, or minimize the negative impacts of the first-order adjustment efforts. These domestic social and political impacts of globalization, and the subsequent policy responses, constitute second-order adjustments in the globalization process.

Among the ASEAN members, for which economic reform was primarily initiated and promoted by governments, the focus and efforts to date have been first and foremost to open the economy and manage the process of reform. Measures were designed to maintain the various aspects of macroeconomic stability, to sequence reform, and to demonstrate clear benefits from reform. However, there is insufficient awareness that the sustainability and the success of the reform process depend not only on positive achievements but also on how well the negative impacts are seen to be dealt with.

Second-order adjustments are, therefore, as important as first-order adjustments. Participation in globalization must be compatible with a country's domestic social and political stability. This requirement becomes more real and urgent in societies with more democratic political systems. In the long run, it is also important for more authoritarian systems. Furthermore, the process of integration into the global economy should not result in domestic social and political disintegration (Rodrik 1997). The urgency to undertake second-order adjustments will be greater for societies that are more heterogeneous.

The challenges of globalization differ among the ASEAN members. Indonesia, the Philippines, Thailand, and Vietnam have all undertaken significant first-order adjustments more quickly than did Singapore and Malaysia, both of which were already well integrated into the world economy by the 1980s. Yet, even among the former four countries, there are observable differences in their managing of and dealing with both first-order and second-order adjustments. Nonetheless, it seems probable that the ultimate policy responses will be similar for each country. One country may have a greater urgency than another country, but the differences might only be a matter of timing or degree.

PERCEPTION, DEBATE, AND RESPONSE

Globalization is not a new phenomenon. However, the ASEAN economies of Indonesia, the Philippines, Thailand, and Vietnam began to globalize only in the mid-1980s, at which time they embarked on significant liberalization of their trade and investment regimes and financial sectors.

First-order adjustments of globalization in these four countries have been based on pragmatism. This strategy of interdependence (Soesastro 1995) was deemed the most viable option to deliver economic growth. The policy is not grounded in ideological considerations but rather on an objective assessment of what other countries (specifically, the newly industrializing economies of East Asia) have achieved. There is also a strong element of competition among the countries in the region—competition to make each economy more attractive to global investment. Such competitive liberalization is in itself a powerful factor of globalization. However, globalization-related reform will only be sustained if it produces economic growth plus achievements in other important areas that are seen to be negatively affected by globalization. These areas include greater equalities (for example, in income parity and in regional distribution of wealth), the survivability of small enterprises, job security, cultural identity, and political sovereignty. The various segments in society—the individual, the community, the government, and the state—attach differing degrees of importance to the wide range of impacts from globalization.

In Vietnam, as in the other ASEAN economies, globalization was initiated by the government. The government actively formulates and manages Vietnam's participation in the globalization process, which is seen as integral to the national development effort. In his survey of Vietnam, Nguyen Hong Ha, acting chief of the Office for Scientific Administration, Institute for International Relations in Vietnam, points out that both the Communist Party of Vietnam (CPV) and the Vietnamese government regard globalization as irreversible and believe Vietnam must respect this trend in formulating its development policy.

Vietnam's policy of globalization has yet to meet any serious resistance or resentment from the populace. Initial opposition within the CPV and the government has weakened considerably with the dramatic improvement in the country's economic performance following the launch of the Doi Moi reform program in 1986. The Vietnamese economy grew at an average of about 8 percent per annum from 1990 to 1996, and its exports increased at an average of 27 percent per annum during the same period. By the end of 1995, approved FDI totaled more than US$18 billion. Support for the policy was further strengthened by the changed international political environment, particularly the end of the cold war, and more recently by Vietnam's membership in ASEAN and its participation in AFTA. However, alleged widespread corruption might well be the cost for sustaining reform.

Vietnam's membership in ASEAN has been given special significance. Through ASEAN, Vietnam believes that it can strengthen its position in the world, and by participating in AFTA it hopes to become more attractive to international investors (resulting in additional FDI). This approach to ASEAN membership is certainly not unique to Vietnam. Vietnam also attaches great importance to ASEAN as a cooperative arrangement that will help the country maintain its national sovereignty in the face of globalization. The introduction of so-called economic zones, or export processing districts, is one strategy designed to minimize the possible effects of globalization on state power and national sovereignty.

Vietnam's government believes that the country can effectively deal with the challenges of globalization. Leaders are confident that the country can turn those challenges into opportunities. Nguyen's survey points to a number of other perceived challenges, namely enhanced competition and rising interdependence as well as challenges in political and cultural fields. Some view the proper response to expanded competition as the reform of industries. Others contend that the government should provide assistance to industries to undertake the necessary reforms, and that a policy of industrial targeting is necessary. As regards growing interdependence, many want the government to be selective in accepting FDI and to adopt a policy of diversifying its export markets.

The political, social, and cultural impacts of globalization are seen as real problems, especially for societies, such as Vietnam, that are undergoing rapid economic development. Living standards have improved significantly, but the gap between rich and poor has widened considerably. This is a major qualitative change from what the society had experienced previously and thus may create resentments. However, the income gap is not widely perceived as a short-term concern, essentially because in general the people feel that they are now better off than before.

A greater concern for Vietnam is the strengthening of its cultural identity in the face of globalization. An open economy and society bring foreign influences and values, only some of which are beneficial. Vietnam contends that such influences, particularly those that derive from outside information flows, should be limited. Another primary concern is the improvement of the country's educational system, as underscored by the 1996 Congress of the CPV, which named education a top priority among the policies it suggested. The government views education as a key to enhancing Vietnam's international competitiveness.

Vietnam is currently preoccupied with managing its first-order adjustments; second-order adjustments, including policies to rectify the widening income gap, while recognized, are not seen as urgent. The benefits of Vietnam's globalization policy appear to far outweigh its perceived costs. However, the disadvantaged segments in the society may lack sufficient channels to express their discontent.

In Indonesia, the government is also the main promoter of globalization. Its policy aims to strengthen participation in international integration and increase the benefits that can be derived from this process. Since 1986, the government has implemented a series of liberalization measures, initially confined to the export sector of the economy and gradually introduced to the economy as a whole. The country's unilateral trade liberalization measures have been supported by its regional and multilateral commitments in such groupings as AFTA, APEC, and the World Trade Organization (WTO). The government argues that Indonesian industries and companies will become internationally competitive only if the domestic economy opens further. However, the government cautions that developing countries such as Indonesia require a longer period of adjustment than the industrialized countries. Both the WTO and APEC accept this principle.

Indonesia's business community feels that in its pursuit of globalization, as manifested in a series of deregulation and liberalization policy packages, the government must do a great deal more to make Indonesian industries and local companies internationally competitive. The existing reforms are viewed as reactive and incoherent, as well as discriminatory. The reforms often exclude certain groups or sectors from deregulation, thus creating an environment of unfair competition. Some have called for a more proactive policy, including some form of industrial targeting. Others stress the need for an anti-monopoly law or some similar form of competition legislation. An urgent need exists for more transparent and coherent rules and regulations. The government, which has responded slowly to these demands, does not view the development of such rules as integral to its first-order adjustments.

The government subscribes to the view that Indonesia cannot isolate itself from the powerful trend toward the global integration of markets, and this is the prevailing view in Indonesia. President Suharto laid to rest doubts about Indonesian participation when he stated, "Whether we are willing or not, and whether we do like it or not, we have to participate in the globalization process." This statement was made in connection with Indonesia's chairmanship of APEC in 1994 and commitments made in the context of APEC liberalization.

The survey of Indonesia by Sukardi Rinakit identifies three other views on globalization. The first view regards globalization primarily as a phenomenon that has resulted from increased global security interdependence. The challenge to such globalization is that existing security arrangements are inadequate to deal with this development. The second view is that globalization is essentially a process in which countries are pressured to adopt the dominant (that is, Western) values and norms. The third view focuses on the intensification of information flows and the advances in communication technology that have resulted in a more compressed world—with all its consequences.

From the perspective of these other viewpoints, Indonesia's government has taken too narrow a view of globalization. However, Indonesia's response in a few areas has been more liberal than that of some neighboring governments. For example, Indonesia has not attempted to control information flows by banning the use of satellite dishes as have Singapore and Malaysia. (Dr. Chia Siow Yue of Singapore points out, however, that there may be greater sensitivities to the problem of information flows in Singapore and Malaysia because a much larger proportion of the population in those countries understands English.) On this more liberal attitude, Indonesians have no reason to complain. The much more rigid regulations on and control of the domestic media are another matter.

The threat of outside pressure to adopt "international" values is a primary concern to nationalist groups with strong ideological orientations. However, such issues as labor rights and human rights are increasingly supported within Indonesian society, particularly among the educated younger generations and the many nongovernmental organizations (NGOs). The development of civil society in Indonesia has increased awareness of the social dimensions of globalization, and this, in turn, has led to greater demands on the government to address these issues more systematically. Rinakit's survey shows that the policy responses of the government in a number of relevant issue areas are perceived as inadequate. A number of areas have been identified as critical, but some—such as improvement of the educational system and the bureaucracy—should be regarded as integral to Indonesia's first-order adjustment efforts. Inadequacies in or the deterioration of the educational system or the bureaucracy were not caused by globalization and are therefore first-order adjustments.

The most important second-order domestic adjustments include the perceived (and actual) asymmetric side effects of globalization in widening gaps or increasing disparities of income and access to economic opportunities between different groups in society, between regions within the country, and between large and medium or small enterprises. These gaps and disparities are caused by a host of factors, but a widespread perception exists that globalization reinforces and magnifies them. Furthermore, the government may assume that its success in undertaking first-order adjustments allows it to take lightly the second-order challenges. However, these challenges will likely become more severe and complex as international integration deepens. Each country must determine its policy response to these challenges, but the burden cannot rest with governments alone. Clearly, a role exists for civil society, and thus the level of cooperation between the government and civil society in dealing with these issues becomes a crucial concern.

In Thailand and the Philippines, civil society is further developed than in other ASEAN members. The Thai economy and society have undergone rapid changes in the past decade, and in response various domestic adjustments have been undertaken.

The survey of Thailand by Chantana Banpasirichote reveals that since 1990 a wide range of people have been involved in discussions on globalization. As in Vietnam and Indonesia, globalization is seen in Thailand mainly as a process of global economic integration. The Thai government has used globalization to justify its economic reform program and to rationalize policy changes in education, information, and technology, as well as culture. Indeed, cultural reforms have likely resulted from the active participation of civil society in the debate on globalization. As the survey suggests, globalization has made policy formation in Thailand more inclusive.

As in Vietnam and Indonesia, the government is at the forefront of promoting globalization in Thailand. Although Thailand's private sector—primarily the business community—is increasingly engaged in the internationalization of its business activities, this sector has not promoted globalization to the country as a whole. In the local language, the official word for globalization has a positive, proactive connotation—to expand globally or to conquer the world (*lokapiwat*). Scholars and the wider public, however, use a term with a more defensive and negative connotation (*lokanuwat* and its many variations).

Chantana's survey of Thailand suggests that globalization has been discussed more widely in this country than in Indonesia and certainly much more than in Vietnam. The debate has been quite healthy, and has led to an understanding that there ultimately must be a balance between economic nationalism and international liberalization. It is somewhat surprising that the issue of foreign cultural domination has entered into the debate in Thailand; Thai society has maintained its cultural identity despite being open to foreign influences for centuries. A major concern is the impact of globalization on the disadvantaged segments of society, particularly the rural population. To what level will the state retain control of the country's development so as to emphasize and allocate resources to strengthen (and perhaps even protect) rural and other disadvantaged populations?

The issue of labor standards arises not in response to the growing pressures from the outside to adopt international standards but primarily from a domestic concern that the country's search for greater international competitiveness may be pursued at the expense of its workers. Thus, civil society has demanded the raising of labor standards and the promotion of labor rights and other human rights. Other issues related to the country's desire to strengthen its international competitiveness include the improvement of the educational system and the bureaucracy, which is also the case in Indonesia, and the improvement of the country's scientific and technological base. The need for greater political transparency and broadened political participation has also been stressed.

However, concrete steps to accomplish these goals are lacking. Efforts to promote the development of science and technology have been given priority as manifested in the establishment of numerous independent research agencies outside the existing bureaucratic structure. This effort too is integral to Thailand's first-order adjustments. Although the debate in Thailand on the impacts of globalization has been much richer than in Vietnam and Indonesia, Chantana's survey shows the absence of a coherent policy that would form the basis for a set of second-order adjustments to globalization, that is, those that deal directly with the social and political dimensions of the challenges.

Among the ASEAN members, the articulation of these challenges perhaps has been strongest in the Philippines. The recent past has also seen significant liberalization efforts by the government. *Globalization,* as Maria Socorro Gochoco-Bautista states in her survey of the Philippines, has become an important buzzword that has been used effectively by the government to justify economic reform. The reform in the Philippines under the Ramos administration appears to have been successful because it is seen as being internally generated, albeit in response to external developments—that is, globalization—rather than being imposed by outside agencies (such as the World Bank or the International Monetary Fund).

The Philippines has also used AFTA domestically to provide an additional push to the government's initiative toward unilateral trade liberalization. Indeed, Executive Order (EO) 470 set most-favored-nation tariffs below AFTA's preferential tariffs. More recently, EO 264/288 set a target of tariff reduction to a uniform rate of 5 percent on most industrial and nonsensitive agricultural products by 2004. This initiative was to a large extent driven by the Philippine chairmanship of APEC in 1996.

The Philippines hosted the APEC meetings in 1996, and various groups in the Philippines used the occasion to voice their concerns over the impact of globalization on Philippine society. APEC was seen as a concrete manifestation of globalization. The issues addressed by these groups vary but include concerns that economic liberalization could displace millions of workers and farmers, that the burden of adjustment will not be equally shared and will fall heavily or solely on the poor, and that globalization could lead to the destruction of societal values. These concerns continue to be expressed in the Philippines, other ASEAN members, and throughout the Asia Pacific region. As the survey indicates, many of these groups do not belong to the usual leftist groups that will oppose APEC anyway, but consist of nonideologically based groups that have adopted a middle-of-the-road stance. Their message was that APEC's agenda should not be confined only to trade and investment liberalization but should include various other efforts aimed to promote a more holistic pattern of sustainable development.

The domestic adjustment efforts facing ASEAN members relative to globalization must go beyond first-order adjustments. Gochoco-Bautista's survey of the Philippines shows that by and large there is acceptance that globalization necessitates the introduction of wide-ranging market-based reforms. However, globalization also necessitates democratization, which should mean the development and enhancement of participatory processes. The importance of this appears to be more clearly articulated and recognized in the Philippines than in the other ASEAN members. Indeed, the Philippines has a longer tradition in the development of such processes, although interrupted by the Marcos years, and a stronger civil society than many other ASEAN members.

CONCLUSION

The surveys reveal that in four ASEAN economies—Indonesia, the Philippines, Thailand, and Vietnam—the challenge of globalization has been taken seriously and that first-order adjustments have been properly focused. However, the success of this policy of globalization, as manifested in economic liberalization, deregulation, and marketization, as well as privatization measures, depends on the success in formulating and implementing second-order adjustments, which still lag.

ASEAN members want the process of economic reform to be sustained. First-order adjustments have been largely initiated and driven by governments. Second-order adjustments will be much more complicated. The more successful the first-order adjustments, leading to deeper international integration, the more complicated the second-order adjustments will be. A political environment is required that allows for wider participatory processes and the development of co-operative mechanisms between governments and civil society. This is an important challenge to the ASEAN members.

BIBLIOGRAPHY

Asia Pacific Economics Group. 1997. *Asia Pacific Profiles.* Vol. 3. London: Financial Times.

Rodrik, Dani. 1997. *Has Globalization Gone Too Far?* Washington, D.C.: Institute for International Economics.

Soesastro, Hadi. 1995. "ASEAN Economic Cooperation in a Changed Regional and International Political Economy." In Hadi Soesastro, ed. *ASEAN in a Changed Regional and International Political Economy.* Jakarta: Centre for Strategic and International Studies.

World Bank. 1996. *Global Economic Prospects and the Developing Countries.* Washington, D.C.: The World Bank.

Developed Countries

3 · Canada

Paul Bowles

THE role of international actors, forces, and institutions has permeated contemporary policy debates in Canada. Indeed, one of the features of globalization is precisely that policy debates concerning globalization are increasingly internationalized and that the distinctions between domestic and foreign/international policy issues become blurred. International issues have been incorporated into Canadian policy debates that might previously have been conducted in exclusively domestic terms, and the impact of changes in the global economy on Canada has itself become a focal point for policy debate.

Although this fusion of domestic and international policy issues has clearly occurred in Canada, the way in which globalization has entered into Canadian policy debates has, in part, been determined by contemporary economic, political, and social issues that might be considered primarily domestic in origin. Although globalization has undoubtedly had an homogenizing influence on policy debates around the world, there nevertheless remain individual country characteristics that are important in explaining how globalization has affected policy debate in different national contexts.

This chapter addresses the following concerns:

- A brief overview of some important contemporary Canadian issues and some historical background on the debate over the nature and terms of Canada's incorporation into the international economy prior to the 1980s.

- An outline of the critical dimensions of globalization that have been identified as having significant influences on Canadian economic and social policies.
- How these dimensions of globalization have affected policy debate in six key areas of Canadian economic and social policy: monetary sovereignty, social policy, labor market policy, trade policy, competition policy, and citizenship and cultural policies.
- An assessment of the current state of the debate on globalization and suggestions as to areas where future comparative and collaborative research may be particularly useful.

THE CANADIAN CONTEXT FOR THE GLOBALIZATION DEBATE

As a highly trade-dependent country, Canada's ratio of exports plus imports as a percentage of gross domestic product (GDP) is over twice that of Japan and the United States and comparable to that of European countries (table 1). As such, Canada's integration into the international economy has been the subject of debate for a considerable period. In general, there are two main positions with respect to Canada's relationship to the international economy. One, which I will call the free trade position, derives from the belief that Canada has benefited enormously from an open international trading system and should pursue efforts to maintain such a system. Canada's current status as a high-income country has resulted from its ability to exploit its comparative advantage (especially in resource-based industries). The benefits of trade to Canada in terms of realizing this comparative advantage—raised productivity and enhanced growth—are significant and warrant the adoption of a free trade policy.[1]

Table 1. Indicators of Trade Openness, G-7 Countries, 1970–1990: Exports Plus Imports/GDP (%)

	Canada	France	Germany	Italy	Japan	United Kingdom	United States	Average
1970	42.9	32.3	25.5	32.7	20.3	45.3	11.0	30.0
1980	55.0	44.3	53.1	47.4	28.3	52.4	20.8	43.0
1990	50.5	45.5	58.5	42.1	21.6	51.5	21.1	41.5

Source: World Bank (1992).

Note: The average is the country average unadjusted for country size.
GDP: Gross domestic product.

A well-articulated and significant body of research argues the second position for a nationalist economic policy. This school views Canada's position as a natural resource exporter as an undesirable long-term development strategy for reasons connected with the Prebisch-Singer terms-of-trade hypothesis (that is, the long-term deterioration of primary goods' prices relative to manufactured goods' prices) and the perceived greater scope for productivity improvements in the manufacturing sector. For these reasons, Canada needs a more interventionist strategy in which the state acts to mediate the forces of international competition and to support an indigenous manufacturing sector. Eden and Molot (1993) document the industry-building policies of successive governments and the nature of the engagement with the international economy that complements these policies. They conclude that there are three identifiable phases of national policy since Canada's formation in 1867.[2] The debate over globalization and Canada's role in the new global economy therefore resonates with the debates of previous periods.

There are also a number of issues that may be thought of as being primarily domestic issues. These issues help to explain why the debate over globalization has highlighted certain aspects more than others and why it has taken on some of the specific characteristics that it has. Four issues dominate the domestic context: debt, employment and inequality, national unity, and federal-provincial relations.

First, Canada's federal and provincial debt levels have reached levels that many policymakers view as serious and requiring sustained action to reduce (Harris 1993). The first step by governments at both levels has been a move to reduce their current operating deficits with balanced budget targets (although achieved by few). The climate is therefore one of fiscal restraint.

Second, Canada has performed poorly, particularly compared with the United States, in generating new jobs and in reducing unemployment, which currently stands at 10 percent (Osberg, Wien, and Grude 1995). Even as unemployment remains high, the quality of new jobs is the subject of much debate spurred by the evidence of increasing earnings' inequality during the 1980s.

These two trends—high debt and high unemployment—have important implications. One is that there are important intergenerational issues: The burden of debt may fall disproportionately on the young, precisely the age group that is having the hardest time finding well-paying employment (Scarth 1996). Another is that the increasing inequality of earnings has not been fully reflected in household income inequality indicators because of the offsetting role of government transfers. However, these transfers are now under threat because of governments' debt-reduction strategies, and the future prospects for the equity of Canadian society therefore remain uncertain.

Third, national unity has come under strain, most obviously because of the political situation in Quebec and the narrowness of the defeat of Quebec sovereignty in the last referendum. Although separatism finds its most dramatic expression in Quebec, other forces weakening federal authority, such as regionalism, can be found in many parts of the country (Gibbins 1995). This regionalism has undoubtedly been reinforced by new patterns of trade and investment that have occurred with greater regional economic integration in North America and the Asia Pacific region (Britton 1996). The dual processes of domestic fragmentation and global economic integration are to some extent evident in Canada as in other parts of the world (Laforest and Brown 1994). The question of what it means to be a Canadian and how to preserve and protect such an identity has risen on the political agenda.[3]

Finally, the result of these political schisms and the weakened role of the federal government as it seeks a way to reduce its budget deficit has been to reopen old questions about the nature of fiscal federalism in Canada (Hobson and St.-Hilaire 1993; Torjman 1993; Banting, Brown, and Courchene 1994). The desire for greater autonomy for the provinces while at the same time protecting national social standards remains an enduring Canadian conundrum (Torjman and Battle 1995).

I have described these issues as being primarily domestic. It would perhaps be more accurate to say that they would be contentious areas of debate if the international economy had remained unchanged and we had not witnessed the increasing integration of the global and North American regional economies evident since the mid-1980s. However, that these changes have occurred has both influenced how these issues are viewed and helped shape the terms in which the debate over the impact of globalization takes place.

FIVE DIMENSIONS OF GLOBALIZATION

Despite the widespread attention given to globalization in the popular media and academic writing, there exists no accepted definition of the term, or agreement on its causes or significance. To facilitate discussion of the impact of globalization, here I will highlight five major and interrelated features of globalization that have been identified in the literature as having significant implications for Canadian policies and institutional structures. These dimensions are the expanding power of international financial markets, the enhanced importance and mobility of long-term capital, changes in production technology, the increasing openness of international trade, and finally, the ever-widening scope of international capitalism following the collapse of the formerly centrally planned economies. These five dimensions of globalization have been caused by a number of factors ranging from technologically determined factors such as declining communication and transportation costs to politically determined factors such as deregulation policies and institutional collapse.

International Financial Markets

An often cited example of the "new globalism" is the rise in the importance and influence of international financial markets. Evidence of extended capital mobility and the increased internationalization of capital markets during the 1980s has been documented by Cosh, Hughes, and Singh (1992). They argue that "the financial markets of the advanced industrial countries have undergone far-reaching changes since the mid-1970s. These changes essentially stem from the following interrelated factors: the progressive deregulation of financial markets both internally and externally in the leading countries; the internationalisation of these markets; the introduction of an array of new financial investments; and the emergence and the increasing role of new players, particularly institutional investors, in the markets" (19).

The reasons for this internationalization of capital markets are identified closely with the policies followed by the major industrial nations in Cosh et al.'s analysis, a point that has also been made forcefully by a number of Canadian scholars, including Bienefeld (1992) and Helleiner (1994b). However, others place more emphasis on reduced transaction costs and the information revolution as central explanations of the trend to capital market internationalization.

The argument refers not only to short-term financial assets (such as bonds and equities) but also to foreign exchange markets. Data on the volume of foreign exchange transactions supports the general argument that international financial markets have increased substantially in importance and power during the past 20 years. For example, Frankel (1996, 5–6) shows that foreign exchange trading advanced rapidly during the 1980s and 1990s, and by April 1995 amounted to approximately US$1.2 trillion per day—some 40–50 times larger than world trade flows per day. The French macroeconomic policy reversal in 1983 served as an early example of the power of international financial markets, but the currency crises that engulfed the British, Italian, and Swedish governments in 1992 as a result of their participation in the European exchange rate mechanism fully illustrated the impotence of national governments in the face of currency flight. The Mexican peso crisis of 1995 offered further evidence of this.[4]

Long-Term Capital Mobility

The importance of long-term capital flows, or foreign direct investment (FDI), has risen sharply in the 1980s and 1990s, and the increasing volume of FDI since 1986 is one of the main factors identified as driving the global integration of production and trade and the diffusion of technology across national borders. Since 1986, the total value of FDI outflows and inflows for Organization for Economic Cooperation and Development (OECD) countries has surged almost fivefold, with FDI outflows from OECD countries in 1995 topping US$250 billion (Witherell 1996, 9). FDI has always been an important source of productive capital in Canada and remains so. Although the trend for OECD

Table 2. Net Direct Investment Flows in Selected OECD Countries, 1993–1995 (US$ million)

	Australia	Canada	France	Germany	Italy	Japan	New Zealand	United Kingdom	United States	All OECD
1993	2,294	−825	−25	−19,317	−3,480	−13,628	3,831	−11,161	−31,493	−62,870
1994	−2,119	1,253	60	−20,593	−2,872	−17,050	−1,989	−18,655	78	−49,223
1995	n.a.	6,400	2,574	−25,878	1,137	−22,225	1,313	−7,929	−22,196	−52,332

Source: Witherell (1996, 9).

Note: Figures are inflows-outflows. A negative figure indicates a net FDI outflow.

countries as a whole is for outflows to exceed FDI inflows, Canada is typically a large net recipient of FDI, and in 1994 and 1995 was the largest net recipient of FDI among OECD countries (table 2).

In addition to the substantial increase in the volume of FDI over the past decade, the mobility of that capital, or the ease with which it crosses national borders, has also expanded significantly. This mobility has resulted from the investment liberalization policies adopted by developed and developing countries alike—sometimes unilaterally, sometimes regionally as part of regional trade and investment agreements, and sometimes through multilateral institutions such as the General Agreement on Tariffs and Trade (GATT).

Changes in Production Technology

The increased volumes of FDI have made multinational corporations increasingly important vehicles for the transmission of technology across national borders. However, the nature of that technology has also changed significantly and constitutes a separate dimension of the process of globalization. Thus, the changing nature of technology, and particularly the shift from Fordist to post-Fordist (or Taylorist to post-Taylorist) technology and to new forms of industrial and work organization, has been argued to be a critical factor driving and shaping globalization (Oman 1996). This has affected spatial patterns of production, market structures, and industrial relations systems throughout the world and led to debates about the nature of "flexible production" and its implications for labor, education, and social policies.

Trade Liberalization

Although the growth in volume of world trade over the past decade has not been as dramatic as the increase in the volume of trading on international financial markets or in FDI flows, trade openness has nevertheless been an important characteristic of globalization. In particular, declining average tariff barriers under the auspices of the Uruguay Round of GATT and the changing structure of world trade with the rapid rise in manufactured exports from developing countries, especially from those in East and Southeast Asia, have led to a more open and competitive international trading system. Regionally based trade agreements have supplemented the system by lowering or eliminating tariffs between member countries. For Canada, this primarily means

Table 3. Canadian Imports and Exports by Country or Country Grouping, 1992–1995 (%)

	United States	Japan	European Union	Other OECD	Other Countries
			Exports		
1992	75.5	5.0	7.8	1.9	9.7
1993	78.4	4.8	6.3	1.7	8.7
1994	79.3	4.7	5.7	1.9	8.2
1995	77.7	5.0	6.8	1.7	8.8
			Imports		
1992	71.5	5.8	9.0	3.0	10.7
1993	73.5	4.8	7.9	2.6	11.1
1994	74.9	4.0	7.9	3.5	9.7
1995	75.0	3.7	8.9	3.5	9.0

Source: Statistics Canada (1998).

the 1989 Canada-U.S. Free Trade Agreement (CUSFTA) and the 1991 North American Free Trade Agreement (NAFTA); the United States is far and away Canada's most important trading partner (table 3). Not surprisingly, many of the arguments over the domestic adjustments required by economic integration are advanced in the context of debate over CUSFTA and NAFTA. Furthermore, part of the debate over Canada's trade policy centers on the relationship between a regionally based trading bloc and multilateral trade policies.

The Global Reach of Capitalism

The characteristics of the new globalism all point to the increased importance of the flows of capital (productive and financial), technology, and goods and services across national borders. One further aspect of globalization points to the fact that the number of nations involved in such flows has increased significantly since the collapse of communism in 1989 and changing development strategies elsewhere. The World Bank summarizes this globalizing trend thus: "In the late 1970s, only a few developing countries, led by some in East Asia, were opening their borders to flows of trade and investment capital. About a third of the world's labour force lived in countries with centrally planned economies, and at least another third lived in countries insulated from international markets by prohibitive trade barriers and capital controls. Today, three giant population blocs— China, the republics of the former Soviet Union, and India—with nearly half the world's labour force among them, are entering the global market, and many other countries from Mexico to Indonesia have already established deep linkages. By the year 2000, fewer than 10 percent of the world's workers are likely to be cut off from the economic mainstream" (1995, 50).[5] This trend not only has had the effect of increasing competition within the global economy for markets and for attracting capital but also has been associated with an ideological shift. The collapse of the formerly centrally planned economies and the move toward liberalization in a range of developing countries have resulted in a general policy disposition toward market solutions, and the associated view of the wisdom of private business and the folly of government.[6]

GLOBALIZATION AND DOMESTIC ADJUSTMENT: POLICY DEBATES

The impact of globalization has profoundly affected the nature of policy debates on Canada's economic and social policies, debates that have involved university researchers, government ministries, independent research institutions, and popular organizations. In this section, I provide an overview of debates in six key areas (fig. 1). The most

Figure 1. Globalization and Domestic Policy Adjustment in Canada

Globalization Pressures	*causing*	Policy Adjustment	*conditioned by*	Canadian Context
International capital markets Trade	⟶	Monetary sovereignty	⟵	Debt
International capital markets Trade FDI Technology	⟶	Social policy	⟵	Unemployment/ inequality Fiscal federalism Debt Unity
Trade FDI Technology	⟶	Labor market policy	⟵	Unemployment/ inequality
Trade FDI	⟶	Trade policy	⟵	Unemployment/ inequality
Trade FDI	⟶	Competition policy		
Technology Post–cold war	⟶	Citizenship and cultural policy	⟵	Unity

relevant features of the Canadian context for each of the policy areas are also indicated in figure 1, and help to explain why the debate in some of the policy areas has taken the form that it has.

Monetary Sovereignty

The expanded scope of international financial markets and the greater openness of trade have led to debates about the institutional basis for, and conduct of, monetary policy in Canada as in many other countries over the past decade. Some of the proposed institutional monetary arrangements include those that point to the need for a closer monetary union with the United States, given the background of CUSFTA and NAFTA and the potential for continentwide financial instability following the Mexican peso crisis (Dorn and Salinas-Leon 1996). Some argue that to take full advantage of worldwide capital markets and increasingly open trade, Canada should enter into a pegged exchange rate regime with the United States or even adopt the U.S. dollar as legal tender. However, the benefits of such a move are by no means accepted even within circles sympathetic to greater openness in international flows (see Crow 1995 for further discussion).

Although these areas of discussion are interesting, perhaps the single most important policy debate concerns the independence and accountability of the Bank of Canada. The debate over central bank independence is by no means confined to Canada. Indeed, in the Asia Pacific region, the accountability of the Federal Reserve has been questioned in the U.S. Congress, the Bank of Japan Law has been revised, China's 1995 Central Bank Law gave greater autonomy to the People's Bank, the relationship between the Bank of Korea and the Ministry of Finance in South Korea has been one of concerted political attention, and New Zealand's central bank contract has received much worldwide attention.

In Canada, the Bank of Canada has assumed greater independence from government, a development associated with the bank's 1988 decision to adopt a zero-inflation target as its sole objective (as a result of the ascendancy of neoconservative/monetarist economic thinking within the bank)[7] and evidenced by the government's reluctance to interfere with its operations. For example, when former Bank of Canada Governor John Crow's term of office came to an end in 1993, the government felt obliged to appoint as his successor his deputy, Gordon Thiessen. Despite widespread criticism of the bank's policies under Crow, the government feared that appointing a new governor from outside of the bank would be interpreted by the international financial markets as a desire to assert political control over the bank and soften its strong anti-inflationary stance.

That the issue of central bank independence should have arisen in so many countries at this historical juncture is in some ways puzzling. The conventional argument for central bank independence is that it lowers inflationary outcomes by removing the temptation for politicians to use discretionary monetary policy to solve short-term political problems. Thus, we might expect debate over the position of the central bank to be characteristic of inflationary periods rather than the current period, when the world economy as a whole and OECD countries in particular are in one of their least inflationary phases. Furthermore, it is now widely recognized, even by central bankers themselves, that the relationship between monetary aggregates and inflation is weak, and thus the current fashion with central bank independence seems even more in need of explanation.

Bowles and White (1994) argue that the issue of central bank independence has arisen, in part, in the context of a debate about appropriate domestic financial institutions for globally integrating financial markets.[8] In particular, given the increased importance and volatility of international financial markets, and their ability to humiliate national governments of whose economic policies they disapprove, many governments have permitted the central bank to enjoy a greater degree of independence to increase the credibility of the bank with the international financial community. Growing constituencies within countries see an independent central bank as a necessary institutional response to minimize the threat of economic malaise posed by international capital flight. The central bank has therefore become a part of the government and at the same time above it, removed from the normal political pressures and requirements of democratic societies.

Coordinated international policies are one possible response that might reduce the power of international financial markets. Indeed, the role that governments have played in promoting the growth of international financial markets through their own policies of domestic

financial liberalization has been significant (see, for example, Bienefeld 1992). As such, the increased power of international financial
markets is not an inevitable process driven purely by exogenous factors such as falling communication costs and the information technology revolution but remains an area in which active government
policy is possible. Thus, the increasing influence of international
financial markets is viewed as a process that could be reversed with
appropriate action by governments acting in concert at the international level. The implementation of policies such as the Tobin tax on
international financial transactions to reduce their speculative nature
have therefore been advanced (Helleiner 1996).

Both the independence of the Bank of Canada and the zero-inflation
policy that it has followed have been subject to considerable criticism
by those for whom the appropriate policy responses are domestic
rather than international. Critics of the zero-inflation policy argue that
the costs in terms of high unemployment and increasing debt are extremely high. For example, Pierre Fortin, recent president of the Canadian Economics Association, argues that the zero-inflation policy
resulted in the interest rate differential between Canada and the United
States rising to historically high levels (Fortin 1996). The result was a
rising value of the Canadian dollar, weakened export performance,
and higher unemployment. The solution proposed by both Fortin and
other critics of the bank's policies, such as the Canadian Centre for
Policy Alternatives in its annual *Alternative Budget*, involves both a
policy change (cutting Canadian short-term interest rates) and an institutional change (restructuring the Bank of Canada to permit greater
control by elected representatives).[9]

In arguing that the Bank of Canada has increased interest rates
to an excessive degree, the critics imply that the bank has exercised
considerable discretionary authority in setting interest rates, that it
has not been subject to pressures to do so by international capital
markets, and that reversing the high interest rate policy will not
have any particular significance for international financial markets.
The importance of the current integration of international financial
markets for constraining national policy autonomy in the area of
monetary policy is therefore essentially denied. It is not that international financial markets are not important, it is that they are not now
more important; as Gillespie argues, "From the 1870s to the 1990s

Canadian governments have been conscious of the role played by international capital markets" (1996, 1).

The debate over the appropriateness of the policies pursued by the Bank of Canada has therefore had important implications for the debate on the effects of globalization. The government and some academics regard a more independent central bank as a requirement for credibility in a world of global capital markets, an institutional change that may be regarded either positively or negatively depending on one's view of the efficiency with which international financial markets operate. Others argue that the discretionary power exercised by the bank remains large, has been abused, and that the bank needs to be brought back under greater (national) democratic control. The debate captures an important tension between the institutional forms required by the imperatives of global market forces and those required by domestic democratic ideals, a tension particularly evident in the debate over the position of the central bank but also evident in other policy areas as well.

Social Policy

The future of the Canadian welfare state—or social programs—occupies a central place in contemporary political and economic debate in Canada. At one level, the welfare state is viewed as a unifying feature of Canada as a nation, differentiating it from the United States and providing a rallying point for those seeking to persuade Quebecers of the benefits of the Canadian federation. The welfare state is, we are told, a part of the very fabric of Canada. At the same time, the welfare state has come under increasing attack as being "too expensive and too extensive" in its current form and in need of restructuring or "reinventing." The reasons for this include the federal government's desire to reduce its total expenditure to meet the deficit-reduction targets that it views as being necessary for domestic political and economic reasons and to prove its fiscal responsibility to foreign creditors. The debate over federal-provincial areas of jurisdiction has also had important implications for the thinking on how to restructure social programs.

The pressures of globalization and North American regional economic integration also have important implications for the future of the Canadian welfare state. Although widespread agreement exists over the importance of globalization, the nature and desirability of its impact is a topic of debate.

One view is that the operations of the global economy have fundamentally changed the nature of the Canadian economy and that the welfare state must be restructured to meet these new conditions. For an example of this type of reasoning, consider the arguments of Canadian economists Courchene and Lipsey. Brown summarizes their position thus: "In their view, the social contract must change to complement the nature of the economy on which it rests. In other words, the welfare state should complement the underlying structure of the economy, and should not—and probably cannot—be used in the long run merely to offset fundamental changes happening there . . . [they] believe that the old social contract has been rendered obsolete by global events beyond the control of any national government. Canada's current dilemmas result partly from the social contract's sluggishness in adapting to the new globalized economy" (1994, 116–117).

The welfare state, therefore, by increasing rigidities in the labor market, has slowed the adjustment of the economy required by globalization and a more extensive international division of labor. Such adjustment gradualism is regarded as harmful as it has led to higher adjustment costs and induced hysteresis in labor markets. The welfare state as it now exists was designed to serve economic and social structures that are no longer relevant, and the "crisis of the welfare state" has resulted, in large part, from the failure of the welfare state to adapt sufficiently quickly.[10] The welfare state, therefore, needs to be reconstituted on a more flexible, less expensive, and less universal basis in which the microeconomic efficiency of social policy receives increased emphasis.[11]

Others agree that globalization has indeed placed increasing pressures on the welfare state, but regard this as an erosion of national policy autonomy and detrimental to Canadian living standards, and, therefore, an argument for taming globalization rather than for dismantling the welfare state. The welfare state, being centrally concerned with redistribution, owes its origin and development to the political support that it has garnered over the course of the past century. The political shifts associated with globalization have been unfavorable to this cause and have resulted in increasing pressures on the welfare state from the forces of global capitalism (Myles 1995; Teeple 1995). The argument that increased capital mobility would limit the welfare state should not be surprising in this context because, as Helleiner argues, the architects of the Bretton Woods agreement, John Maynard Keynes and Harry Dexter White, originally regarded capital controls as necessary to preserve the "political autonomy of the welfare state" (1994a, 165). With increasing openness to trade and capital flows, the result will be pressures on states with more extensive social programs to reduce them to the level of the lower spenders. In other words, we would expect to see downward harmonization, or a race to the bottom, in social spending.[12]

Certainly, there has been considerable concern in Canada that CUSFTA would result in downward pressure on Canada's social programs, even though social programs, as such, were excluded from CUSFTA. Banting summarizes the arguments thus: "First, it was argued that if Canada establishes social programs and related taxes that raise the costs of production above those in the United States, investment will drift south, Canadian business will lobby for lower taxes, and Canadian governments will have little choice but to reduce their social commitments. Second, it was argued that if Canada establishes programs and tax policies that lower the costs of production by socialising costs that are borne by employers in the United States, such programs might be interpreted in the United States as subsidies and subjected to countervail and other trade action. In either case, the result would be convergence between the two social policy regimes, with the burden of adjustment falling on Canada" (1992, 22).[13]

Indeed, labor and environmental side agreements were explicitly negotiated as part of NAFTA to prevent the downward harmonization of standards in these areas. Some argue that the appropriate policy response to these downward pressures in the social policy as well as other spheres is the inclusion of effective social (and labor standards) clauses in all trade agreements to ensure that Canadian living standards, particularly those of the poorest, are adequately protected (Robinson 1995).

Ironically, Courchene and Lipsey's "new global realities" (identified as a reason to reinvent the welfare state on a less extensive basis) have also been used as an argument for the expansion of social programs. According to this argument, it is agreed that the welfare state was designed in a different era—one in which governments had a commitment to full employment and where Fordist production implied a social structure based on a male breadwinner and a traditional family.[14] However, the change to post-Fordist methods of production, and the associated globalization of production, have transformed the nature of production and employment. In particular, there has been a rise in part-time workers, a feminization of the labor force, and increasing disparities between core and peripheral workers as a result of production methods variously referred to as "flexible," "lean," or "Japanese" (see Morris 1991). These changes, together with the end of government commitment to full employment, have led the current period to be denoted as one of economic insecurity. One of the primary purposes of the welfare state, it is argued, is precisely to provide a collective insurance policy against economic insecurity, and as the latter has increased, as a result of globalization, then so has the need for an extensive welfare state.[15]

This type of argument was recently given additional intellectual credence from evidence reported by Rodrik (1996). Rodrik finds a strong positive statistical relationship between size of government and degree of trade openness in a sample of over 100 countries. He concludes that "not only is openness an important determinant of government consumption levels across countries, openness in the early 1960s turns out to be a significant predictor of the expansion of government consumption in the subsequent three decades" (8). Rodrik suggests that the explanation for this statistical finding can be found in the role that government spending plays in reducing the role of external risk to which economies are exposed. Because more open economies have higher degrees of such risk, they compensate by having larger public sectors. Rodrik says that "societies seem to demand (and receive) a larger government sector as the price for accepting larger doses of external risk" with the result that "globalization may well require big, not small, government" (1, 26).

The welfare state occupies a central place in contemporary Canadian policy debate. However, there are a variety of positions being advanced on the relationship between social policy and globalization. To some, an outdated welfare system hampers the realization of the benefits of globalization; to others, globalization and regional integration threaten a much needed and valued system of collective social insurance.

Labor Market Policy

The preceding discussion of social policy is obviously connected with labor market and employment policies. Indeed, these two policy areas are increasingly conflated with discussion flowing freely across the two areas. For example, a recent publication by Adams, Betcherman, and Bilson (1995) on labor law appeared in the C. D. Howe Institute's Social Policy series with the following explanation: "Why a volume on labour law in a series on social policy? On first reflection, debates over the scope of union and management powers may seem far removed from policy debates on topics such as housing, welfare and unemployment insurance. But, as the saying goes, 'the best social policy is a good job.' In that sense, all government policies bearing on the level of employment and the distribution of market earnings are integral to social policy."

Thus, much of this discussion on labor market policy resonates with the debates over social policy. One of the principal forces linking these two areas is the impact of new production technologies and particularly the shift to post-Fordist production technologies. Workers need to be more "flexible" and "adaptable," a view that has important implications for labor and training policies. In particular, with individuals likely to hold five or six different jobs in an average working life, the need for adaptable skills has been emphasized. Increased skill levels are also important given the disappearance of well-paid blue-collar jobs with changing technology and import competition from lower wage economies. In these ways, through changing technology and increasing trade integration, globalization affects the employment choices and outcomes of Canadians.

The emphasis at the level of government policy therefore is on increasing the skill levels of workers and on responding to how Canada might adapt to the new knowledge-based global economy (Courchene 1994). Such an emphasis affects retraining programs for unemployed workers; in this context, "workfare" arises as a policy instrument, that is, requiring welfare recipients to participate in training programs or public works.[16] This phenomenon represents another instance of social and labor market policy integration; the social policy objective of income maintenance adapts to include a training component because the expectation is no longer that the unemployed will necessarily return to the same or similar employment. Structural changes to the economy, in large part caused by the forces of globalization, require that the unemployed retrain for the jobs of the future.

The role of postsecondary education is also affected. For example, the British Columbian provincial government recently responded to a report that it commissioned titled "Training for What?" with a policy shift toward supporting more vocationally based postsecondary programs and institutions.[17] Comparative work with the United States on the efficacy of various retraining and education programs has been particularly evident.

Although substantial agreement exists on the need for training programs and developing the skills necessary to compete in the new global economy, skepticism remains in some quarters about the ability of such programs to deliver a reasonable standard of living for all Canadians. In particular, some argue that too much emphasis has been placed on the ability of these supply-side measures to solve the problems of increasing income disparities and unemployment. Osberg, for example, argues that traditional demand-side policies are also needed to generate the jobs needed by retrained workers: "There is little point in improving training programs or increasing work incentives if there are no jobs available for the retrained and remotivated. The federal government controls macroeconomic policy, while provincial governments administer social assistance and deliver most training programs. In the absence of a commitment to full employment by the federal government, social policy reform at the provincial level is doomed to failure" (1996, 124). This is interesting because it again suggests that globalization has not irrevocably eroded the ability of national governments to utilize Keynesian-inspired demand management policies to address these problems in the way that some interpreters of globalization argue. Others argue that the triumph of globalization in this sphere is the triumph of a corporate agenda that has sought to reorient education and training policies to better fit corporate, rather than individual, aspirations, and has undermined the independence of the education system.

Increasingly, the responses to the pressures from globalization are coming from provincial-level governments.[18] Here, we find an interesting diversity of labor market institutions and approaches to training policies. For example, in British Columbia the social democratic government's response has been heavily influenced by Robert Reich's (1991) argument that in a modern economy it is the relatively immobile factors of production of infrastructure and highly educated and trained work forces that are the key to attracting high-quality jobs.[19] An expansion in postsecondary education, an emphasis on vocational skills, and investment in infrastructure are seen as possible ways to attract foreign investment to British Columbia, particularly from the Asia Pacific region. In Ontario, the neoconservative model has been adopted and is based on reducing business regulations and the levels of support to the unemployed and to social safety nets, and follows a free market route to competing in the global economy. In New Brunswick, a mixture of neoconservative social policy (including workfare) and activist government policy in training and seeking to attract new high-tech industries to the province has been adopted (see Milne 1996 for an assessment). In Quebec, a social corporatist approach has been taken involving highly public meetings of government, business, labor, and other groups in an attempt to forge a consensus on how to tackle the province's economic problems. A comparison of these strategies, their economic and social bases, and their relative successes could provide important information on the types of strategies that work in the global economy.

Trade Policy

Just as labor and social policy have become fused in important respects, so too trade policy has become linked with other important policy areas, such as industrial, competition, and environmental policies. Perhaps the most contentious of these has been the trade and environmental policy linkage. This linkage is important at the global level and increasingly so in Canadian trade policy discussion.[20] There are perhaps three main positions here. One is that, to quote Perroni and Wigle, "trade liberalisation and environmental protection may be treated as separable objectives" (1994, 552). Although there may be some interaction between trade and environmental policies, they should not be viewed as strong, and environmental protection is not best dealt with through trade policies. This counters a second strand

in the literature, which argues that the same sort of downward harmonization pressures that are evident in the social policy area are also
present in the case of the environment. That is, trade liberalization,
on its own, will lead to a competing downward harmonization of environmental standards, and it is necessary to ensure that trade policies
take this into account. A third position is more concerned that environmental regulations may be used as nontariff barriers to trade and may
adversely affect the goal of trade liberalization.

CUSFTA and NAFTA dominate the debate of trade policy "proper"
in Canada. Trade policy discussions focus almost entirely on free trade
agreements, a topic of considerable importance given that it fundamentally challenges the interventionist economic nationalism position that had influenced policy-making circles prior to the 1980s. The
free trade debate was so important that it is not an exaggeration to say
that the 1988 federal election was in fact the "free trade election."

Accounts of the debates over the free trade deal with the United
States and the subsequent, somewhat less fervent, debate over NAFTA
can be found elsewhere (see, for example, Grinspun and Cameron
1993 and Lipsey 1994). There are some important issues related to
trade law that I will also leave aside.[21] Here, I will take the trade agreements as given and consider Canada's post-NAFTA trade policy. In
contrast to the United States, where some prominent free trade supporters, such as Jagdish Bhagwati, argued that NAFTA should be seen
as a part of a trend toward a regionalization of the global economy
that could seriously undermine the multilateral process, Canadian
free traders were strongly behind CUSFTA and NAFTA and argued
that they were consistent with advancing the multilateral process. Although, technically, neither CUSFTA nor NAFTA contradicts Article
24 of GATT, the argument being made was stronger than this. Much
of the post-NAFTA period has therefore been spent considering how
Canadian policy could ensure that the outcome of NAFTA was not
a "Fortress North America" but rather a contribution to a more open
international trading system (see Smith and Steger 1994), a position
that accords with Canada's longstanding support for multilateralism.[22]

This debate has taken the forms of (a) arguing that NAFTA offers a
model of an open trading arrangement that can contribute to our understanding of how subglobal trading agreements can contribute to

the goal of freer global trade, and relatedly (b) supporting and promoting other trade liberalization initiatives. In both of these areas, there has been a strong Asia Pacific, and more narrowly East and Southeast Asian, dimension.

Consider the first argument. Soon after Canada signed NAFTA, then–Prime Minister Brian Mulroney visited Singapore to reassure Asia that NAFTA was not an exclusionary club but one whose members were keen to remain open to trade and investment flows. This argument was recently advanced, again in Singapore, by prominent free trade supporter and economist Richard Lipsey. He argued that "the EU and NAFTA are very different institutions. In particular, the former is a trading block while the latter is not. In what follows, I shall argue that although there is some cause for concern over the behaviour of the EU and the US, there is little reason to believe that the NAFTA—and the WHFTA (Western Hemispheric Free Trade Area) that may follow it—will contribute to the development of trading blocks or to rising protectionism. On the contrary, they should contribute to general trade liberalization and other new regional arrangements would do well to copy this model rather than that of the EU" (Lipsey 1996, 24).

The argument is, therefore, that NAFTA is an outward-looking, trade liberalizing agreement. To provide proof of this, Canada has followed strategy (b) of actively pursuing trade agreements with other countries. For example, Canada has signed bilateral free trade deals with Israel and Chile, has publicly raised the possibility of an EU-NAFTA trade deal, is involved in the WHFTA discussions, and is a member of the Asia-Pacific Economic Cooperation (APEC) forum. Thus, the current phase of regionalism in the world economy is characterized by what I have termed elsewhere "multiple regionalism" (see Bowles 1997). That is, countries are not simply members of one trade bloc but members of several, some of which are overlapping in membership (for example, NAFTA and APEC). Furthermore, these trade initiatives have been matched by high-profile trade missions to several countries in Asia.

To the free trade constituency, and those who supported NAFTA, such initiatives are important because they demonstrate that NAFTA is not an example of closed regionalism but is consistent with trade liberalization initiatives with a broad range of countries. At the same time, some Canadian policymakers and trade policy commentators are concerned that Canada might suffer from being in a hub-and-spoke relationship with the United States, and they are therefore keen to expand Canada's membership of trading clubs.[23] Perhaps paradoxically, therefore, having entered into CUSFTA and NAFTA with the United States, Canadian policy has increasingly focused on the Asia Pacific region as a way to avoid being too reliant on trade with the United States. However, this approach leaves unresolved the broader relationship between regionalism and globalization as forces in the world economy.

Competition Policy

A recent survey of Canadian business executives revealed that the most often cited change in their business operations over the previous five years was the increase in competition that they faced from both domestic and international sources (see Betcherman et al. 1994, 13).The survey results indicate the importance of increasing global competition in business concerns and operations.

In Canada, as in many countries, this increased competition and opening to global markets resulted from regulation (or more accurately deregulation) policy.[24] Deregulation policies were adopted both actively as a means of increasing competitive pressures on businesses and therefore complementary to trade and capital liberalization measures, and passively as a response to comply with international trade agreements. The technological changes and the information revolution that have accompanied globalization have also meant that new areas of business have arisen in which government regulatory regimes are playing catch up.[25]

One prominent argument contends that with capital more mobile internationally, the national regulatory environment can be an impediment to attracting FDI and to realizing the advantages of a more extensive international division of labor. Sauve and Schwanen (1996), for example, argue that investment rules may hinder the efficient flow of capital across national borders and examine ways in which investment rules might be changed to facilitate globalization. Hirshhorn and Gautrin's (1993) collection examines the relationship between government regulation, investment decisions, and economic performance outcomes, whereas Benedickson, Doern, and Olewiler (1994) consider specifically the effects of environmental regulation on investment decisions. Thus, so it is argued, regulation policies must accord with those found elsewhere.

Harmonization pressures have also come as a result of trade agreements. In Canada, discussion has ensued over how best to ensure the promotion and protection of fair competition in CUSFTA and NAFTA. In particular, attention has focused on whether competition policy can be used as a trade remedy instrument rather than having to rely on antidumping and subsidy measures. For example, competition policy could be used to address anticompetitive practices such as discriminatory and predatory pricing instead of using antidumping measures. Thus, as Doern argues, "Because of the onset of free trade and the evidence of the protectionist nature of antidumping cases, the economic conclusion increasingly is that antidumping laws are unnecessary and should be replaced by competition law. Competition law would be more appropriate, because its policy rationales and procedures are more geared than is antidumping law to promoting competition rather than to protecting competitors" (1995, 170). The example of the Australia-New Zealand Closer Economic Relations Trade Agreement has been used to support this argument.

Although economists have advanced such arguments, others have raised the political problems of implementing them. The options for implementing such a policy range from piecemeal changes in specific parts of competition policy to a move toward greater harmonization of Canadian and U.S. competition policies and even the establishment of a supranational competition agency as in the European Union. Although all of these options remain discussion points at this stage, they indicate how competition policy has broadened in scope as a result of regional economic integration, and how issues of political sovereignty in decision making have arisen in tandem.

Citizenship and Cultural Policies

The effects of North American regional and global economic integration are contributing to the angst over defining and protecting Canadian identity. This takes a number of different forms. First, there is the debate over the protection of Canadian cultural activities. These are defined not simply as activities but as industries, thereby indicating their commodification and that they are therefore potentially subject to the usual rules of trade nondiscrimination. For this reason, cultural industries were specifically excluded from NAFTA. However, widespread concern exists that changes in competition policy as well as World Trade Organization (WTO) regulations are making it increasingly difficult for Canada to control, for example, its own media.

Second, national identity is in part linked to national industries, and the development of such industries historically has been a part of the process of nation building. In Canada, this has typically taken the form of the transportation (whether railroad or airline) and energy industries. Global competition as well as the nondiscrimination provisions of international trade agreements are seen as threatening some of these operations, and their demise is viewed not simply as an economic outcome but also as one affecting Canada as a political entity.[26]

Third, the right to Canadian citizenship itself has been commodified through recent changes to immigration policy, which is increasingly no longer seen simply as a humanitarian issue but also as a tool of economic policy. The new global marketplace for entrepreneurs has led to changes in Canadian immigration policies. In particular, the "independent business investor" category for immigrants has become more important, with both the federal and some provincial governments cooperating in actively making Canadian citizenship purchaseable to those willing to invest a specified sum in Canada (DeVoretz 1995).

Fourth, the extended mobility of companies has led to the increasing revolt against "shareholder primacy"—the view that companies are answerable only to their shareholders, must do whatever is in their shareholders' best interests, and owe nothing to the local communities in which they operate. Although clashes between the interests of the shareholders of a company and the workers that it employs are, of course, nothing new, there is an increasing trend toward clashes between shareholder and local community interests. The desirability of restraints on shareholder primacy has been taken up in some business schools, most notably at the Clarkson School at the University of Toronto. The ideological premise that "private business is always right," which was strengthened by the collapse of communism, has perhaps found its most serious challenge here.

Each of these areas indicates a deeper tension from the promotion of the economic over the political, or the promotion of "consumer sovereignty" or "shareholder primacy" over the "rights and duties of the citizen." The constitution enshrines the role of the "citizen," but the role of such an individual is increasingly seen as threatened by the pressures emanating from the global marketplace. In this respect, Canada shares many of the same features as some other Asia Pacific countries where globalization has also threatened national identity.

ASSESSMENT AND FUTURE RESEARCH AREAS

In surveying the debates over the impact of globalization on Canadian domestic policy considerations, it is evident that there are a number of unresolved issues and areas where future collaborative research would be useful. I have identified four areas that would be particularly useful areas for future work and areas in which the Canadian experience and the contribution of Canadian researchers could be significant. These areas concern (a) globalization and the nation-state; (b) globalization, citizenship, and economic growth; (c) globalization and the national context; and (d) the relationship between globalization and regionalization.

Globalization and the Nation-State

There are some fundamental differences about the role that the nation-state does and should play in response to the process of globalization. I briefly review three key schools of thought here, each with its own methodology, assessment of the implications of globalization, and implications for state behavior.

The first of these schools of thought I will call the "globalization as an opportunity" school. Its fundamental proposition is that the process of globalization is one that is welfare enhancing for all countries. This proposition rests on the theoretical framework supplied by neoclassical economics in which globalization, by leading to a more globally efficient allocation of resources and an increased spread of technology, promotes efficiency and increases economic growth. All countries can be expected to gain in this process. The nation-state adapts domestic institutional structures and adopts economic and social policies that will permit the process of globalization to proceed as smoothly as possible; the state's role is therefore one of a facilitator. The main obstacle to the state's effective pursuit of this role is the presence of losers in the globalization process who may have the ability to block or impede facilitating policies by organizing around their special interests. Although the process of globalization may lead to generally increasing levels of welfare, these benefits are widely dispersed, and those who may lose in the process tend to be concentrated in certain industries, regions, or social groups. The task of government becomes to design appropriate policies to ease the negative effects on these groups and to provide the leadership necessary to construct a broad coalition in favor of globalization-facilitating measures. In this sense, this school relies on a political economy approach, now familiar in many adjustment-related debates, which emphasizes the need to overcome special interest groups' opposition to policy measures.[27] This school of thought can be readily identified in the social policy, labor market policy, competition policy, and trade policy debates.

The second school of thought can be characterized as taking a "globalization as a threat" position. It also utilizes a political economy approach, but one that draws more heavily on the Marxist tradition in which certain forces are given primacy; the neo-Gramscian variant, which stresses the process of creating and maintaining ideological hegemony, is particularly well developed in Canada. In this case, the process of globalization serves the interests of capital and the capitalist class. Its purpose is to free capital accumulation from national state control, a process that weakens the social structures that were constructed on a nation-state basis in the post–World War II period. The process of globalization has dramatically changed the relation of states to the international economy; whereas states could previously be seen as "gatekeepers," insulating domestic economies from the ravages of the international economy, their policy has now been reduced to the point where they have in fact become the agents transmitting the requirements of the globalizing economy onto the domestic economy. The state therefore plays the role of reforming the domestic economy to meet the needs of the international economy. As Cox puts it, there is a "process whereby national policies and practices have been adjusted to the exigencies of the world economy of international production" (1987, 253).

The outcome of this, in terms of the aforementioned policy debates, is that Canada, which for most of this century and particularly in the postwar period has through social and political pressure built a welfare state, has been transformed by the pressures of globalization into the competitor state, where the emphasis is not on redistribution and so-cial equity but on policies to compete in the global economy.

The third school of thought can be characterized as the "globaliza-tion as a nonbinding constraint" school. This school recognizes that globalization is taking place but does not regard this as constituting a qualitative change. In the Canadian context, this means a recognition that the Canadian economy has always been an open economy, sub-ject to external pressures, and that the new globalism is a continuation of this without necessarily being associated with a qualitative change in the ability of national governments to intervene in their economies. Thus, the state remains a viable agent for implementing national poli-cies connected with, for example, employment and social policy ob-jectives. This position was also in evidence in the debate on monetary sovereignty.

It seems to me unlikely that differences between these three schools of thought are likely be resolved through empirical evidence alone, because they are based on different methodologies, analytical catego-ries, and worldviews. However, comparative studies on the effects of globalization on the role of the nation-state in Asia Pacific countries might be fruitful for assessing the robustness and general applicability of the three schools.

Globalization, Citizenship, and Economic Growth

The argument that globalization increases national welfare, an argu-ment of the "globalization as an opportunity" school, has been ad-vanced most prominently in Canada by economist Richard Lipsey. The argument, based on the results of the Canadian Institute for Advanced Research, which Lipsey directs, is that globalization facilitates the flow of technology across national borders, and it is technology, advanc-ing in Schumpeterian discontinuous waves, that is the basis of cur-rent living standards. Therefore, a positive relationship exists between globalization and economic growth.

However, Lipsey's growth theory is not the only one on offer. An increasing amount of attention has been given to the role of "social capital" in enhancing growth. This is a nebulous and varying term, initially used by political scientist Putnam (1993) in a study of Italy and now used widely to the extent that it has permeated the World Bank (1996), whose Social Task Group recommends "investing in social capital," and bearing comparison with Abramowitz's (1986) argument that the ability of countries to catch up with the technological leaders through international openness depended on their "social capabilities." Although a precise definition of this term may be elusive, it usually implies some degree of social organization and social empowerment and commitment that translates into better economic performance, and the presence or absence of social capital explains different growth outcomes.[28] However, it is precisely this social capital, this empowerment, this degree of social organization that others have argued, in the Canadian context, to be threatened and undermined by globalization. That is, if citizenship is undermined by the absence of effective democratic control as a result of globalization, then the quantity of social capital must decline (see Robinson 1995).

Globalization, therefore, has contradictory implications for these two growth processes. Whether and how globalization facilitates the spread of technology but undermines citizenship and social capital is interesting but currently unexplored territory.[29]

Globalization and National Contexts

I have argued that the debate over the impact of globalization on national policies has depended, in part, on that national context itself (fig. 1). However, little research has been done on how different national contexts affect policy debates on globalization. One line of argument is that we are witnessing "policy convergence." However, the causes of this convergence, if such it be, could be many: greater information available from other countries on best practices, elite networking or "epistemic communities," or the pressures of globalization.[30] Furthermore, such policy convergence has received most attention within the context of OECD countries. The opportunity to look at the issue of the importance of national contexts could be particularly illuminating for Asia Pacific countries. Including Canada in comparative studies could be interesting here.

In particular, the following two questions might be explored. First, to what extent is the debate over monetary sovereignty in Canada conditioned by sensitivities over the level of Canadian debt? Are the same concerns with monetary sovereignty expressed by creditor countries in the Asia Pacific region? Second, to what extent is the globalization debate in Canada conditioned by the fact that earnings inequality and income polarization have occurred? Some argue that import competition from low-wage countries has adversely affected the economic position of less skilled workers in industrialized countries (see especially Wood 1994). Although rising inequality is well documented in Canada, there are few empirical examinations of the extent to which the globalization of trade has been responsible for this in the Canadian case (see MacPhail forthcoming for an exception). Nevertheless, it is worth asking whether the possible negative effects on unskilled workers in Canada and on income equality are mirrored by positive effects on unskilled workers and income distribution in developing countries in the Asia Pacific region.

These questions explore more deeply whether globalization should be seen primarily as an homogenizing force leading to common outcomes and converging policy responses or whether national contexts still play an important, and differentiating, role.[31] In particular, could the distinctions between debtor/creditor and developed/developing countries be used to identify symmetric outcomes and policy responses to globalization?

Globalization and Regionalization

Those supporting free trade in Canada point to NAFTA as an open trading arrangement capable of being used as a stepping stone to freer global trade. This points to the important theoretical question of the relationship between regionalization and globalization. For some, the same forces essentially propel the processes of regionalization and globalization, namely, the desire of capital to expand on a multinational basis with reduced state control. At the level of state policy, some argue that countries adopt regional strategies to ensure their participation in the global economy; the two strategies should be seen as complementary. For others, however, regionalization and globalization remain potentially antagonistic forces, with the potential as much to divide as to integrate the world economy. Some of the differences here relate to the former theorists viewing capital flows as the most important dimension of globalization, whereas in the latter case it is the direction of trade flows that has received the most attention. Thus, just as globalization has several dimensions, so does regionalization; understanding the relationship between the two is therefore a complicated task.

Added to which, we are not dealing with a clearly identifiable regionalization. The occurrence of "multiple regionalism" is by no means confined to Canada; in fact, it is a widely shared condition in Asia Pacific countries with NAFTA, AFTA, WHFTA, APEC, and the Australia-New Zealand Closer Economic Relations Trade Agreement all prominent. Understanding the relationship between these regional arrangements and between them and the process of globalization is another area where comparative work in the Asia Pacific region would be useful.

NOTES

1. For a review of the contributions by Canadian economists supporting the case for free trade over the past 30 years see Wonnacott (1993).

2. The three phases of Canadian national policy identified by Eden and Molot are (a) defensive expansionism, 1867–1940; (b) compensatory liberalism, 1941–1981; and (c) market liberalism, from 1982 onward.

3. This debate has been further complicated by the arguments made by some groups, most notably First Nations groups, that they require differential rights in order to preserve their cultural identity within Canada. For discussion, see Fierlbeck (1996).

4. It is not only national governments whose reserves are small relative to the size of international capital movements. Sachs, Tornell, and Velasco argue that "the magnitude of international capital movements clearly swamps what the IMF can do under existing arrangements" (1995, 32).

5. Defining globalization by the extent of global trade has led Anton (1995) to argue that globalization can be traced back to the Spanish conquest of the Americas.

6. As Hart notes, "in practice there is now almost universal acceptance of the efficacy of the market in organizing economic activity and of the more limited role of governments in regulating its operation. The implication of this development is revolutionary" (1996, 1).

7. See Drainville (1995) for an analysis of why Canadian policymakers were so receptive to monetarism.

8. See Siklos (1994) for an introduction to the Canadian case.

9. See Laidler and Robson (1995) for the counterargument that the Bank of Canada should avoid being dragooned into solving the government's budgetary problems.

10. In this respect, Canada is seen as suffering from "Eurosclerosis," the term coined by critics of the European welfare state to denote the effects that

it has had on causing high levels of unemployment and labor market rigidities.

11. See also Boadway, Breton, Bruce, and Musgrave (1994) for the view that governments need to be more selective in their objectives as a result of globalization pressures.

12. See Bowles and Wagman (1997) for an empirical test of this and other hypotheses on the relationship between globalization and the welfare state.

13. See also Grinspun, who argues that "the increased mobility of capital with the United States and Mexico, promoted by the free trade, creates strong pressures for harmonization of public policies across the border" (1993, 110).

14. See Reynolds (1993) for a collection on how demographic technological, social, and labor market changes have altered perspectives on how best to assist the employable unemployed.

15. See also Bakker (1996) for studies which argue that while these labor market changes have led to a convergence of male and female job experiences, the needs of women for the provisions of the welfare state have increased and that the reductions in social programs are particularly harmful to women.

16. See Sayeed (1995) for analysis.

17. See also Hum and Simpson (1996) for discussion of the relationship between employer-based training and Canada's competitive position globally.

18. See Brown and Fry (1993) for subnational governmental responses to globalization in North America.

19. For discussion of the implications of this for national policy see Mintz and Preston (1993).

20. See Kirton and Richardson (1992) for a collection of papers exploring trade and environment links in the Canadian and global contexts. See also Whalley (1991) and Smith (1995).

21. See Feltham (1996) for review.

22. See Black and Sjolander (1996) for an analysis of how this support has been a self-interested one and how bilateral agreements, such as CUSFTA and NAFTA, have, in the authors' view, challenged Canada's commitment to multilateralism.

23. For Canada's relationship with other countries, especially the United States, in a world of trading blocs see Hart (1994) and Wonnacott (1996).

24. For discussion of this in the case of the telecommunications industry see Stanbury (1996).

25. The "information superhighway" is one such area. See Globerman (1995) for discussion.

26. This view has been advanced by the Council for Canadians, a populist nongovernmental organization.

27. This school therefore can be seen as part of the "political economy of rent seeking" approach which is found prominently in the work of the international financial institutions and many neoliberal economists.

28. See Helliwell (1996) for an attempt to use the concept of social capital to explain economic growth rates in Asia.

29. It could also be argued that globalization may undermine authoritarian regimes and may therefore *increase* social capital by increasing participation in the political system. Thus, the effects of globalization on social capital may differ depending on existing political institutions; this points to the fact that the effects of globalization may depend on national context.

30. See Smith in Courchene (1995) for discussion of policy convergence.

31. There is relatively little work that compares Canada with developing countries in this respect. One important exception is the collection edited by Morales-Gomez and Torres (1995), in which the parallels of social policy reform in Canada and Latin America are analyzed.

BIBLIOGRAPHY

Abramowitz, Moses. 1986. "Catching Up, Forging Ahead, and Falling Behind." *Journal of Economic History* 46(2): 385–406.

Adams, Roy, Gordon Betcherman, and B. Bilson. 1995. *Good Jobs, Bad Jobs, No Jobs: Tough Choices for Canadian Labour Law.* Toronto: C. D. Howe Institute.

Anton, Danillo. 1995. *Diversity, Globalization and the Ways of Nature.* Ottawa: International Development Research Centre.

Bakker, Isabella, ed. 1996. *Rethinking Restructuring: Gender and Change in Canada.* Toronto: Toronto University Press.

Banting, Keith, Douglass Brown, and Thomas Courchene, eds. 1994. *The Future of Fiscal Federalism.* Kingston, Ont.: School of Policy Studies, Queen's University.

Benedickson, Jamie G., Bruce Doern, and Nancy Olewiler. 1994. *Getting the Green Light: Environmental Regulation and Investment in Canada.* Toronto: C. D. Howe Institute.

Betcherman, Gordon, N. Leckie, K. McMullen, and C. Caron. 1994. *The Canadian Workplace in Transition.* Kingston, Ont.: Industrial Relations Centre Press, Queen's University.

Bienefeld, Manfred. 1992. "Financial Deregulation: Disarming the Nation State." *Studies in Political Economy* 37: 31–58.

Black, David, and C. Sjolander. 1996. "Multilateralism Reconstituted and the Discourse of Canadian Foreign Policy." *Studies in Political Economy* 49: 7–36.

Boadway, Robin, A. Breton, N. Bruce, and R. Musgrave. 1994. *Defining the Role of Government: Economic Perspectives on the State.* Kingston, Ont.: School of Policy Studies, Queen's University.

Bowles, Paul. 1997. "ASEAN, AFTA and the New Regionalism." *Pacific Affairs* 70(2): 219–233.

Bowles, Paul, and B. Wagman. 1997. "Globalization and the Welfare State: Four Hypotheses and Some Empirical Evidence." *Eastern Economic Journal* 23(3): 317–336.

Bowles, Paul, and G. White. 1994. "Central Bank Independence: A Political Economy Approach." *Journal of Development Studies* 31(2): 235–264.

Britton, John, ed. 1996. *Canada and the Global Economy: The Geography of Structural and Technological Change.* Montreal: McGill-Queen's University Press.

Brown, Douglass. 1994. *Economic Change and New Social Policies.* In W. Watson, J. Richards, and Douglass Brown, eds. *The Case for Change: Reinventing the Welfare State.* Toronto: C. D. Howe Institute.

Brown, Douglass, and Earl Fry, eds. 1993. *States and Provinces in the International Economy.* Kingston, Ont.: School of Policy Studies, Queen's University.

Cosh, A., A. Hughes, and A. Singh. 1992. "Openness, Financial Innovation, Changing Patterns of Ownership, and the Structure of Financial Markets." In Tariq Banuri and Juliet B. Schor, eds. *Financial Openness and National Autonomy: Constraints and Opportunities.* Oxford, England: Clarendon Press.

Courchene, Thomas, ed. 1994. *Stabilization, Growth and Distribution: Linkages in the Knowledge Era.* Kingston, Ont.: School of Policy Studies, Queen's University.

———, ed. 1995. *Technology, Information and Public Policy.* Kingston, Ont.: School of Policy Studies, Queen's University.

Cox, Robert. 1987. *Production, Power and World Order: Social Forces in the Making of History.* New York: Columbia University Press.

Crow, John. 1995. *Two and a Half Cheers for Canadian Monetary Sovereignty.* Toronto: C. D. Howe Institute.

DeVoretz, Donald, ed. 1995. *Diminishing Returns: The Economics of Canada's Recent Immigration Policy.* Toronto: C. D. Howe Institute.

Doern, G. 1995. *Fairer Play: Canadian Competition Policy Institutions in a Global Market.* Toronto: C. D. Howe Institute.

Dorn, J., and Roberto Salinas-Leon. 1996. *Money and Markets in the Americas: New Challenges for Hemispheric Integration.* Vancouver: The Fraser Institute.

Drainville, A. 1995. "Monetarism in Canada and the World Economy." *Studies in Political Economy* 46: 7–42.

Eden, Lorraine, and M. Molot. 1993. "Canada's National Policies: Reflections on 125 Years." *Canadian Public Policy* 19(3): 232–251.

Feltham, I., ed. 1996. *International Trade and Dispute Settlement: Implications for Canadian Administrative Law.* Ottawa: Centre for Trade Policy and Law.

Fierlbeck, K. 1996. "The Ambivalent Potential of Cultural Identity." *Canadian Journal of Political Science* 29(1): 3–22.

Fortin, Pierre. 1996. "The Canadian Fiscal Problem: The Macroeconomic Connection." In L. Osberg and Pierre Fortin, eds. *Unnecessary Debts.* Toronto: James Lorimer.

Frankel, Jeffrey A. 1996. "How Well Do Foreign Exchange Markets Function: Might a Tobin Tax Help?" NBER Working Paper No. 5422. Cambridge, Mass.: National Bureau of Economic Research.

Gibbins, Roger. 1995. *The New Face of Canadian Nationalism.* Kingston, Ont.: School of Policy Studies, Queen's University.

Gillespie, W. 1996. "A Brief History of Government Borrowing in Canada." In L. Osberg and Pierre Fortin, eds. *Unnecessary Debts.* Toronto: James Lorimer.

Globerman, Stephen. 1995. "Economics of the Information Superhighway." In Thomas Courchene, ed. *Technology, Information and Public Policy.* Kingston, Ont.: School of Policy Studies, Queen's University.

Grinspun, Ricardo. 1993. "The Economics of Free Trade for Canada." In R. Grinspun and D. Cameron, eds. *The Political Economy of North American Free Trade.* Montreal: McGill-Queen's University Press.

Grinspun, Ricardo, and D. Cameron, eds. 1993. *The Political Economy of North American Free Trade.* Montreal: McGill-Queen's University Press.

Harris, Richard, ed. 1993. *Deficits and Debt in the Canadian Economy.* Kingston, Ont.: School of Policy Studies, Queen's University.

Hart, Michael. 1994. *What's Next: Canada: The Global Economy and the New Trade Policy.* Ottawa: Centre for Trade Policy and Law.

———. 1996. "A Multilateral Agreement on Foreign Direct Investment—Why Now?" Occasional Paper No. 37. Ottawa: Centre for Trade Policy and Law.

Helleiner, Eric. 1994a. "From Bretton Woods to Global Finance: A World Turned Upside Down." In Richard Stubbs and Geoffrey Underhill, eds. *Political Economy and the Changing Global Order.* Toronto: McLelland and Stewart.

———. 1994b. *States and the Reemergence of Global Finance.* Ithica, N.Y.: Cornell University Press.

———. 1996. "Post-Globalization: Is the Financial Liberalization Trend Likely to Be Reversed?" In Robert Boyer and Daniel Drache, eds. *States against Markets: The Limits of Globalization.* London: Routledge.

Helliwell, John. 1996. "Economic Growth and Social Capital in Asia." NBER Working Paper No. 5470. Cambridge, Mass.: National Bureau of Economic Research.

Helliwell, John, and Robert Putnam. 1996. "Social Capital and Economic Growth in Italy." *Eastern Economic Journal* 21(3): 295–307.

Hirshhorn, Ronald, and Jean-François Gautrin, eds. 1993. *Competitiveness and Regulation.* Kingston, Ont.: School of Policy Studies, Queen's University.

Hobson, Paul, and F. St.-Hilaire. 1993. *Reforming Federal-Provincial Fiscal Arrangements: Toward Sustainable Federalism.* Montreal: Institute for Research on Public Policy.

Hum, Derek, and Wayne Simpson. 1996. *Maintaining a Competitive Workforce: Employee-Based Training in the Canadian Economy.* Montreal: Institute for Research on Public Policy.

Kirton, John, and Sarah Richardson. 1992. *Trade, Environment and Competitiveness.* Ottawa: National Roundtable on the Environment and the Economy.

Laforest, Guy, and Douglass Brown, eds. 1994. *Integration and Fragmentation: The Paradox of the Late Twentieth Century.* Kingston, Ont.: School of Policy Studies, Queen's University.

Laidler, David, and W. Robson. 1995. *Don't Break the Bank!: The Role of Monetary Policy in Deficit Reduction.* Toronto: C. D. Howe Institute.

Lipsey, Richard. 1994. *The NAFTA: What's In, What's Out, What's Next?* Toronto: C. D. Howe Institute.

———. 1996. "NAFTA and Other Regional FTAs: Threat or Promise?" *Journal of the Asia Pacific Economy* 1(1): 23–38.

MacPhail, Fiona. Forthcoming. "What Caused Earnings Inequality to Increase in Canada during the 1980s?" *Cambridge Journal of Economics.*

Milne, W. 1996. *The McKenna Miracle: Myth or Reality?* Toronto: Canadian Centre for Public Management.

Mintz, Jack, and Ross Preston, eds. 1993. *Infrastructure and Competitiveness.* Kingston, Ont.: School of Policy Studies, Queen's University.

Morales-Gomez, Daniel, and A. Mario Torres. 1995. *Social Policy in a Global Society.* Ottawa: International Development Research Centre.

Morris, J. 1991. "A Japanization of Canadian Industry?" In Daniel Drache and Meric Gertler, eds. *The New Era of Global Competition: State Policy and Market Power.* Montreal and Kingston: McGill-Queen's University Press.

Myles, John. 1995. *The Market's Revenge: Old Age Security and Social Rights.* Ottawa: Caledon Institute of Social Policy.

Oman, Charles. 1996. "The Policy Challenges of Globalization and Regionalisation." Policy Brief No. 11. Paris: OECD Development Centre.

Osberg, Lars. 1996. "Social Policy, Macro Policy, and the Debt." In L. Osberg and Pierre Fortin, eds. *Unnecessary Debts.* Toronto: James Lorimer.

Osberg, Lars, Fred Wien, and Jan Grude. 1995. *Vanishing Jobs: Canada's Changing Workplaces.* Toronto: James Lorimar.

Perroni, C., and R. Wigle. 1994. "International Trade and Environmental Quality: How Important Are the Linkages?" *Canadian Journal of Economics* 27(3): 551–567.

Putnam, Robert. 1993. *Making Democracy Work: Civic Traditions in Modern Italy.* Princeton, N.J.: Princeton University Press.

Reich, Robert. 1991. *The Work of Nations.* New York: Vintage Books.

Reynolds, Elisabeth, ed. 1993. *Income Security in Canada: Changing Needs, Changing Means.* Montreal: Institute for Research on Public Policy.

Robinson, I. 1995. "Globalization and Democracy." *Canadian Centre for Policy Alternatives Monitor* 2(7): 13–15.

Rodrik, Dani. 1996. "Why Do Open Economies Have Bigger Governments?" NBER Working Paper No. 5537. Cambridge, Mass.: National Bureau of Economic Research.

Sachs, Jeffrey, A. Tornell, and A. Velasco. 1995. "The Collapse of the Mexican Peso: What Have We Learned?" NBER Working Paper No. 5142. Cambridge, Mass.: National Bureau of Economic Research.

Sauve, Pierre, and Daniel Schwanen, eds. 1996. *Investment Rules for a Global Economy.* Toronto: C. D. Howe Institute.

Sayeed, A. 1995. *Workfare: Does It Work? Is It Fair?* Montreal: Institute for Research on Public Policy.

Scarth, William. 1996. *Beyond the Deficit: Generation X and Sustainable Debt.* Toronto: C. D. Howe Institute.

Scott, Anthony. 1993. "Does Living in Canada Make One a Canadian Economist?" *Canadian Journal of Economics* 26(1): 26–38.

Siklos, P. 1994. *Money, Banking and Financial Institutions: Canada in the Global Environment.* Toronto: McGraw-Hill Ryerson.

Smith, Murray, and D. Steger, eds. 1994. *Trade Policy in the 1990s.* Ottawa: Centre for Trade Policy and Law.

Smith, M., ed. 1995. *International Trade and Sustainable Development.* Ottawa: Centre for Trade Policy and Law.

Stanbury, William, ed. 1996. *Perspectives on the New Economics and Regulation of Telecommunications.* Montreal: Institute for Research on Public Policy.

Statistics Canada. 1998. *Imports and Exports of Goods on a Balance of Payments Basis.* < http://www.statcan.ca/english/Pgdb/Economy/ International/gblec02a.htm > (24 September 1998).

Teeple, Gary. 1995. *Globalization and the Decline of Social Reform.* Toronto: Garamond Press.

Torjman, Sherri, ed. 1993. *Fiscal Federalism for the 21st Century.* Ottawa: Caledon Institute of Social Policy.

Torjman, Sherri, and Ken Battle. 1995. *Can We Have National Standards?* Ottawa: Caledon Institute of Social Policy.

Whalley, John. 1991. "The Interface Between Environmental and Trade Policies." *Economic Journal* 101(405): 180–189.

———. 1996. "Why Do Countries Seek Regional Trading Agreements?" NBER

Working Paper No. 5552. Cambridge, Mass.: National Bureau of Economic Research.

Witherell, William H. 1996. "An Agreement on Investment." *The OECD Observer*, no. 202(October/November): 6–9.

Wonnacott, Ronald. 1993. "Trade Liberalisation: Canadian Contributions since the 1960s." *Canadian Journal of Economics* 26(1): 14–25.

———. 1996. "Free Trade Agreements: For Better or Worse?" *American Economic Review* 86(2): 62–66.

Wood, Adrian. 1994. *North-South Trade, Employment and Inequality: Changing Fortunes in a Skill-Driven World.* Oxford, England: Clarendon Press.

World Bank. 1992. *World Tables 1992.* Washington, D.C.: World Bank.

———. 1995. *World Development Report 1995: Workers in an Integrating World.* New York: Oxford University Press.

———. 1996. "The World Bank Invests in Social Capital: Interview with the Head of the Social Task Group." *Transition* 7(9–10): 11–12.

4 · Japan

Takenaka Heizō
Chida Ryōkichi

THE Japanese economy has faced many structural adjustments in the past. For a country that pulled itself out of the ashes of World War II to achieve the kind of prosperity it enjoys today in an unprecedentedly short time, adjustments in economic structure would seem to be commonplace. With its dependence on foreign suppliers for most of its energy, adapting to changes in the international economic environment is Japan's fate, as the two oil crises of the 1970s illustrated. Indeed, the government's annual white papers on the Japanese economy are filled with references to structural adjustments.

Since the 1980s, however, and particularly after the stratospheric rise of the yen in the late 1980s, adjustment of the domestic economy has become the subject of a larger policy debate. The increased global interdependence of economies has driven this debate. These issues affect not just Japan but also the entire world. Both developed and developing countries must adjust their structures to take advantage of new opportunities for development in newly competitive markets.

There are also unusual factors at work in Japan's economy, and these factors have an undeniably large influence on the domestic policy debate over structural adjustment. As globalization deepens the interdependence of economies worldwide, it exposes the contradictions and problems in domestic economies and societies, generating domestic debate.

This chapter surveys the domestic adjustments that Japan will require to adapt to globalization and the policy debates that have taken place so far. We examine the basic factors behind the policy debates from three perspectives: (a) the perception of the Japanese public that its economy is "small and frail," (b) the existence of a two-tiered economic structure, and (c) the decline in the potential growth rate caused by a combination of structural factors. These factors have been extremely influential in the domestic policy debate on globalization. We examine four aspects of globalization that are deeply intertwined with economic structural adjustments: (a) volatile exchange rates caused by the increase in capital movements, (b) active outgoing direct investments and the consequent international linkage of production, (c) the growing pressure from all sides for freer trade, and (d) technological change, particularly the rapid advances in communications and information, and the paradigm shifts in production technology.

The domestic policy debate is surveyed in five areas: (a) deregulation, (b) the Big Bang reforms for financial market liberalization, (c) jobs, (d) macroeconomic balances, and (e) taxation. The domestic Japanese debate on globalization in the 1980s has leaned toward the resolution of external economic friction. In the 1990s, new difficulties have led to recognition of the need to be actively involved in globalization to revitalize the Japanese economy.

WHAT IS GLOBALIZATION TO JAPAN?

Three factors in the Japanese economy and society are important background issues to the domestic adjustments required by globalization.

Perception of the Japanese Public that Its Economy Is "Small and Frail"

Many Japanese perceive that they live in a "small and frail country." This may seem odd in light of the Japanese economy's large presence on the world stage, where it accounts for one-quarter of total production. Whether measured in terms of per capita income, trade values, or official development assistance, the Japanese economy is undeniably mammoth. Moreover, a large domestic sector supports this economy. Japan depends on trade for only 14.4 percent of its economy (1994), which is low in comparison with the rest of Asia and even with the other developed countries. Wakasugi (1988) has analyzed the relationship between the appreciation of the yen in the late 1980s and trends in the industrial structure and corporate behavior. He finds that the Japanese economy is, essentially, a self-sustained and autonomous entity and argues that even before the yen appreciated Japan's dependence on foreign economies was not high. Nishikawa (1985), on the other hand, claims that Japan is resource-poor and must therefore promote exports to be able to import the raw materials that it needs. This, he says, has caused the people of Japan to heed foreign economic relations ever since the Meiji Period (1868–1912). Something in the mentality of the Japanese people makes them anxious over their economic future because the majority of their energy and natural resources are imported.

This perception of frailty gives debates on Japanese economic policy two different biases. First, the Japanese accept that internationalization and globalization cannot be avoided because it is impossible to cut off economic interaction with the outside world. When used in Japan, the terms *internationalization* and *globalization* have a progressive and advanced nuance and have become part of the daily lexicon. Second, there exists a form of anxiety and at times panic—even flat-out rejection—over domestic adjustments. The debate over the need for structural adjustments has not always been adequate. Some sectors, such as agriculture, reject the need for internationalization and globalization, and argue that Japan's resource dependencies require them to be as self-sufficient as possible.

Nakatani (1987) sees the reaction of the Japanese public to internationalization and globalization as a sensibility that has been with Japan since it sealed itself off to the outside during the Edo Period (1603–1868). Nakatani says:

> The Japanese have a surprisingly deep feeling for "Japan." . . . The Japanese are enormously concerned about "Japan," to the point that how Japan is perceived by other countries is a question of intense interest to them. Japan is probably the only one among the developed countries . . . that can use the word

"internationalization" so frequently and feel such romance in this strange (?) coinage. . . . The reason the Japanese are so extraordinarily interested in foreign countries and indeed exhibit such tension about the subject is that they have never really had any interaction with foreigners on a day-to-day basis and therefore have never really experienced the truism that foreigners are, ultimately, members of the same tribe as the Japanese themselves. (62)

Two-Tiered Structure of the Japanese Economy

A second factor that must be understood to make sense of the domestic Japanese policy debates on economic globalization is the two-tiered structure of the economy. All economies have some industrial sectors that are extremely productive and enjoy a high degree of international competitiveness and others that are less productive and less internationally competitive. In Japan, the contrasts between these groups historically have been pronounced. A handful of highly competitive industries (for example, textiles in the 1960s, steel in the 1970s, and transportation and electrical equipment since the 1980s) have accounted for a large portion of exports. Having started to industrialize later than other developed countries, Japan refined competitive industries by concentrating its resources in specific promising sectors (however, the experts disagree about whether this was successful) while protecting domestic industries. Because of this two-tiered structure, there are large differences in the content and direction of the economic policy debate depending on which sectors of the economy are considered. More important still is the fact that as international competitive pressures increased in the 1980s and beyond, the contrasts became more manifest between those industries that adapted to competition positively and those that have felt greater need to hide behind the regulations of the past.

According to Harada (1996), statistics show there are only four industries in Japan—transport machinery, electric machinery, primary metals, and chemicals—that are more productive in absolute value than the same industries in the United States. These highly productive industries occupy only 20 percent of the overall economy, while the remaining 80 percent of the economy comprises low-productivity industries shielded by various protective measures and regulations.

Harada clearly shows the negative correlation between the degrees of restrictions and the growth rates of productivity in Japanese industries.

Lower Potential Growth Rate

Since the 1980s, the Japanese economy has gone through several structural adjustments that have had nothing to do with globalization per se. These adjustments have lowered its potential growth rate (Japan Development Bank Research Department 1994), and that lower growth rate—the third factor—now serves as an important macroeconomic assumption in discussions of globalization and the economy. Unlike other countries, Japan has experienced this decline in the growth rate during the most intense period of globalization. During the high-growth period of the 1960s, Japan had average annual real growth of 10.1 percent. The twin oil crises of the 1970s brought down the annual rate to 4.6 percent for that decade, still fairly high as growth rates go. In the 1980s, the rate slid to 4.0 percent, and the latest government economic plan, the 1995 interim report by the Subcommittee of the Economic Council, forecasts a potential real annual growth rate of 3.5 percent.

These large declines in the potential growth rate coincided with the formation and collapse of the bubble economy in the late 1980s and early 1990s, and therefore the actual growth rate fell even faster. During the bubble period (1986–1991), the average real economic growth rate was 4.7 percent, and stock prices grew by an average of 5.3 percent per year. From 1992 to 1995, economic growth slowed to 1.2 percent per year, and stock prices declined by 6.2 percent annually. In other words, it was not just a slowdown, but a strong negative acceleration. Furthermore, during this period the population aged far faster than previously predicted, further reducing growth expectations (Obuchi 1997). The National Institute of Population and Social Security Research (1997) finds that the decline in the birthrate is far more dramatic than had been forecast, which has meant that the aging of the population is also proceeding more rapidly. The institute predicts that total population will peak in 2007 and begin to decline thereafter.

Meanwhile, Japanese companies' use of lifetime employment and seniority wage systems has kept the unemployment rate extremely low. This, in turn, has caused Japan to be inordinately wary of job losses. The result has been to increase public anxieties about the structural adjustments that are being triggered by globalization, and to possibly blunt the country's willingness to move forward positively with domestic adjustments so as to improve overall economic welfare.

ASPECTS OF GLOBALIZATION

The term *globalization* is commonly used in Japanese economic debates, but its meaning is extremely complex and nebulous. Four aspects, however, appear most closely related to economic structural adjustment.

The first is the volatile exchange rates caused by the increase in capital movements. It is axiomatic that changes in relative prices will be the most influential factor in economic structural adjustments. In the 1980s and 1990s, changes in exchange rates were the most important factor in altering the relative prices in economies around the world. In Japan, this involved an incredible 224 percent rise, from ¥260.24 against the dollar just prior to the Plaza Accord of 1985 to ¥80.3 at the peak in 1995. The yen also appreciated against major Asian currencies, as is seen in the 608.1 percent rise against the yuan.

Over the short term, volatile foreign exchange markets became a policy problem because export industries were depressed and a high-yen slump ensued. In concrete terms, the government was forced to resort to frequent stimulus packages to alleviate the slump. These economic programs eventually expanded the fiscal deficit and produced problems in the fiscal structure. Longer term, the rise of the yen has become an important force in promoting changes in consumption and industrial structures.

Outgoing direct investments and the consequent international linkage of production constitute the second aspect. The new activity in outgoing direct investments and the consequent international linkage of production are directly related to exchange rates. Kojima provides a comprehensive analysis and explanation of globalization in which he states, "Economic globalization, especially after the eighties, was sharply accelerated by the rapid expansion of international capital movements, including outgoing direct investments. . . . Under the GATT system, free trade expanded and the economies of the world became more interdependent, but capital movements, and particularly direct investments in offshore production, integrated the world more than even trade" (1990, iv). Indeed, Japan's offshore production rate (the ratio of foreign production to domestic production) has reached 8.6 percent (1994), which is lower than the United States' 25.2 percent (1993) or Germany's 21.3 percent (1993), but a vast expansion from only 3.2 percent in 1986. In essence, Japan transferred a large portion of its productive facilities to other countries in a short period of time.

Third is trade liberalization. Increased pressure for freer trade has been brought to bear by three routes. First was liberalization through international organizations such as the General Agreement on Tariffs and Trade (GATT) and its successor, the World Trade Organization (WTO). Second was the promotion of more liberal trade by regional economic arrangements such as the North American Free Trade Agreement (NAFTA), the European Union, and the Asia-Pacific Economic Cooperation (APEC) forum. Third were bilateral negotiations on freer trade. The debate still rages on which of these is the most desirable technique for promoting free trade, but the most cogent view is probably that the "triple track" approach of global, regional, and bilateral negotiations supplement each other to contribute to greater liberalization overall. Clearly, other countries will use all three to pressure Japan.

The pressure for liberalization grew as former socialist states began to move toward market economies, expanding the size of the global market. Takenaka (1995) estimates that in the mid-1970s the market economy had a population of about 2.7 billion people and finds that it has roughly doubled today to about 5.5 billion. In Japanese policy debates, talk of greater worldwide pressure for trade liberalization and the expansion in the size of the market economy is often accompanied by the term *megacompetition*. The increase in competitive pressure works through market mechanisms to expose, in different forms, the distortions in systems and policies, and therefore has the effect of underscoring for society the need for structural adjustment.

Technological change, particularly rapid advances in communications and information technology and the change in production technology paradigms, is a fourth dimension to globalization. Advances in communication and information technology have vastly changed the nature of market transactions in the financial sector by making it possible to move large amounts of capital instantaneously. In addition, today's high-tech industries, and indeed many other important industries, are subject to economies of scale and economies of networks that give a predominant advantage to those companies that are successful in capturing and expanding their share of a market early and using that position to reduce their average costs. Furthermore, this competition for market share takes place on a global scale and creates in its wake global standards and benchmarks. This, in turn, necessitates changes in competition and technology policies.

The paradigm shift for production technology has both accelerated the competition in global markets and changed the nature of that competition. A first mover's advantage creates technology lock-ins that bring positive feedback to competition. Recognition of these changes caused Kojima to conclude, "Changes in the economic and eventually political structures of the world will necessitate changes in the rules that govern this system. The most important change will be the revisions that are mandated in the concepts of the traditional state and sovereignty. The system of interdependence and globalism is a system that demands a partial relinquishment of sovereignty" (1990, v–vi).

DOMESTIC POLICY DEBATE ON GLOBALIZATION

Globalization influences the Japanese economy in many different ways and is central to many domestic policy debates. This is particularly true of those structural adjustments that rest primarily on deregulation. There is recognition that the top priority must be to adapt the economy to globalization and restore its vigor, but there is also deeply ingrained skepticism about the market mechanisms on which the deregulation argument is based.

Deregulation

Reforms to Japan's economic structure have been debated since the early 1980s. The initial impetus to the argument that emphasized the need for deregulation-driven structural reform came from the Maekawa Report, published by a private advisory group to then–Prime Minister Nakasone Yasuhiro in 1986. This report focused on how to deal with Japan's external surpluses, and it was much criticized for its attempt to posit external surpluses as a policy objective. The Japanese economy performed well during the late 1980s, so there was no pressing need perceived for the structural reforms advocated by the report. The situation changed dramatically when the economy began to slow in the 1990s. Reinvigorating the economy with deregulation-driven structural adjustments became the most important challenge for Japanese policymakers. Today, structural reform is discussed not because of the need to remedy external imbalances, but from the broader perspective of how to adapt the Japanese economy to the march of globalization.

Markets versus Regulations Many commentators emphasize the need to deregulate the economy, but Itō (1992) provides perhaps the most succinct positioning of deregulation within the larger Japanese framework. In examining deregulation's theoretical underpinnings, he points out that there are reasons for regulation other than market failure. Excessive competition, for instance, may serve as a reason for regulations that limit market entry. Itō also argues that the Japanese economy is clearly overregulated, but a large gap exists between seeking to move in the direction of deregulation and the simplistic arguments that ascribe all power to the markets.

Many of those who argue in favor of deregulation share Itō's perceptions. In contrast, Uchihashi (1995) has consistently opposed deregulation. He criticizes simplistic faith in all-powerful markets, and uses the deregulation of the U.S. airline industry to argue that the facts do not support the contention that deregulation lowers prices. Uchihashi (1997) has compiled a collection of dialogues between himself and other economists who are either negative or skeptical about deregulation. Among them, Sawa Takamitsu argues that "we should get rid of regulations on market entrance, but there are other regulations like those on the environment that we should tighten"(85). This is in one sense an objection to the idea of "universal deregulation." Uzawa Hirofumi contends that "there is a mechanism for maintaining the stability of society that exists somewhere between state management and market functions. . . . Social overhead capital should be managed according to community standards and at the community level, as close to the residents as possible"(20). Sawa's position is not all that far from Itō's, and Uzawa too takes issue with regulation led by the central government.

Others consider deregulation from the position of comparative institutional analysis. Aoki and Okuno (1996) note that systems and institutions are dependent on their history and that even the U.S. economy, which seems to take deregulation as its goal, is still regulated (if in a different form than Japan). They then argue, "The most important message of comparative institutional analysis is that there are many different kinds of systems—the current system is not set in stone, it changes" (12). When moving to a new system, "the most important point to emphasize is the dynamism that exists within the system" because this "produces competition, which enables new institutions and mechanisms to be discovered and built" (13). Although Aoki and Okuno emphasize competition, they do not limit themselves to the competition created by neoclassical market mechanisms.

The Impact of Deregulation   Another economic debate focuses on the domestic-foreign price differential, which is one of the primary reasons given for deregulation. Here, there is a significant empirical literature. For example, Maki (1996) uses a consumer demand function to verify how high Tokyo price levels are in comparison to those of cities in other countries. He found that in 1993 prices in Tokyo were about 30 percent more than those in New York and about 40 percent higher than in London, Berlin, and Paris. In a similar vein, Sazanami, Urata, and Kawai (1995) find that if the gap between import prices and domestic producer prices is considered to be a handicap—that is, a trade barrier—then in 1989 alone tariff and nontariff barriers cost Japanese consumers ¥10 trillion to ¥15 trillion. When producer profits and tariff revenues are deducted, the total loss to the Japanese economy was ¥1.1 trillion to ¥2.4 trillion.

Kimura, Kawai, and Tanaka (1996) use a similar technique as Sazanami et al. to find that imperfect competition and trade barriers exist for the domestic production of materials industries such as chemicals, petroleum and coal products, glass and ceramics, and steel. Moreover, these broadly defined barriers have expanded over the past 10 years for most imported goods. This finding indicates that Japan has not made any progress in opening its markets.

Most empirical analyses view deregulation as contributing greatly to reinvigorating the Japanese economy because of the productivity gains engendered. The Economic Planning Agency (1994) says that competition promotion would raise productivity to four-fifths of the U.S. levels in five years and add 1.6 percentage points to Japan's gross domestic product (GDP) growth rate. The Industrial Structure Council (1994, 1995) says that Japan could expect real GDP growth rates of 3.0 percent per year from 1996 to 2000, but warns that growth will be only 1.6 percent if reforms are postponed. The Economic Planning Agency (1997) argues that from fiscal 1998 to fiscal 2003, deregulation would increase growth by an average of 0.9 percentage point a year, which would add 5.8 percent to real GDP levels in 2003. Meanwhile, the consumer price growth rate would decline by an average of 1.2 percentage points a year, so that consumer prices would be 7.3 percent lower in 2003. This would occur without any change in the unemployment rate, the agency says, because deregulation of the labor market would enhance the adjustment function for the supply and demand of labor.

Kawai (1996, 1997) performs detailed analyses of the impact of deregulation on specific sectors. Simulations with his general equilibrium model, which includes 162 industrial sectors, yield the following conclusions: First, deregulation will increase productivity in all industries, bringing down prices and expanding consumption and investment. This will add 10.8 percent to the GDP, or the equivalent of an ¥800,000 per household increase in the consumer surplus in the long run. Second, the effects of deregulation will be greatest in the agriculture, forestry, and fishing; wholesaling; and transportation and telecommunications sectors. It will also have an income redistribution effect because the price reduction will most benefit low-income households. Third, there will be labor movement involving 8.4 percent of the total work force. If movement is impossible, however, this will translate directly into unemployment. In particular, the elderly will lose jobs in the agriculture, forestry, and fishing as well as wholesaling sectors.

Incoming Direct Investment　Globalization has brought an increase in cross-border activities, and many Japanese companies have been quick to move overseas. Few foreign companies, however, have set up operations in Japan. Inasmuch as foreign companies have different kinds of expertise and strengths than Japanese companies, their movement into Japan would invigorate domestic markets. Their absence presents a serious problem for the future of the Japanese economy.

Two chief analyses have been done on this point. Urata (1996) did a cross-country analysis of Organization of Economic Cooperation and Development (OECD) members to confirm that direct investment into Japan from 1990 to 1993 was only 18 percent of expected levels. Shinozaki and Endō (1997) use cross-country data in a regression analysis that confirms that from an international perspective, investments into Japan are indeed low. Both studies point to the same factors as possible impediments: high costs (for rent, wages, raw materials, and taxes); demanding user standards; culture (language), business practices, and other customs; difficulty in attracting talented staff because of the illiquidity of the labor market; and the lack of specialist institutions and people to provide mediation, support services for the public (legal, regulatory), and business information.

Financial Market Liberalization: Japan's Big Bang Reforms

A more specialized debate focuses on the financial sector. There has recently been much talk of the need for financial system reform and many recommendations have been made. This activity stems from recognition of the potential for instability and regulation to hollow out Japan's financial markets. Japan's Big Bang reforms are a policy response to this argumentation.

The Economic Council (1996) recommends a detailed and comprehensive liberalization and deregulation program, contending that globalization necessitates the removal of the barriers that compartmentalize the financial services industry, financial holding companies being allowed, the regulations on asset transactions being lifted, and the government moving to a rules-based administrative style. It calls on the government to complete all of these reforms by 1999. Horiuchi (1997) argues that the legal and regulatory frameworks that define the Japanese financial system and the mechanisms that actually operate on rapidly growing financial and capital markets lack consistency. He takes issue with traditional regulatory practices, for instance, seeking consensus on the introduction of new products; the tax system, as exemplified by the securities trading tax; insufficient information disclosure; and the firewalls between different sectors of the financial services industry. He also points to the moral hazard problem—the more serious the bad-debt crisis becomes, the riskier it is for financial institutions to do anything at all, and the greater the chance that they will procrastinate, thus driving up the ultimate costs.

Komine (1997) believes that the globalization of finance has produced an international "competition among systems" that necessitates a shift from traditional financial services to areas requiring more advanced expertise. Japanese finance, he warns, is losing in this competition. He describes analytical findings that suggest that the economic effect of the Big Bang reforms would raise the total factor productivity of the financial services industry by 27.9 percent in four years. Finance would benefit more than other industries. Komine also suggests that Japanese finance has lacked international competitiveness because it has been too heavily regulated. Absent the regulations, it has the potential to be among the world leaders, just like Japanese manufacturing.

Suzuki (1997) sees grave problems with the sequencing of the liberalization measures. Suzuki asserts that the amendments to the Foreign Exchange and Foreign Trade Control Law, which took effect in April 1998, are essential to preventing the hollowing of Japanese finance and reestablishing Japan to a position alongside New York and London as one of the world's three most influential international financial centers. However, Suzuki contends that amending the Foreign Exchange Law as the first step of the Big Bang reforms could prove problematic. Interest rates will still be regulated (the fixed issuing rate for short-term government securities), stock trading fees and other fees will still be fixed at what by international comparison are high rates, the securities trading tax and the exchange tax will still raise trading costs, and withholding taxes will still be deducted from the interest received by nonresidents. In short, domestic markets will remain just as difficult and expensive to trade in as ever. Without other reforms, Japan residents will be encouraged to transfer their assets to settlement and investment accounts overseas and this, Suzuki says, could indeed promote financial hollowing. He urges that domestic regulations be relaxed quickly to avoid this.

Tachibanaki, Yamamoto, and Kasamatsu (1996) have made recommendations concerning the tax system that take a different approach than Suzuki's. They attempt to quantitatively verify whether the financial markets are hollowing. The value of trading handled by the Tokyo Stock Exchange was in excess of US$1 trillion from 1987 to 1990, but has slumped in the 1990s and is now lower than that of the

London market. Foreign companies turn to other markets for listing, and some have even delisted their shares in Tokyo. On foreign markets, Samurai bond (yen-denominated foreign bonds) issues have slumped, whereas Euroyen bond issues are up sharply. Foreign exchange trading in 1993 was only at about 70 percent of 1989–1990 levels. The authors find four reasons for this hollowing: (a) the high cost of doing business (wages, rent, fees, corporate taxes); (b) regulations and customs that make new product approvals and licensing unbearably slow; (c) differences in accounting systems; and (d) other drawbacks such as language, lack of infrastructure, and lower living standards.

However, Tachibanaki et al. also point out that the effective corporate tax rate is low, as is taxation on interest and dividend incomes. Tax systems are, at any rate, determined by domestic conditions, and Tachibanaki et al. warn against facilely linking them to the debate on hollowing. They also look askance at arguments that companies are fleeing to the cheaper markets of Hong Kong and Singapore, or that Japan's securities trading tax is causing a problem. Singapore and Hong Kong, they point out, have little choice but to hinge their fortunes on finance. Japan has an internationally competitive manufacturing sector and is thus in a different position. Therefore, Japan does not need to follow Singapore and Hong Kong in making policy decisions. Rather, Japan should carve out a position for itself that is complementary to its markets. Tachibanaki et al. propose lowering listing standards and relaxing other regulations to bring down fees, and bringing accounting standards and disclosure requirements in line with international norms.

Employment Issues

Employment issues have already surfaced several times in this survey of the deregulation debate. As cited earlier, Kawai (1996, 1997) contends that one of the negative effects of deregulation will be the movement of 8.4 percent of the work force, and warns that unless labor movement is possible, this will translate directly into unemployment. The job losses will be heaviest among older workers in the agriculture, forestry, and fishery as well as wholesaling sectors, which means that jobs for the elderly will be an important issue alongside facilitating labor movements, diversifying employment patterns, and developing human resources. Yashiro and the Japan Economic Research Center (1995) find that if deregulation reduces the relative unit labor costs of nonmanufacturing compared with manufacturing to U.S. levels, it will result in 12.55 million excess workers. If these excess workers are absorbed by the new demand for labor created by deregulation, then real GDP will increase by 18.7 percent, they claim. Shimada's (1997) simulation analysis suggests that the rectification of the domestic-foreign price differential will result in 11.2 million excess workers, but the decline in prices (and other factors) will increase demand and create 10.1 million new jobs. The Economic Planning Agency (1997) likewise finds that productivity gains will reduce the demand for labor over the short term, and notes that the unemployment rate in 2003 will be slightly higher than it would have been had structural reforms not been made.

Regardless of whether deregulation goes forward, the movement of production offshore will have a serious impact on domestic jobs. Fukao (1995) analyzes the possible impact of overseas production on domestic employment. He finds that the long-term effects will be primarily on the labor share, and according to his calculations (which come with limitations and conditions) the effect will not be that large. Over the short- and medium-term, however, an analysis of the electrical machinery industry indicates that an increase in overseas production will have a negative impact on domestic production. This has not yet caused a serious job problem in Japan because the overseas production rate in the manufacturing sector is still low, but if Japanese manufacturers continue to move into Asia, there is indeed the potential for job problems. Fukao also points out that serious adjustment problems from offshore expansion could affect specific industries, job categories, and geographical regions. By contrast, Kuwahara (1994) underscores the large impact that globalization has had on jobs, particularly those for unskilled workers, in other developed countries. Japan's performance has been comparatively good so far, but Kuwahara warns that jobs can no longer be taken for granted. The Industrial Structure Council (1996) says that if nothing is done, manufacturing will shed 1.24 million jobs in the next five years. In its 1994 report, the council calculated that if Japan failed to deregulate and make other reforms, 4.85 million people would be out of work in the year 2000; with reforms, there would be only 1.7 million without jobs.

All these studies indicate that globalization will likely have an impact on jobs. Although deregulation will have a negative impact on jobs, the Industrial Structure Council (1994) finds that the impact will be even more serious if deregulation and other reforms are not made. The development of programs to smooth out the employment adjustments must also be addressed.

To improve the supply-and-demand adjustment functions of the labor market, the Industrial Structure Council (1995, 1996) and Keidanren (Japan Federation of Economic Organizations) (1996) advocate encouraging paid job referral services, liberalizing temporary job agencies, and bringing greater flexibility to working hours. The Economic Council (1996) and Shimada (1997) support self-improvement programs for white-collar workers, who do not take well to group training and referral services, and the creation of a system to evaluate the aptitudes and abilities of these individuals and provide appropriate information based on these evaluations.

These programs to enhance the supply-and-demand adjustment functions of the labor market would also help to remove impediments to incoming direct investment, and would encourage foreign companies to set up operations in Japan. Deregulation-oriented labor market reform is also an important component in policies to adapt to globalization. Labor market reform will, of course, encourage changes in such Japanese-style labor practices as lifetime employment and seniority wages, but Seike (1996) argues that such reforms cannot be made all at once because they impinge deeply on the life planning of the individual. For example, under the seniority wage system, young workers tolerate low wages because they expect higher pay when they reach middle age. It would be unfair to these workers once they reach middle age to decide to pay them commensurate with their current contribution to the company. Seike advocates introducing employment and wage reforms as early as possible, but enacting them slowly.

Macroeconomic Balances

Structural reform that is driven by globalization and deregulation influences both macroeconomic balances and the effectiveness of macroeconomic policy. Here, we review structural reform as it affects the investment and savings balance, and look at studies of financial liberalization and macroeconomic policy, and of the need for policies to control total demand.

Investment and Savings Balance and Structural Reform   The Maekawa Report advocated deregulation-driven structural reform to cut external surpluses. Komiya (1994) takes issue with this from the perspective of the investment and savings balance. He argues that the current account can be divided into a "trend portion" and a "cyclical portion." The difference between trend savings and investment will determine the trend current account, and the effective exchange rate (read, "terms of trade") between two countries will have no influence in determining the investment and savings balances among countries. Were Japan to throw wide open its markets and imports increase as a result, the exchange rate would move in the direction of a weaker yen, which would offset the impact on the current account. Komiya therefore concludes that the current account surpluses posted by Japan since the 1980s are structural, and that they cannot be reduced by structural adjustments that promote imports or by an appreciation of the yen.

Komiya's argument is countered by Akabane (1993a, 1993b), who claims that Japan has foreign surpluses because its industries are internationally competitive, and that these surpluses produce net savings. Koo (1995) also believes that the increase in net exports pushing up the GDP causes high savings. Both conclude that structural adjustments could be used to increase imports, which would shrink the current account surplus and relieve the excess savings.

Yoshikawa (1994) argues that the accuracy of the neoclassical investment and savings balance theory employed by Komiya depends on how great a role the trend portion of the current account actually plays. If the cyclical portion is greater, then Keynesian theory will be more effective, which would indicate that higher export competitiveness expands the current account surplus and import promotion will contract it. Hanazaki (1996) grants that the supply side determines the trend portion and the demand side the cyclical portion, but notes that both sides are closely related and doubts that the clear divisions used by Komiya are theoretically viable.

Ultimately, the conclusions one reaches on the relationship between structural adjustment and external surpluses will depend on the economic model employed. Takenaka, Chida, Hamano, and Miyagaki (1987) use a world model in which demand-driven domestic models are linked to trade and capital matrixes in an attempt to quantitatively measure the effect of structural adjustment. They find that by changing the income elasticity of exports and imports, significant portions of the external deficits of the United States and the external surpluses of Japan could be erased.

The purpose of deregulation-driven structural adjustments has shifted from reducing external surpluses to reinvigorating the domestic economy (though even the Maekawa Report was not concerned exclusively with external surpluses). However, Japan's external surpluses remain huge, and although the argument about them may be on a back burner, no solution has yet been reached. External imbalances are an issue that cannot be ignored in discussions of deregulation.

Financial Liberalization and Macroeconomic Policy   The liberalization and internationalization of financial markets will have a vast impact on the effectiveness of macroeconomic policy. Using the Mandel-Flemming model, which is the simplest available and assumes the perfect substitutability between domestic and foreign assets, fiscal policy has no effect whatsoever. Fiscal expansion will invite higher exchange rates, causing net exports to decline. The key point is, of course, whether domestic and foreign assets can be substituted for each other. Chida and Takenaka (1986) confirm that whether fiscal policy expands or contracts, exchange rates will depend to a large extent on whether domestic and foreign assets can be substituted for each other. More open financial markets can be expected to increase the substitutability of domestic and foreign assets, which will probably reduce the effectiveness of domestic fiscal policy in controlling aggregate demand. However, Asako (1997) maintains that reasons other than those pointed to in the Mandel-Flemming model could explain the decline in the multiplier, so even were a decline to occur it would be difficult to identify the cause with any precision.

Aggregate Demand Control Policies   Aggregate demand control policies are expected to play some role in alleviating the negative influence that globalization will have on jobs. Takenaka sees globalization as providing a positive supply shock to an economy and therefore finds an "undeniable need to manage aggregate demand in a manner that is commensurate with the increase in supply capacity" (1996, 156). He goes on to say that "proactive aggregate demand control policies will be required in order to take advantage of this (positive supply shock)" (157). Shimada advocates "government support for the creation of demand" on a scale that would enable full employment to be maintained. This is necessary, he says, to shut out the deflationary effects of the falling prices that will be brought about by structural reform. Simulation analyses suggest that a ¥100 trillion increase in government investments between now and the end of the century would create more jobs than would be lost to reform.

Taxation

The globalization of the economy has made it easier for people, goods, and money to move across borders, and this makes it possible for companies to locate in countries with lower tax burdens. Therefore, countries where the tax burdens are markedly higher than the norm or where there are structural problems in the tax code risk industrial hollowing. Moreover, personal income tax rates that are extraordinarily high or extremely progressive will undermine the motivation to work and therefore impair economic vigor. In addition, the globalization of the economy and the liberalization of financial flows will diversify cross-border transactions and give them more of a service component. Customs officials, who have traditionally been concerned with taxing goods, are unable to fully monitor cross-border service transactions, and therefore new systems will be required.

In a globalizing Japan, the corporate tax code is seen as most in need of reform. Corporate taxes account for about 24 percent of Japan's tax revenues, which is extremely high compared with Germany, Great Britain, the United States, and other countries. There is little difference between France, Germany, Great Britain, Japan, and the United States in terms of the corporate tax rate, but Japan's effective tax rate, at 49.98 percent, when local corporate taxes are included, is extremely high by comparison. Studies indicate that Japan is high even when the marginal effective tax rate is considered (Business Policy Forum 1986).

Most of the newly industrializing Asian and Association of Southeast Asian Nations (ASEAN) countries have extremely low corporate tax rates, which makes it attractive for Japanese companies to move their operations there. Some worry that this may cause a hollowing of domestic industry. Simultaneously, taxes inhibit foreign companies from locating and investing in Japan. For example, Maekawa (1997) analyzes the direct investments made by the Japanese electrical equipment industry in five ASEAN countries and China over a 10-year period extending from 1985 to 1994. She finds that the closer one comes to the present, the less important wage differences are as a determining factor in direct investments and the more important capital costs adjusted for corporate taxation become. This finding indicates that the hollowing caused by distortions in the Japanese tax structure could become serious indeed.

Industry has demanded a reduction in corporate tax rates, and the government has generally agreed to move in that direction. A report issued by the Corporate Taxation Subcommittee of the Tax Commission in November 1996 says that the current rate of 37.5 percent should be cut to about 35 percent. However desirable this may be, the report also points out that Japan is in difficult fiscal straits and "not in a situation that would allow substantial tax reduction policies to be implemented at this time." Instead, the report advocates widening the tax base and reforming the Article 38 items (by, for example, eliminating the reserve against bonuses) so as to provide funding for a reduction in the basic rate. Reduction of the real tax burden is "an issue for the future."

Although the current national corporate tax rate of 37.5 percent is somewhat higher than in other countries, it is not that much higher. The effective tax rate is high because of local corporate taxes and corporate residential taxes. Hashimoto (1996) argues that local corporate taxes should be included in any discussion of reducing the tax burden on companies. Given the mounting pressure to decentralize authority to local governments, this will necessitate a debate on how tax resources are to be divided between the central government and individual regions. Others point out the need to widen the tax base from the perspective of economic neutrality as well as reducing the tax burdens on companies. Even the Tax Commission report notes the need to eliminate a plethora of reserves and to "organize and rationalize" tax breaks.

Another issue raised by globalization and corporate tax reform is the taxation of companies with losses. At present, the 37.5 percent tax rate applies only to the largest companies, which make up less than 1 percent of all incorporated entities (about 2.4 million). Nonetheless, the taxes paid by these large companies account for about 60 percent of total corporate tax revenues. Honma and Saitō (1997) maintain that this tax structure has exacerbated industrial hollowing. Large companies that bear extremely heavy tax burdens have a strong incentive to move overseas, whereas it is advantageous for lightly taxed smaller companies to remain at home.

In addition, about 63 percent of these 2.4 million companies operate in the red. Some argue that companies with losses should also be taxed, but the reason why there are so many such companies in the first place is because Japan has an extremely progressive tax code that creates a marginal tax rate on personal income that is high by international standards. Thus, incorporation is a means of avoiding income tax. Therefore, a reform of corporate taxation will eventually entail a reform of income tax as well (Miyaguchi 1997).

FUTURE TASKS

The Japanese economy contains sectors that have already been baptized into globalization and are making efforts to adjust to it and sectors that have yet to be globalized. This two-tiered structure has become more prominent in the 1990s. Manufacturing is the obvious representative of a sector that has already globalized. With expanding exports, the switch from exporting to overseas production, and the establishment of an international division of labor, the history of Japanese manufacturing parallels the history of Japan's adaptation to globalization. The financial services industry, on the other hand, is only now coming to grips with globalization as it prepares for the Big Bang reforms. The image of the Japanese banking industry being crushed by onerous Bank of International Settlement (BIS) burdens is an accurate reflection of the perception among the Japanese public that Japan has an economy that is small and frail. Even those banks for which international operations are not essential have found adapting to globalization (clearing BIS standards) unavoidable. The cost of the domestic adjustments has surfaced in the form of the recent credit crunch.

The extremely low levels of incoming direct investments point to the directions that will be taken in future globalization. Purely statistical comparisons show a large gap between Japan and other developed countries in terms of incoming direct investments. Therefore, any further globalization of Japan will likely bring with it an expansion in such investments. As Toys "R" Us has demonstrated, foreign companies can enter and have a vast impact on the domestic market. Productivity gains are often pointed to as one of the positive effects of deregulation, but how much is gained will depend to a great extent on whether there are new entrants into the market in the form of foreign companies with superior managerial resources.

Three points are crucial to any discussion of globalization and the domestic adjustments involved: (a) declines in the long-term potential growth rate, (b) the timing and speed of globalization, and (c) the cost of domestic adjustments. All are interrelated.

We have examined the argument that falling long-term potential growth rates tracked the trend toward globalization in Japan. Indeed, Japan's potential growth path shifted lower during the prolonged low growth of the 1990s. The speed with which the population is aging makes it clear that low real GDP growth rates are to be expected over the long term. Japan has already experienced a downward shift in its potential growth rate following the high-growth period. That shift coincided with soaring energy prices, so Japan responded to the lower growth path by energy-conserving adjustments that allowed it to use scarce resources more efficiently. In the future, aging demographics will mean that labor is the scarce resource. If Japan can efficiently use its labor resources, it should maintain growth on a per capita GDP basis, even with no growth in total GDP. Domestic deregulation, international divisions of labor, and the entrance of foreign companies—in short, globalization—will contribute to the more efficient use of labor resources.

However, an argument persists over the short-term timing and speed of globalization. Unlike oil shocks, the aging population problem has emerged slowly, and there are options in the timing and speed of the response to it. The domestic adjustments required by globalization will have a substantial short-term deflationary effect through employment and other mechanisms. Almost all empirical analyses agree on this point. Shimada (1997), for example, advocates a large government stimulus to create the demand that would mitigate these deflationary pressures. A recession is looming in Japan, and this may cause some to conclude that now is not the time to make domestic adjustments such as deregulation. Certainly, the costs of domestic adjustment would have been smaller in the late 1980s when the economy was roaring, but as long as the economy is expanding steadily there is little incentive to initiate adjustments that may well undermine the boom. We also examined the issue of technological change and noted that the speed of adjustment was an important factor in capturing a first mover's advantage. Ultimately, it will be difficult if not impossible to simultaneously achieve the three objectives of short-term economic stimulus, long-term structural reform, and the other long-term challenge, fiscal construction. A political judgement must be made on which receives priority. Shimada (1997), for example, advises that fiscal construction be temporarily deferred.

Even taking into account the deflationary effect of domestic adjustments, the costs of globalization will be large. The signs of this happening could already be seen at the end of 1997 when two large financial firms collapsed. However, if incoming direct investments increase and more foreign companies enter the Japanese market, there will also be new job opportunities. Unfortunately, the low liquidity in the labor market remains an impediment to incoming direct investments. Enhancing the labor market's ability to adjust supply and demand would contribute both to reducing the costs of direct investments in Japan and to easing the entry of foreign companies, thereby mitigating the overall cost of adjustment. Labor market reform is therefore urgent. However, as Seike (1996) argues, care must be taken with the age groups who have accepted low wages under the traditional seniority wage system.

Globalization of the economy is not itself the ultimate goal. Rather, we must ask how much this will contribute to the stabilization and improvement of living standards. There are few who would completely reject the significance of globalization. But opinions differ as to the timing and sequencing of globalization, the costs of domestic adjustments to globalization, and how those costs should be paid. The globalization of the Japanese economy has so far involved expanding exports, expanding imports, and expanding foreign production. The globalization of the future will likely involve an increased presence in Japan of companies from other countries.

BIBLIOGRAPHY

"Action Plan for Reforming and Recreating the Economic Structure." 1997. Cabinet decision (16 May).

Akabane Takao. 1993a. "Sakadachi shita kuroji chochiku chōkarongi" (Standing the surplus/savings argument on its head). *Shūkan Tōyō Keizai* (28 August).

———. 1993b. "Aiesu baransuron no gokai" (Misunderstanding investment and savings balance theory). *Nihon Keizai Sentā Kaihō* (1 November).

Aoki Masahiko and Okuno Masahiro. 1996. *Keizai shisutemu no hikaku seido bunseki* (Comparative institutional analysis of economic systems). Tokyo: Tokyo Daigaku Shuppankai.

Asako Kazumi. 1997. "Zaisei/zaiseiseisaku to makuro keizai" (Fiscal spending, fiscal policy and macroeconomics). In Asako Kazumi, Fukuda Shin'ichi, and Yoshino Naoyuki, eds. *Gendai makuro keizai bunseki: tenkanki no Nihon keizai* (Contemporary macroeconomic analysis: the Japanese economy at a transition). Tokyo: Tokyo Daigaku Shuppankai.

Business Policy Forum. 1986. *Waga kuni kigō zeisei no hyōka to kadai* (Japanese corporate taxes: assessment and challenges). Tokyo: Kigyō Katsuryoku Kenkyūsho.

Chida Ryōkichi and Takenaka Heizō. 1986. "Kogata sekai moderu no kaihatsu to seisaku shumirēshon bunseki" (Development of a small world model and policy simulation analysis). *Nihon Keizai Kenkyū*, no. 16: 15–28.

Economic Council. 1996. *Kōdō Keikaku Iinkai wākingu gurūpu hōkokusho* (Report of the working group to the Activities Planning Committee). Tokyo: Economic Planning Agency.

Economic Planning Agency. 1994. *Gendai no rakuichi-rakuza: kiseikanwa to keizai kasseika* (A modern "free market": deregulation and economic invigoration). Tokyo: Ministry of Finance, Printing Bureau.

———. 1997. *Keizai hakusho* (Economic white paper). Tokyo: Ministry of Finance, Printing Bureau.

Fukao Kyōji. 1995. "Nihon kigō no kaigai seisan katsudō to kokunai rōdō" (Overseas production activities of Japanese companies and domestic labor). *Nihon Rōdō Kenkyū Zasshi*, no. 424: 2–12.

Hanazaki Masaharu. 1996. *Amerika no bōeki akaji, Nihon no bōeki kuroji* (America's trade deficit and Japan's trade surplus). Tokyo: Tōyō Keizai.

Harada Yutaka. 1996. *Nihon keizai no haiboku* (The defeat of the Japanese economy). Tokyo: Tōyō Keizai Shinpōsha.

Hashimoto Tōru. 1996. "Keizai gurōbaruka to zeisei" (Globalization of the economy and taxation). In *Keizai gurōbaruka to zeisei* (Globalization of the economy and taxation). Tokyo: Japan Taxation Research Association.

Honma Masaaki and Saitō Shin, eds. 1997. *Dōsuru hōjinzei kaikaku* (What to do about corporate tax reform?). Osaka: Federation of Taxpayers Associations.

Horiuchi Akiyoshi. 1997. "Kinyū shijō to kinyū gyōsei no seigōka ga kyūmu" (Urgent need for consistency in financial markets and financial regulation). *Nihon Keizai Kenkyūsentā Kaihō* (1 June): 12–16.

Industrial Structure Council. 1994. *Nijūichi seiki no sangyō kōzō* (Industrial structure in the twenty-first century). Tokyo: Ministry of International Trade and Industry, Industrial Policy Bureau.

———. 1995. *Nijūichi seiki eno Nihon keizai saiken no shinario* (Scenario for rebuilding the Japanese economy in the twenty-first century). Tokyo: Ministry of International Trade and Industry, Industrial Policy Bureau.

———. 1996. *Sōgōbukai kihon mondai shō-iinkai chūkan torimatome* (Interim report of the Basic Problems Subcommittee). Tokyo: Ministry of International Trade and Industry, Industrial Policy Bureau.

Itō Motoshige. 1997. *Zemināru kokusai keizai nyūmon* (Introductory seminar on international economics). Tokyo: Nihon Keizai Shimbun Press.

Itō Takatoshi. 1992. *Shōhisha jūshi no keizaigaku* (Consumer-oriented economics). Tokyo: Nihon Keizai Shimbun Press.

Japan Development Bank Research Department, ed. 1994. *Nihon no senzai seichōryoku* (Japan's latent growth capacity). Tokyo: Nihon Keizai Shimbun Press.

Kawai Hinoki. 1996. "Shijōkaihō no ippan kinkō bunseki" (A general equilibrium analysis of market liberalization in Japan). *Nihon Keizai Kenkyū*, no. 31: 133–165.

———. 1997. "Naigai kakakusa to shijō kaihō no keizai kōka" (Domestic-foreign price differentials and the economic effect of market opening). *The Keizai Seminar* (September): 40–45.

Keidanren. 1996. "'Miryokuaru Nihon' no sōzō (Creating an attractive Japan). Tokyo: Tōyō Keizai Shinpōsha.

Kimura Fukunari, Kawai Hinoki, and Tanaka Iwao. 1996. "Naigai kakakusa to bōeki shōheki" (Invisible trade barriers and price differentials: evidence from Japanese export, import, and domestic price data). *Mita Journal of Economics* 89(2): 85–100.

Kojima Akira. 1990. *Gurōbarizashon* (Globalization). Tokyo: Chūō Kōronsha.

Komine Takao. 1997. "Kinyū no gurōbarizashon to Nihon bigguban" (Financial globalization and the Japanese Big Bang). *Kokusai Kinyū* (1 August): 16–21.

Komiya Ryūtarō. 1994. "Kokusai shūshi mondai ni tsuite no oboegaki" (Memo on balance of payments issues). In Itō Motoshige, Ministry of International Trade and Industry, and Training Institute of International

Trade and Industry, eds. *Bōeki kuroji no gokai: Nihon keizai no dokoga mondaika* (Misunderstanding the trade surplus: where the problems are in the Japanese economy). Tokyo: Tōyō Keizai Shinpōsha.

Koo, Richard. 1995. "Aiesuron no jubaku, 'Nichibei' madowasu" (The spell of investment and savings balance theory confuses Japan and the U.S.). *Nihon Keizai Shimbun* (18 May).

Kuwahara Yasuo. 1994. "Gurobaruka ga umu shitsugyō no kyōi" (The threat of unemployment brought by globalization). *Ekonomisuto* (12 July): 54–59.

Maekawa Satoko. 1997. "Kigyō no kaigai shinshutsu to hōjinzei futan" (The movement of companies overseas and corporate taxation). Mimeograph.

Maki Atsushi. 1996. "Nihon shijō no heisasei: naigai kakakusa no reishō" (The price gap between domestic and international markets: theoretical cost of living index approach). *Nihon Keizai Kenkyū*, no. 31: 85–106.

Miyaguchi Sadao. 1997. In Honma Masaaki and Saitō Shin, eds. *Dōsuru hōjinzei kaikaku* (What to do about corporate tax reform?) Osaka: Federation of Taxpayers Associations.

Nakatani Iwao. 1987. *Bōdaresu ekonomī* (Borderless economy). Tokyo: Nihon Keizai Shimbun Press.

National Institute of Population and Social Security Research. 1997. *Nihon no shōrai suitei jinkō* (Population projections for Japan). Tokyo: National Institute of Population and Social Security Research.

Nishikawa Shunsaku. 1985. *Fukuzawa Yukichi to sannin no kōshintachi* (Fukuzawa Yukichi and Three Juniors). Tokyo: Nippon Hyōronsha.

Obuchi Kan. 1997. *Shōshika jidai no Nihon keizai* (The Japanese economy in an age of low birth rates). Tokyo: NHK Press.

Sazanami Yōko, Urata Shūjirō, and Kawai Keiki. 1995. *Naigai kakakusa no keizaigaku* (The economics of domestic-foreign price differentials). Tokyo: Tōyō Keizai Shinpōsha.

Seike Atsushi. 1996. "Rokujūgo sai keizoku koyōsei ga naze hitsuyōka" (Why do we need continuous employment to 65?). *Ronsō* (November): 112–121.

Shimada Haruo. 1994. "Shin sangyō koyō sōshutsu keikaku wo isoge" (Hurry up with the new industry and jobs creation plan!) *Chūō Kōron* (January): 48–62.

———. 1997. *Nihon saifujō no jirenma* (Concepts for reinvigorating Japan). Tokyo: Tōyō Keizai Shinpōsha.

Shinozaki Akihiko and Endō Kazumi. 1997. *Tainichi chokusetsu tōshi to gaishikei kigyō no bunseki* (Analysis of income: direct investment and foreign companies). Chōsa No. 225. Tokyo: Japan Development Bank.

Suzuki Toshio. 1997. *Bigguban no jirenma* (The dilemma of the Big Bang). Tokyo: Tōyō Keizai Shinpōsha.

Tachibanaki Toshiaki, Yamamoto Yōko, and Kasamatsu Hiromitsu. 1996. "Tokyo kinyū shijō kasseika eno michi" (The road to revitalizing the Tokyo financial markets). *Fainansharu Rebyū* (January): 60–77.

Takenaka Heizō. 1995. *Minfuron* (Theory of wealth). Tokyo: Kodansha.

———. 1996. "'Seisaku ron' to shite no Keinzu keizaigaku" (Keynesian economics as a "policy debate"). In Kanamori Hisao and Japan Economic Research Center, eds. *Keinzu wa hontō ni shindanoka* (Is Keynes really dead?). Tokyo: Nihon Keizai Shimbun Press.

Takenaka Heizō, Chida Ryōkichi, Hamano Yutaka, and Miyagaki Jun'ichi. 1987. "Saiteki Seisaku Kyōchō no keiryō bunseki—Sakkusu gata sekai moderu ni yoru gaisō shumirēshon" (Quantitative analysis of optimal policy coordination: forecasting simulation using a Sachs-style world model). *Fainansharu Rebyū* (May): 36–56.

Uchihashi Katsuhito. 1995. *Kisei kanwa toiu akumu* (The nightmare of deregulation). Tokyo: Bungei Shunjū.

———. 1997. *Keizaigaku wa dare no tame ni aruka* (Economics for whom?). Tokyo: Iwanami Shoten.

Urata Shūjirō. 1996. "Tainichi chokusetsu tōshi no genjō to sogai yōin" (Why is foreign investment in Japan so low?). *Nihon Keizai Kenkyū*, no. 31: 66–84.

Wakasugi Takahira. 1988. "Ristorakucharingu to Nihon kigyō no kōdō" (Restructuring and Japanese corporate behavior). In Itō Motoshige, Ueda Kazuo, and Takenaka Heizō, eds. *Pāsupekutibu Nihon keizai* (Perspectives on the Japanese economy). Tokyo: Chikuma Shobō.

Yashiro Naohiro and the Japan Economic Research Center. 1995. *2020 nen no Nihon keizai* (The Japanese economy in 2020). Tokyo: Nihon Keizai Shimbun Press.

Yoshikawa Hiroshi. 1994. "Keijō shūshi no bunseki—Keinzu riron no tachiba kara" (Current account analysis: from a Keynsian perspective). In Itō Motoshige, Ministry of International Trade and Industry, and Training Institute of International Trade and Industry, eds. *Bōeki kurogi no gokai: Nihon keizai no dokoga mondaika* (Misunderstanding the trade surplus: where the problems are in the Japanese economy). Tokyo: Tōyō Keizai Shinpōsha.

5 · New Zealand

Paul Dalziel

N EW ZEALAND provides an important case study of the way in which countries can choose to respond to the economic and social forces of globalization. After several decades of economic policies intended to isolate New Zealand's producers and consumers from global trends (Hawke 1985, chap. 9), the New Zealand government decided in 1984 to internationalize the domestic economy, and supported this decision over the following 10 years with a program of economic and social reforms that left no aspect of public policy unexamined. Radical changes in the foreign exchange market, overseas investment and immigration policies, import licensing and tariffs, assistance to agriculture and industry, market regulation, fiscal and monetary policies, industrial relations law, government trading departments, competition law, social welfare income support, and the funding of health and education were all motivated, at least in part, by the desire to address issues that had been raised either by the decision to make New Zealand a more open and internationally competitive market economy or in response to global trends that were seen as unavoidable.

Furthermore, because the government initiated these reforms, a considerable amount of official material is available that explains the fundamental principles used to guide each policy change. The preambles of landmark pieces of legislation such as the Commerce Act 1986, the State-Owned Enterprises Act 1986, the Reserve Bank of New

103

Zealand Act 1989, the Employment Contracts Act 1991, and the Fiscal Responsibility Act 1994 set out the major objectives of these reforms, and the government's annual budget statements are a rich source of information.

Throughout the reform process, a number of books were published examining aspects of the new policy framework (for example, Bollard and Buckle 1987; Boston and Holland 1990; Sandrey and Reynolds 1990; Boston and Dalziel 1992; Duncan and Bollard 1992; Harbridge 1993; Hyman 1994), and four recent volumes provide an overview of the entire period (Massey 1995; Silverstone, Bollard, and Lattimore 1996; Dalziel and Lattimore 1996; Kelsey 1996; see also the article in the *Journal of Economic Literature* by Evans, Grimes, and Wilkinson 1996). Not all of these commentators have been supportive of the reforms (the volume by Kelsey, for example, is particularly critical), but much of the material written in New Zealand has been prepared with an international audience in mind. The New Zealand reforms have attracted considerable worldwide attention, both from those who urge other governments to implement similar policies and from those who argue that the reforms have widened social and economic divisions in the country that should serve as a warning to others.

In New Zealand, globalization generally refers to the spectacular growth in economic activity (particularly business decisions concerning investment and production) that is planned at a global level rather than at the local, regional, or national levels. Globalization has been made possible by recent technological advances that have accelerated the longstanding trend toward the free flow of commodities, manufactured goods, services, financial capital, labor, information, and environmental degradation across national borders. New Zealand policymakers generally take for granted that they have no influence over globalization per se, but can only choose the extent to which domestic producers and consumers will be required or permitted to participate in the process.

The term given to a country's policy of increasing the exposure of its economy to globalization is internationalization (see, for example, Britton 1991; Le Heron 1993; Walker and Fox 1996). Internationalization, in turn, pressures policymakers to introduce policies of domestic adjustment to take full advantage of the opportunities (or to minimize the economic threats) created by globalization, and it is these domestic adjustment policies that are the focus of this chapter. The chapter consists of four parts:

- The events and debates that led to the 1984 decision to internationalize the New Zealand economy after decades of relatively isolationist policies.
- An outline of the policy reforms that were introduced from 1984 to 1994, at least in part to support the internationalization process.
- The major institutions that were involved in providing policy advice and commentary during the reforms, and which continue to pursue a research agenda that includes globalization issues.
- The relationship between globalization and political sovereignty. In the author's opinion, the most fundamental issue raised by New Zealand's response to globalization is the impact it has had, or potentially will have, on political sovereignty. There are widely divergent views within New Zealand about these impacts and whether they are beneficial or contrary to the interests of specific subgroups of the New Zealand population.

THE DECISION TO INTRODUCE REFORM

In the 1950s and 1960s, New Zealand enjoyed one of the highest levels of per capita gross domestic product (GDP) in the world. Economic policies were based on a preferential trade agreement with the United Kingdom, under which New Zealand exported large volumes of meat and dairy products to that country at favorable prices. This arrangement produced sufficient foreign exchange to pay for imported raw materials for processing by an expanding manufacturing sector, which was highly protected from international competition by a strict system of import licensing. The government played an important role in the economy. Not only did it directly regulate much economic activity, but it was also involved as a major provider of services in industries as diverse as banking, insurance, legal services, superannuation services, railways, air travel, bus travel, shipping, engineering and construction, architectural services, port and airport services, electricity and gas, telecommunications, primary produce marketing, coal mining, forestry, oil refining, steel production, printing, broadcasting, hotel accommodation, computing services, postal services, and weather forecasting. Wages were set by annual negotiations between employer organizations and occupation-based trade unions, and the government absorbed any unemployment through increased employment in its various trading activities.

As the United Kingdom moved toward closer integration with the European Union (formally joining the then-named European Economic Community on January 1, 1973), New Zealand lost its favored trading status. Considerable pressure was also created by the first oil shock in 1973–1974. The initial reaction of the New Zealand government was to increase the level of government direction of economic activity. In particular, the government initiated a series of expensive Think Big energy projects in an attempt to reduce the country's level of dependence on imported fuels. It increased subsidies and tax exemptions to farmers and other exporters, boosted its own level of expenditure accommodated by monetary expansion, and raised the amount of regulatory intervention in the economy, culminating in a two-year freeze on all prices, wages, dividends, professional charges, directors' fees, rents, interest rates, and exchange rates from June 1982.

In June 1984, the government called an early general election for July 14, 1984. There was a sustained run on the New Zealand dollar during the election campaign, but the prime minister insisted the Reserve Bank defend the dollar by entering the forward exchange market. On the day after the election, which produced a landslide victory for the opposition Labour Party, the governor of the Reserve Bank announced that New Zealand had exhausted its foreign exchange reserves. The new prime minister devalued the currency by 20 percent, and the Reserve Bank subsequently estimated the cost of defending the overvalued dollar during the election campaign equivalent to 2.25 percent of the year's GDP. At the time, the foreign exchange market was arguably the most effectively regulated market in the economy because all transactions had to be approved by the Reserve Bank; nevertheless, the government incurred a substantial loss through its unsuccessful efforts to resist domestic adjustment to international changes.

There were other symptoms of the failure of the isolationist policies prior to 1984. The government's financial deficit had increased to 6.5 percent of GDP, the current account of the balance of payments had been continuously in deficit since the early 1970s, unemployment had risen to approximately 4.5 percent of the labor force (after being less than 1 percent before 1978), inflation rebounded quickly after the end of the 1982–1984 price freeze, and there had been no sustained growth over the previous 10 years. The New Zealand government convened a three-day economic summit of business, union, and community leaders, who issued a unanimous communiqué at the end of the proceedings. Particularly relevant for the program of reforms that followed was the following paragraph:

> The Conference accepts that we cannot isolate ourselves from the international market place. While the domestic market is very important for employment and income stability, the size of our market means that any increase in living standard would be very limited without external trade. Export earnings provide the means for employment growth. Success in exporting or import substitution with only reasonable assistance provides a test of our efficiency in using resources. (Economic Summit Conference 1984, 304–305)

This unanimous acceptance that New Zealand could no longer remain isolated from the international marketplace set the scene for two significant policy changes that internationalized the New Zealand economy to an extent not known for 50 years or more. The first change was a decision to phase out the system of import licensing that restricted the flow of manufactured goods into New Zealand. Import licensing was introduced in December 1938 as a mechanism to reduce chronic balance-of-payment deficits, but had come to be used as an instrument for protecting domestic manufacturing industries. At the change of government in 1984, approximately 24 percent of imports required a license (Rayner and Lattimore 1991, 47). Five years later, this ratio had been reduced to 5 percent, and the last licenses were removed in June 1992 (Lattimore and Wooding 1996, 331). Thus, there are now no quantitative restrictions on imports into New Zealand, and this internationalization of domestic production (reinforced by reforms to New Zealand's tariff structure) contributed to a 15 percent fall in mainstream manufacturing employment from 1984 to 1995 (Hazledine and Murphy 1996, 359).

The second change involved a substantial liberalization of international capital flows in and out of New Zealand. In the early 1980s, exporters were required to sell foreign exchange to the Reserve Bank of New Zealand within six months of receipt, and there were strict regulations that restricted short-term overseas borrowing by domestic companies and domestic borrowing by overseas-owned companies (Buckle 1987, 241). These requirements and restrictions were all lifted by the end of 1984, so that financial capital could freely flow in and out of the country without hindrance. On March 4, 1985, New Zealand moved to a floating exchange rate regime, and New Zealand's finance sector subsequently has been thoroughly integrated into global financial markets.

THE REFORMS

A wide range of economic reforms accompanied the internationalization of the New Zealand economy through the deregulation of capital and commodity flows from 1984 to 1994. The overall strategy can be described using budget documents presented to Parliament on July 2, 1992 (fig. 1). Although these budget documents were relatively late in the program of reforms, they nevertheless provide a good guide to the model of reform adopted by policymakers throughout the decade. Each of the key elements of the strategy is linked to "international linkages." Richardson described these linkages as follows:

> Through international linkages such as foreign direct investment, New Zealand firms can access the latest technology and knowledge. This helps raise productivity and skill levels, enabling New Zealand firms, regardless of size, to meet the highest quality standards. This in turn makes New Zealand more attractive as a location for overseas firms and New Zealand products more marketable overseas. . . .
>
> There are strong ties between having a stable macro-economy and better international links. The more stable the economy, the easier it will be to attract foreign capital and invest in developing overseas markets. A stable local economy helps firms perceive and adjust to the inevitable shocks from the world economy with the least disruption—perhaps even turning some of them to advantage by dealing with them better than do overseas

Figure 1. The New Zealand Government's Strategy for Economic Growth, June 1992

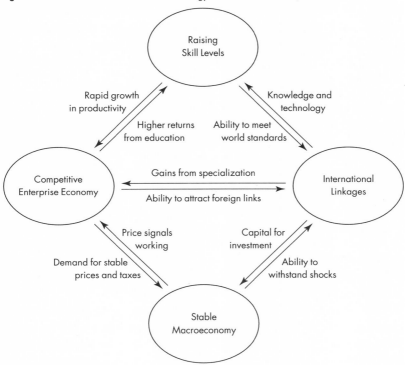

Source: Richardson (1992, 11).

competitors. Access to world sources of capital means that New Zealand is not limited to the levels of domestic savings.

International trade allows New Zealand firms to export what they do best and to import products that can be produced less well here. This scenario heightens competition, enables domestic firms to raise overall productivity, and helps the whole economy—not just the businesses directly concerned. In turn, the more competitive are local businesses, large and small, the greater the likelihood of them attracting foreign investment or developing other sorts of overseas contacts. (1992, 12)

Figure 1 and the budget text just quoted illustrate how the logic of globalization was an integral part of the policies of domestic adjustment implemented in New Zealand after 1984. The above linkages are well understood by economists, of course, and often advocated to policy-makers. New Zealand, however, has been unique in applying this model so consistently and across such a broad range of policy areas in such a short period of time, despite considerable resistance by the electorate at different times.

Equalizing Domestic Prices to International Prices

Prior to 1984, a number of government policies meant that New Zealand producers and consumers did not face international prices. The government gave significant subsidies to farmers (both for outputs and for some inputs) and tax exemptions to nontraditional manufacturing exporters, levied tariffs at different rates on imported goods, imposed ceilings on domestic interest rates, and operated a fixed exchange rate regime in which the international value of the New Zealand dollar was determined by the minister of finance. Within 12 months of the beginning of the reforms in July 1984, all of these subsidies and regulations were either abolished or a timetable for their withdrawal announced.

Thus, the budget on November 8, 1984, announced the progressive elimination of subsidies and tax exemptions to agricultural producers, exporters of manufactured goods, and the state-owned suppliers of electricity and coal. The government also accelerated a process already under way to reduce tariffs across all imported commodities. In 1981, the average tariff was estimated to be 28 percent, but had been reduced to about 7 percent by 1996. The 1995 Budget of the Government announced a further review of tariff levels in 1998, with the aim of moving to zero tariffs at some unspecified future date.

The removal of interest rate controls was one of the first actions of the new government after the July 1984 election, and took place in two stages on July 18 and August 30 that year. Financial institutions were no longer required to meet minimum reserve asset ratios, and the banking sector was opened to new entrants. These financial deregulation policies (amounting to "a transformation which in terms of its scope and rapidity has probably been unequalled in any other country in the OECD region" [Deane 1986, 7]) were in part designed to increase the volume of daily transactions in the New Zealand foreign exchange market until the market was judged to be large enough to support a freely floating exchange rate. The New Zealand dollar was floated in March 1985, and the Reserve Bank has not directly intervened in the foreign exchange market since.

Promoting Competition in Markets

The dismantling of import licenses and the lowering of tariffs increased significantly the competition faced by New Zealand producers in the tradable sector, but several other policies were introduced to promote competition in domestic markets. The government removed restrictions on entry into a number of specific industries and occupations (for example, domestic air travel, road transport, banking, taxi drivers, foreign exchange dealers, and property conveyancers), but more generally the government reformed the Commerce Act so that its purpose was simply "to promote competition in markets within New Zealand" (Commerce Act 1986, Preamble).

In keeping with this objective, Section 27 of the Commerce Act declares that "no person shall enter into a contract or arrangement or arrive at an understanding, containing a provision that has the purpose, or has or is likely to have the effect, of substantially lessening competition in a market." Similarly, Section 36 declares that "no person who has a dominant position in a market shall use that position for the purpose of: (a) restricting the entry of any person into that or any other market; or (b) preventing or deterring any person from engaging in competitive conduct in that or in any other market; or (c) eliminating any person from that or any other market." Later in the act, Section 66 seeks to prevent mergers and takeovers that would create or strengthen a dominant position in a market, unless it "would be likely to result in a benefit to the public which would outweigh any detriment. . . ."

Responsibility for enforcing these competitive provisions lies with the Commerce Commission, subject to appeal to the High Court. The Commerce Commission has significant powers of investigation and enforcement, and is permitted to grant an exemption only if it would likely result in a benefit to the public that would outweigh the lessening in competition. The act does not define "benefit to the public," but the commission has tended to emphasize gains in efficiency that can occur when a larger scale of operation reduces unit costs (economies of scale) or when technological advances allow lower prices.

Corporatizing and Privatizing State-Owned Enterprises

At the change of government in July 1984, the public sector of New Zealand was very large and covered a number of trading activities organized as government departments, each of which was responsible to a minister of the Crown. In December 1985, the government announced that these departments would be converted into state-owned enterprises (SOEs) based on five principles: (a) responsibility for non-commercial functions would be separated from SOEs; (b) managers would be given a principal responsibility of running the SOEs as successful business enterprises; (c) managers would be given the power to make decisions on how to meet agreed performance objectives so that they could be held accountable; (d) unnecessary barriers to competition would be removed; and (e) individual SOEs would be reconstituted under the guidance of boards of directors comprising, generally, members appointed from the private sector.

Twelve months later, these principles were given legislative effect in the State-Owned Enterprises Act 1986. Section 4 of the act states that "the principal objective of every State enterprise shall be to operate as a successful business and, to this end, to be: (a) as profitable and efficient as comparable businesses that are not owned by the Crown; and (b) a good employer; and (c) an organisation that exhibits a sense of social responsibility by having regard to the interests of the community in which it operates and by endeavouring to accommodate or encourage these when able to do so" (1986). Fourteen SOEs (including five organizations, such as Air New Zealand, that were already operating within a corporate structure) were established under this legislation on April 1, 1987, and since then all of the government's trading departments have been corporatized.

In the following years, many of these SOEs were sold to the private sector (privatized), and many of the new owners were overseas companies. Most important among these transactions was the sale of Telecom in September 1990 to a consortium of two American companies (Ameritech Corporation and Bell Atlantic Corporation) for NZ$4.25 billion, the largest sale in the Southern Hemisphere and the fourth largest in the world that year (Duncan and Bollard 1992, 146). The

New Zealand electorate has thus seen a large number of public assets pass into foreign ownership, which has at times been a source of considerable political controversy.

Decentralizing Labor Contracts

Since 1984, labor law in New Zealand had been based on three key principles. The first principle was that employed workers should belong to some union, normally on the basis of the worker's occupation ("compulsory unionism"). The second principle was that the minimum terms and conditions of employment negotiated at a national level by the relevant union and employers' organizations (known as "awards") should be compulsory for all employers of workers in the award occupation ("blanket coverage"). The third principle was that the state should provide a mechanism for resolving industrial conflicts that arose either in the negotiation of awards or in subsequent enforcement of their provisions ("compulsory arbitration"). After another change of government in October 1990, the new government decided that these principles were no longer appropriate in an internationally competitive market economy.

The preamble of the new labor legislation, the Employment Contracts Act 1991, states that its purpose is "to promote an efficient labour market." Although the act explicitly protects freedom of association, the previous principles of compulsory unionism and blanket coverage were replaced by a principle of voluntary negotiation between individual parties (who may choose to enter into a collective agreement, but cannot bind any other parties to it). Under previous legislation, the primary employment relationship was between the union (to which an employee was obliged to belong) and the employers' organization (whose agreements bound all employers); the new act makes the primary employment relationship to be between the individual employee and the individual employer, with neither party able to force a collective agreement on the other.

The main objective of this legislation is to increase the flexibility of individual companies and workers to negotiate the terms of their employment to allow productivity gains to be identified, implemented, and rewarded in a way that is not easily achieved with centralized bargaining. The legislation provides for certain minimum conditions to be part of every employment contract (a minimum number of statutory holidays, for example, and the explicit outlawing of offenses such as discrimination or sexual harassment), but otherwise the terms of any contract are a matter for negotiation by the employer and employee. Compulsory arbitration no longer exists, although the state continues to sponsor a specialist Employment Court and an Employment Tribunal.

Reforming the Welfare State

New Zealand's welfare state is based on the principle that general taxation will pay for the public provision of education, health services, superannuation, and social welfare income support (unemployment, sickness, widows, and domestic purposes benefits). As the economic reforms proceeded, policymakers became more and more concerned about the disincentive effects of high marginal tax rates for income earners and of high replacement ratios for social welfare beneficiaries. In a major reform of the taxation system in 1986, income tax rates were reduced from up to 66 cents on the dollar to no more than 48 cents on the dollar at the same time as a new comprehensive indirect value-added tax was introduced (the Goods and Services Tax, or GST, which is currently set at 12.5 cents per dollar). Further tax cuts in 1989 reduced the top income tax rate to 33 cents on the dollar.

In December 1990, the government announced that it was reducing social welfare income support by 2.9 percent to 24.7 percent for different classes of recipients. This policy, which took effect from April 1, 1991, increased the income gap between social welfare beneficiaries and those in paid employment, and also caused considerable poverty among beneficiaries, reflected in a large surge in demand for assistance from private charities such as food banks. The cuts were anticipated to generate savings in social welfare transfer payments of NZ$1.275 billion in its first full fiscal year (1991–1992), or about 1.7 percent of GDP. In February 1996, the government announced further tax cuts, primarily achieved through a reduction in the middle income tax rate, but chose not to reverse any of the benefit cuts it had imposed in 1991.

The government has also sought to reform health, education, and superannuation policies on the broad principle that "the top third of all income earners can be expected to meet most of the cost of their social services" (New Zealand Government 1990, 20). There has been strong electoral opposition to this strategy, however, and a number of policy announcements along these lines were either not implemented or quickly reversed. Critics who argue that New Zealand's reforms did not go far enough often point to these areas as priorities for further action so that New Zealand can enhance its international competitiveness through private enterprise (see, for example, Evans, Grimes, and Wilkinson 1996, 1,894).

Maintaining Aggregate Price Stability

Prior to 1984, monetary policy in New Zealand tended to be generally accommodating of inflationary pressures (in part, owing to the decision by the government to monetarize growing fiscal deficits in the 1970s and early 1980s), and also showed a clear political business cycle (that is, monetary expansion was strongest in election years). As a result, any gain in international competitiveness by a devaluation of the exchange rate was quickly eliminated by high domestic inflation.

Monetary policy could be used in attempts to engineer political advantage to the party in government rather than for the economic well-being of the country for two reasons: First, the responsibility for setting monetary policy under the previous act was given to the minister of finance, who could communicate changes in policy to the governor of the Reserve Bank by private correspondence, and, second, the objectives for monetary policy provided great latitude for policy changes, because policy was obliged to have regard "to the desirability of promoting the highest level of production and trade and full employment, and of maintaining a stable internal price level" (Reserve Bank of New Zealand Amendment Act 1973, Section 5). Thus, in an election year, the minister could instruct the governor to relax monetary policy to promote production, trade, and full employment, and then the following year instruct the governor to tighten monetary policy to promote price stability.

To eliminate this temptation to the party in power, the 1988 Budget Speech announced a major reform of the Reserve Bank of New Zealand Act. The resulting legislation passed with the support of both the Labour Government and the National Opposition in 1989. There were many important aspects of the new legislation, but there were two critical elements for monetary policy. First, a clear distinction was made between the role of the government (which now defines the objectives of monetary policy) and the role of the Reserve Bank (which now designs the policies to pursue those objectives). Thus, it is no longer possible for a minister of finance to instruct the governor on how monetary policy should be implemented. Furthermore, any changes in monetary policy objectives must be made public by requiring the assent of Parliament and the signature of the governor general.

Second, the legislation defines the normal objective of monetary policy to be the single goal of "achieving and maintaining stability in the general level of prices." This change was justified not only on the basis that having a single objective made the Reserve Bank more readily accountable for the outcomes of its policies, but also on the basis of economic theories that suggest the best contribution monetary policy can make to the promotion of production, trade, and full employment is to maintain price stability.

This reform attracted considerable support from farmers and manufacturers, who had been frustrated by years of high inflation reducing their international competitiveness. In 1996, however, the steps taken by the Reserve Bank to control domestic inflationary pressures caused domestic interest rates to rise. This attracted a large capital inflow, which pushed up the value of the New Zealand dollar, causing considerable hardship to exporters once their forward cover had expired.

Legislating for Fiscal Discipline

At the change of government in 1984, the financial deficit of the government was 6.5 percent of GDP. The elimination of producer subsidies, the broadening of the tax base, the reduction in social welfare spending, general policies of fiscal restraint, and a strong recovery in economic activity after 1991–1992 restored an operating surplus in 1993–1994, which expanded to 3.1 percent of GDP in 1994–1995. In June 1994, the government sought to solidify these gains by passing the Fiscal Responsibility Act. Section 4 of the act sets out five principles of responsible fiscal management: (a) total Crown debt must be kept to prudent levels; (b) operating expenses must not exceed operating revenue on average, over a reasonable period of time; (c) a positive value for Crown net worth must be maintained to provide a buffer against adverse shocks; (d) fiscal risks must be managed prudently; and (e) the level and stability of tax rates should be reasonably predictable for future years. The act does not prescribe exactly what

NEW ZEALAND • 117

a prudent level of total Crown debt is, but the government has indicated that the standard it has adopted is net public debt in the range of 20 percent to 30 percent of GDP.

The act also sets out a precise cycle of financial reporting, beginning with a budget policy statement before March 31 each year specifying the government's long-term objectives and short-term strategies for fiscal policy and explaining how these objectives and strategies are consistent with the principles of responsible fiscal management contained in Section 4 of the act. The budget speech in June or July must be accompanied by an economic and fiscal update that provides Treasury forecasts for the next three years, and by a fiscal strategy report that explains how the budget is consistent with the budget policy statement. The speech also projects trends in the key fiscal variables to show whether they are consistent with the long-term objectives. Finally, in December each year or prior to a general election, Treasury must publish another economic and fiscal update.

The act sets strict standards for financial reports. In particular, all of the Crown's financial reports must use generally accepted accounting practice and must disclose any policy decisions or other matters that may affect the future fiscal situation. Statements that these requirements have been observed must be signed by the minister of finance and the secretary of the treasury at the beginning of every economic and fiscal update. This act is the first of its type in the world, and has introduced a high degree of integrity and transparency into New Zealand's public accounts.

An important role of the Fiscal Responsibility Act, and of the Reserve Bank of New Zealand Act, is to legislate macroeconomic stability to set a framework within which the private sector can undertake efficient investment and resource allocation decisions in competitive, open markets. However, this revises the concept of macroeconomic stabilization that was adopted by earlier policymakers, because the aim is not to offset fluctuations in output over the business cycle, but rather to ensure that monetary and fiscal policy maintain price stability, fiscal balance, and stable tax rates.

Summary

Taken one at a time, each of the above reforms made radical changes to economic management in New Zealand (see table 1). Together, the

Table 1. New Zealand Macroeconomic Data, 1980–1996

Year Ending March	Real Per Capita GDP (1991 $)	Real GDP Growth (%)	GDP Deflator Inflation (%)	Change in Employment (%)	Survey Unemployment Rate (%)	BoP Current Deficit (% GDP)	Total Overseas Debt (% GDP)	Government Fiscal Deficit (% GDP)	Net Public Debt (% GDP)	Nominal Interest Rate (%)	Real Wage of Firms (Index)	Labor Productivity (%)	Real Imports (% GDP)	Real Investment (% GDP)
1980	19,764	2.6	13.8	1.3	n.a.	4.2	36.6	2.1	16.3	13.8	143	1.0	21.8	17.2
1981	19,921	1.1	14.9	-0.1	2.5	3.6	35.4	3.9	17.8	15.4	147	0.8	20.1	15.2
1982	20,804	4.9	15.6	1.6	2.8	5.8	38.5	4.4	21.2	16.5	149	4.3	21.3	18.3
1983	20,751	0.6	11.9	-1.1	3.3	6.1	48.6	4.6	28.4	17.3	139	0.1	21.6	18.7
1984	21,049	2.7	8.0	1.1	4.4	5.5	48.9	6.5	31.6	12.9	134	4.0	20.8	19.3
1985	21,893	4.9	7.6	-2.0	3.5	8.5	69.8	5.0	40.5	17.5	127	1.7	22.1	19.5
1986	21,967	0.8	14.2	7.6	3.1	8.9	66.8	2.6	42.2	19.9	136	-2.5	22.3	20.7
1987	22,372	2.1	18.4	-0.9	4.0	5.1	77.0	3.3	46.2	20.5	135	3.5	22.3	19.1
1988	22,276	0.4	12.1	0.4	4.3	3.8	65.2	2.1	40.9	16.6	137	0.7	24.1	19.7
1989	22,126	-0.4	8.2	-2.9	6.2	0.8	59.2	1.4	44.5	15.2	134	3.7	24.1	18.9
1990	22,158	0.7	5.8	-0.5	7.1	3.9	75.9	1.3	50.0	14.9	131	2.8	27.2	20.2
1991	21,820	-0.4	2.4	-0.9	8.4	2.7	83.0	3.2	46.7	12.6	136	0.1	27.3	19.2
1992	21,285	-1.2	1.2	-2.5	10.6	2.6	86.6	2.6	52.1	9.9	136	1.1	26.6	16.0
1993	21,305	1.2	2.0	0.5	10.1	1.7	94.0	2.4	49.3	8.9	133	2.4	28.2	16.4
1994	22,374	6.2	1.6	4.8	9.3	1.3	86.3	-0.9	44.3	7.9	132	1.3	28.7	18.1
1995	23,237	5.3	1.6	5.7	7.5	3.9	80.8	-3.1	37.9	11.0	131	0.5	31.1	19.9
1996	23,712	3.1	2.8	3.5	6.2	4.0	83.6	-3.6	31.5	11.5	133	-0.2	32.1	20.8

Source: All series are from the updated database of Dalziel and Lattimore (1996).
GDP: Gross domestic product.

reform program integrates New Zealand into the global marketplace, based on a commitment to the efficient allocation of resources within competitive labor and commodity markets open to international prices. A framework of monetary and fiscal stability protected by statute supports these markets, whereas New Zealand's traditional system of social welfare provision is reduced, particularly in the area of income support, to improve the economic incentives and rewards for individual effort and enterprise.

RESEARCH INSTITUTIONS

Research institutions in New Zealand that have undertaken published research into aspects of globalization and its impact on domestic economic and social policies are grouped in this discussion under eight headings: (a) the New Zealand Treasury, (b) other government policy departments, (c) university departments, (d) academic centers, (e) the New Zealand Institute of Economic Research, (f) the New Zealand Business Roundtable, (g) the New Zealand Council of Trade Unions, and (h) other nongovernmental organizations.

The New Zealand Treasury

The New Zealand Treasury is the principal economic and financial advisor to the government, and employs about 150 economic and financial analysts for this purpose. It plays a large role in policy advice, because it must report on most expenditure proposals placed before the government and is often asked to participate in official policy reviews. Treasury staff monitor and analyze developments in the global economy, with a particular focus on New Zealand's major trading partners, as well as in the domestic economy. Under the Fiscal Responsibility Act 1994, it must publish a cycle of economic and fiscal outlooks every year, and these documents are influential in defining public policy debates in New Zealand. The Treasury's *Briefing to the Incoming Government* in 1984, 1987, and 1990 were important publications in explaining and promoting the program of economic reforms implemented after the 1984 election. The New Zealand Treasury is strongly globalist in its analysis, and its documents often present international case studies of policies in other countries that are recommended for adoption in New Zealand. The following quotation from a chapter entitled "Adjusting to International Change" in its 1990 briefing papers captures the Treasury's response to globalization:

> In short, New Zealand producers should be maintaining an outward focus and be looking to develop interdependency with other countries. If this is to happen, it is crucial that the government remove barriers to growth and international competitiveness. The whole economy needs to be open to competition, so that all managers face incentives to improve productivity, invest in new techniques, and upgrade quality and skills. For a small economy to attract investment, the overall stability and quality of policy is important. Given our insignificance relative to the much larger markets of the world, our economic policies need to err on the side of being better and more effective than those of other countries. (Treasury 1990, 36)

Other Government Departments

Apart from the Treasury, there are 43 other government departments in New Zealand (as of June 30, 1997; see New Zealand Government 1997, 116). None of these departments maintains an overview of global trends to the extent performed by the Treasury, but in almost all cases they analyze how domestic policymakers must take into account international trends. This is obviously true of departments with a focus on international trade such as Agriculture and Foreign Affairs and Trade, but it is also true of such departments as Labour and Social Welfare, which must advise their ministers on how domestic policies affect New Zealand's position in international markets. Policy advice units in these departments produce a wide range of official publications, and in recent years both the departments of Labour and Social Welfare have begun publishing journals containing articles by advisors, consultants, academics, and practitioners in relevant policy areas (the *Labour Market Bulletin* and the *Social Policy Journal of New Zealand,* respectively).

The Reserve Bank of New Zealand is part of the Crown in New Zealand but is not a government department. Instead, it has its own legislation (the Reserve Bank of New Zealand Act 1989) and significant autonomy in implementing policy to achieve its statutory objectives.

The bank maintains a small but highly qualified Economics Department, which engages in economic monitoring and analysis on a wide range of monetary issues. It publishes a quarterly *Reserve Bank Bulletin,* a series of more technical *Discussion Papers,* and occasional pamphlets for distribution to the general public. The governor of the Reserve Bank, Don Brash, is a strong advocate for New Zealand's program of economic reforms and for the benefits to be obtained from higher levels of foreign investment by overseas residents.

University Departments

Compared to some of their counterparts overseas, New Zealand university departments are very small. As of March 31, 1996, for example, the number of staff in the economics departments of New Zealand's seven universities were 18 in Auckland, 10 in Canterbury, 13 in Lincoln, 11 in Massey, 15 in Otago, eight in Waikato, and 22 in Victoria (Bairam 1996). These small numbers, plus the requirement that each department cover the wide syllabus of modern economics, mean that academic economists in New Zealand are rarely involved in sustained multiperson programs of research in topics such as globalization and its impacts. However, some universities are seeking to establish a reputation for excellence in particular research areas (see, for example, the summary in Thomson 1995). There is also a strong tradition of academic freedom that encourages individuals to pursue their own chosen line of research. Courses in international economics are taught in every department, and every department normally includes members with a research interest related to globalization or its impact on domestic economic and social policies. Their research is published in international and domestic journals (*New Zealand Economic Papers,* for example).

Economists, of course, are not the only academics with a research focus on globalization, and important pieces of New Zealand research on this topic have been undertaken in the departments of geography, history, law, political science, social policy, and sociology (see, for example, Britton 1991; Kelsey 1996; Le Heron and Pawson 1996). New Zealand academics generally have the reputation of being considerably more cautious in their assessment of the benefits of globalization, and more aware of disparities in the burden of domestic adjustment to global trends, than their colleagues in the New Zealand Treasury (see, for example, the exchanges in Zanetti et al. 1984; Zanetti 1985; Treasury 1985; Dalziel 1991, 1993; Gorringe and Bushnell 1992).

Academic Centers

Although academic research in New Zealand tends to be individualistic and discipline-based, an attempt has been made to produce coordinated research programs through the funding of academic centers. Two such centers—the New Zealand Asia Institute at the University of Auckland and the Institute of Policy Studies at Victoria University of Wellington—maintain an ongoing research capability related to globalization. Both institutes are located in particular universities, but both also work hard to strengthen networks with academics from other parts of the country and overseas. In addition, the APEC Study Centre (University of Auckland), the New Zealand Centre for Japanese Studies (Massey University), the Centre for Strategic Studies (Victoria University), the Industrial Relations Centre (Victoria University), and the International Trade Policy Research Centre (Lincoln University) are involved in the research of one or more aspects of globalization.

The New Zealand Asia Institute was established in May 1995, based on a network of 80 staff members at the University of Auckland. The following extract from its 1995 annual report describes its context:

> The decision to establish the Institute is a response to the growing importance of Asia to New Zealand politically, economically and culturally. Any New Zealand or Australian University which wishes to enter the next century as an internationally-recognised centre of excellence has to give primary attention to the furtherance of the study of Asia, its international relationships in the region, the development of government foreign policy and the university's own changing cultural context. The New Zealand Asia Institute is positioned to take advantage of the many opportunities for long-term academic links with major Asian universities, research institutions, government and multilateral organisations. (5)

One of the New Zealand Asia Institute's key objectives is to build a core of specialists on New Zealand–Asia policy issues and to provide a forum for the presentation and discussion of such issues. It is planning a series of seminars and conferences on major issues in New Zealand–Asia relations or Asia-related community issues covering topics ranging from international trade to Asian immigration and Treaty of Waitangi issues. It also acts as a center for networking academics and others working on such topics.

The Institute of Policy Studies exists to promote the study, research, and informed discussion of current issues of public policy, both foreign and domestic. The institute has four major themes in its research program, one of which is "New Zealand's Place in the World." Under this theme, it has commissioned studies on topics such as New Zealand and the Association of Southeast Asian Nations (ASEAN) (O'Brien and Holmes 1995; Vasil 1995), Asian immigration and investment in New Zealand (Cremer and Ramasamy 1996; McKinnon 1996), and the impact of trade on the environment (Hewison 1995). Like the New Zealand Asia Institute, the Institute of Policy Studies acts as a center for networking academics and others working on a particular policy issue, and both institutes have been used by the Asia 2000 Foundation in New Zealand for this purpose.

The New Zealand Institute of Economic Research

The New Zealand Institute of Economic Research, founded in 1958, is an independent nonprofit incorporated society, which aims to be the preeminent center in New Zealand for economic research and forecasting. The institute is under the direction of a Board elected by its members, and membership is open to any person or corporate body. It has a staff of about a dozen research economists, and conducts research in cooperation with universities and kindred bodies. The institute publishes the *Quarterly Survey of Business Opinion, Quarterly Predictions,* and the *Research Monographs* series and prepares private consultancy reports for its clients on a contract basis. The first objective of the institute is "to conduct research into economic problems affecting New Zealand, especially in connection with economic growth," and in this capacity it regularly comments on international trends and domestic policies (particularly in *Quarterly Predictions*). Recent research monographs on topics related to globalization include Duncan, Lattimore, and Bollard (1992); Colgate and Stroombergen (1993); Duncan and James (1994); Campbell-Hunt and Corbett (1996); and Chapple (1996).

The New Zealand Business Roundtable

The New Zealand Business Roundtable is an organization of the chief executives of around 60 of New Zealand's largest companies (see Cullinane 1995). Roundtable membership is by invitation, and the group employs a small secretariat in Wellington, headed by its executive director, Roger Kerr. The Business Roundtable both undertakes research itself and commissions research from domestic and overseas expert consultants. It is a strong believer in promoting public debate about what it considers to be the key issues, and so publishes numerous reports from its commissioned research (Bates 1996; Epstein 1996; Green 1996; Henderson 1996; New Zealand Business Roundtable 1996a) and collections of speeches by its members (New Zealand Business Roundtable 1994, 1995, 1996b). The organization "endorses the concept of an open, competitive market economy and a medium term policy orientation" (Cullinane 1995, 236), and is one of the most enthusiastic supporters of New Zealand's economic reforms in this direction. It continues to exhort the government to take further steps to reduce its expenditure as a percentage of GDP, privatize government businesses, eliminate excessively costly forms of regulation, reform at a fundamental level New Zealand's systems of education and training, and further integrate New Zealand with the world economy (New Zealand Business Roundtable 1996a, 4–8).

The New Zealand Council of Trade Unions

The New Zealand Council of Trade Unions is the central institution of organized labor in New Zealand (there is also a smaller Trade Union Federation, formed in 1993). It maintains a small secretariat in Wellington, which provides commentaries and other material on trends in the New Zealand economy as they affect workers. It has sought to form a network of links with New Zealand academics who share some of the council's views, reflected in the work of the Gamma Foundation (1993) and Harbridge and Hince (1995). The council's most recent publication (Council of Trade Unions 1996) provides an assessment of priorities for economic policies after the October 1996 general election. This document argues that "economic change has been accompanied by a massive and unequal redistribution of wealth, an erosion of the manufacturing base of the economy, the underdevelopment of the infrastructure, and the underdevelopment of skills" (5). Thus, the council does not accept that the economic reforms to integrate New Zealand into the global economy will lead to sustainable growth with equity, and argues strongly that the government and the trade union movement have roles to play in actively managing economic development.

Other Nongovernmental Organizations

A number of community-based organizations in New Zealand have maintained a largely critical stance toward globalization and the government's economic reforms in response. Those that have produced publications on their research and policies on this subject include the Maori Congress Foreign Policy Committee, CORSO (Council of Organisations for Relief Service Overseas), the Christian World Service, the Campaign Against Foreign Control of Aotearoa, and GATT Watchdog.

The Maori Congress is a national pan-tribal Maori organization that aims among other things to provide a forum for its member tribes to discuss tribal, national, and international issues. In July 1990, the Maori Congress set up a Foreign Policy Committee with an objective to ensure that the international personality of Aotearoa New Zealand is consistent with the Treaty of Waitangi (signed by representatives of the British Crown and of Maori tribes at the beginning of organized European settlement, February 6, 1840). In June 1994, this committee hosted a roundtable meeting on global indigenous strategies for self-determination and development (Mead 1994). The report recognized that "the perspectives of Indigenous peoples at international events are often not sought both at national preparatory and international levels" (5), and recorded the final statement of the gathering: "The Indigenous Peoples Roundtable Meeting, convened by Maori Congress and held in Whakatane, Aotearoa New Zealand, June 1994, unanimously affirms the natural inherited and inalienable right of all indigenous peoples to their self-determination over their lives, livelihoods, lands, territories and all other gifts/assets of their heritage" (14).

CORSO and the Christian World Service (CWS) are two of the many agencies in New Zealand involved in providing emergency relief and acting in partnership with overseas agencies in the Third World to work for economic and social development. These agencies produce material that strongly condemns trends in international debt and natural resource transfers that have widened the income gap between the Northern and Southern Hemisphere countries (see, for example, CORSO/CWS 1994), and argues that New Zealand should not be involved in promoting institutions that produce such adverse outcomes for large numbers of the world population.

The Campaign Against Foreign Control in Aotearoa monitors and opposes the rising amount of new investment and takeovers in New Zealand by foreign-owned transnational corporations (see, for example, Horton 1996). It is thus opposed to one of the fundamental tenets of globalization, namely, the free flow of international capital to wherever the returns are highest. The organization also lobbies against other aspects of globalization, particularly the use of international agreements such as the General Agreement on Tariffs and Trade (GATT) to promote free trade (Small 1996). This organization publishes *Foreign Control Watchdog* three times a year.

GATT Watchdog campaigns against the extension of GATT and against regional trade agreements such as the initiatives of the Asia-Pacific Economic Cooperation (APEC) forum (see, for example, Choudry 1996a, 1996b; GATT Watchdog 1996). This organization also publishes a regular publication, *The Big Picture*. The following quotation from a statement made to oppose an APEC Trade Ministers Meeting in July 1996 illustrates this organization's protest:

> Economic growth and promotion of trade are not ends in themselves. Genuine development must be centered on the needs of people and nature, and deliver real social and economic justice. The form of indiscriminate, unregulated economic growth and trade which APEC advocates delivers the opposite of this—its consequences are socially unjust and ecologically unsustainable; it imposes irreversible social and environmental costs; and it enables governments to abdicate their responsibilities to their citizens and leave them at the mercy of transnational corporations and international financial institutions who are accountable to no one. (GATT Watchdog 1996, 3)

GLOBALIZATION AND POLITICAL SOVEREIGNTY

During the past 10 years, the above organizations have produced a wealth of material analyzing aspects of New Zealand's program of economic reform, often in a global context. It is impossible to summarize that literature here. Instead, the chapter concludes with a discussion of a controversial and fundamental issue within New Zealand about the program of reform as a whole, particularly as the program relates to globalization in the Asia Pacific region. That issue is the relationship between globalization and political sovereignty (see, for example, Kelsey 1995).

There does not appear to be any disagreement that removing controls on international capital movements, reducing barriers to imported goods and services, signing up to international agreements on free trade, deregulating the financial sector, imposing statutory limitations on fiscal and monetary policy, corporatizing and privatizing government trading departments, and encouraging greater private purchases of social services have reduced the ability of the New Zealand government to implement policies in response to domestic political pressures. For example, one of the justifications for the substantial reduction in social welfare income support announced on December 19, 1990, was that the international credit rating agency Standard and Poor's was contemplating a two-step downgrade in New Zealand's credit rating. This would have increased the risk premium paid on New Zealand's overseas debt, and would have affected the borrowing cost of finance faced by New Zealand companies (which cannot have better credit ratings than their national government). The minister of finance flew to New York for a special four-hour meeting with the agency "making submissions to the rating agency on the strength of the government's political will to carry through the December 19 reforms" (that is, the benefit cuts; see Dalziel 1992, 29).

More recently, New Zealand's first general election under a mixed-member proportional representation system produced a government that wished to increase public expenditure on health and education. The governor of the Reserve Bank warned that this would raise domestic inflationary pressure. That would require a monetary response from the Bank, thereby increasing interest rates and accentuating the net capital inflow into the country. This, in turn, would tend to raise exchange rates, putting more pressure on farmers and other exporters. Consequently, the governor urged the coalition partners to practice fiscal restraint, by considering "deferring some part of the tax cuts already announced if there is to be any net increase in government expenditure" (Brash 1996, 64). This advice was duly accepted.

The controversy arises over whether this loss of political sovereignty is a good or a bad thing for the people of New Zealand. Advocates of the reforms, such as the New Zealand Business Roundtable and the New Zealand Treasury, argue that this outcome is highly beneficial, because it imposes a market-based discipline on the government and prevents the government from introducing unfunded expenditures that lower total social welfare. Indeed, the Business Roundtable consistently argues that if New Zealand is to remain internationally competitive, it must continue to reduce the size of government to allow room for greater private enterprise to create wealth and raise prosperity. Critics of the reforms, including the Council of Trade Unions and community-based organizations, argue that the partial withdrawal of government from its formerly accepted roles has allowed greater disparities in income and wealth to be produced within New Zealand. Furthermore, this widening of the gap between rich and poor is viewed as a global trend within and among other countries that will require political initiatives, rather than unregulated market forces, to reverse.

The fundamental question being asked in this debate is whether citizens can rely on deregulated and open markets to produce desirable social outcomes, or whether some government involvement is required at the national or regional economy level to ensure that the poorest and most vulnerable citizens have access to adequate housing, health care, education, and economic opportunity. Related to this question are the issues of whether the market power of transnational corporations is such that citizens may reasonably choose to require a democratic government to exercise countervailing power on their behalf and the trade-offs this creates between market failure and government failure. These issues are the subject of much debate in New Zealand because of the dramatic increase in visible poverty in the community since the economic reforms were initiated in 1984 (New Zealand Council of Christian Social Services 1996), and this is often attributed to the policy changes.

In a specifically New Zealand context, two illustrations can be given of these general issues, arising out of domestic debates about the relationship between indigenous Maori tribes and the Crown and about immigration and foreign investment into New Zealand.

In 1840, representatives of the Queen of England and representatives of the Maori tribes signed the Treaty of Waitangi in which complete government was given to the Crown, but the Maori tribes were guaranteed the unqualified exercise of chieftainship over their lands, villages, and treasures. In recent years, profound constitutional arguments have arisen about the implications of these clauses for the exercise of sovereignty within New Zealand, and whether the Crown can enter into international arrangements such as the Trade-Related Intellectual Property Rights (TRIP) Agreement. TRIP is a Western intellectual property rights regime that might directly conflict with the way Maori authorities might choose to own, control, regulate, and protect indigenous resources in their tribal areas (see, for example, Mead 1994; Heremaia 1996).

During New Zealand's election campaign in 1996, one of the political parties (New Zealand First) raised the issue of whether the rate of immigration and foreign investment is too high for New Zealand to absorb. The specific concern about immigration was that an inflow of wealthy immigrants had increased the demand for quality housing in the city of Auckland, which had contributed to inflationary pressure and hence tight monetary policies by the Reserve Bank. The specific concern about foreign investment was that control of local companies was passing out of domestic ownership in a way that was perceived by some parts of the electorate as reducing economic security in New Zealand. In both cases, the New Zealand First Party proposed that political processes should be used to interrupt global economic processes that were judged to be undesirable, and this attracted significant popular support (in the postelection coalition between the New Zealand First Party and the National Party, however, it was agreed not to pursue these policies during the next Parliamentary term).

These two examples illustrate the immediate relevance in New Zealand of the more general question of the relationship between globalization and political sovereignty, and other examples could be given. Perhaps these issues have been thrown into sharper relief in New Zealand because of the pace and extent of the economic reforms implemented since 1984, but other countries will have their own examples of the tension produced by the international pressures of globalization and domestic aspirations for political autonomy and sovereignty. Therefore, this topic may be one of the fundamental questions that could usefully be researched in an international context, sponsored and coordinated by agencies, such as the Japan Center for International Exchange, which are responding to the "challenge of strengthening and broadening networks among policy research institutions and intellectual leaders involved in Asia Pacific community building" (Yamamoto 1995, xiii).

BIBLIOGRAPHY

Bairam, Erkin. 1996. "Research Quality and Productivity in New Zealand University Economics Departments, 1988–1995." Discussion Paper No. 9608. Dunedin: Department of Economics, University of Otago.

Bates, Winton Russel. 1996. *The Links Between Economic Growth and Social Cohesion.* Wellington: New Zealand Business Roundtable.

Bollard, Alan, and Robert Buckle, eds. 1987. *Economic Liberalisation in New Zealand.* Wellington: Allen and Unwin.

Boston, Jonathan, and Paul Dalziel, eds. 1992. *The Decent Society? Essays in Response to National's Economic and Social Policies.* Auckland: Oxford University Press.

Boston, Jonathan, and Martin Holland, eds. 1990. *The Fourth Labour Government.* Auckland: Oxford University Press.

Brash, Donald. 1996. "Monetary and Fiscal Policy and Their Impacts on Exporters." Speech to Federated Farmers, Southland, summarized in Monetary Policy Statement, December 1996. Wellington: Reserve Bank of New Zealand.

Britton, Stephen. 1991. "Recent Trends in the Internationalisation of the New Zealand Economy." *Australian Geographical Studies* 29(1): 3–25.

Buckle, Robert. 1987. "Sequencing and the Role of the Foreign Exchange Market." In Alan Bollard and Robert A. Buckle, eds. *Economic Liberalisation in New Zealand.* Wellington: Allen and Unwin.

Campbell-Hunt, Colin, and Lawrence Corbett. 1996. *A Season of Excellence? An Overview of New Zealand Enterprise in the Nineties.* Wellington: New Zealand Institute of Economic Research.

Chapple, Simon. 1996. *Full Employment: Whence It Came and Where It Went.* Wellington: New Zealand Institute of Economic Research.

Choudry, Aziz, ed. 1996a. *Aotearoa/New Zealand Country Report*. Christchurch: GATT Watchdog.

———. 1996b. "APEC, Free Trade and Economic Sovereignty." Paper presented to the Manila People's Forum on APEC, November 1996. Christchurch: GATT Watchdog.

Colgate, Pat, and Joselyn Stroombergen. 1993. *A Promise to Pay: New Zealand's Overseas Debt and Country Risk*. Wellington: New Zealand Institute of Economic Research.

Commerce Act. 1986. *The Statutes of New Zealand 1986*. Volume 1, Act No. 5. Wellington: New Zealand Government.

CORSO/CWS. 1994. "Banking on Poverty." Pamphlet produced by CORSO and Christian World Service as part of a global mobilization against the policies of the International Monetary Fund and the World Bank. Christchurch: CORSO/CWS.

Council of Trade Unions. 1996. *Post-Election Priorities—A Union View*. Wellington: New Zealand Council of Trade Unions.

Cremer, Rolf, and Bala Ramasamy. 1996. *Tigers in New Zealand: The Role of Asian Investment in the Economy*. Wellington: Institute of Policy Studies.

Cullinane, Tim. 1995. "The Business Roundtable in 1995." In *Growing Pains*. Wellington: New Zealand Business Roundtable.

Dalziel, Paul. 1991. "The Rhetoric of Treasury." *New Zealand Economic Papers* 25(2): 259–274.

———. 1992. "National's Economic Strategy." In Jonathan Boston and Paul Dalziel, eds. *The Decent Society? Essays in Response to National's Economic and Social Policies*. Auckland: Oxford University Press.

———. 1993. "The Rhetoric of Treasury: Reply." *New Zealand Economic Papers* 27(1): 91–99.

Dalziel, Paul, and Ralph Lattimore. 1996. *The New Zealand Macroeconomy: A Briefing on the Reforms*. Auckland: Oxford University Press.

Deane, Roderick. 1986. *"Preface" to Financial Policy Reform*. Wellington: Reserve Bank of New Zealand.

Duncan, Ian, and Alan Bollard. 1992. *Corporatization and Privatization: Lessons from New Zealand*. Auckland: Oxford University Press.

Duncan, Ian, and D. James. 1994. *Tourism Investment in New Zealand: Opportunities and Constraints*. Wellington: New Zealand Institute of Economic Research.

Duncan, Ian, Ralph Lattimore, and Alan Bollard. 1992. *Dismantling the Barriers: Tariff Policy in New Zealand*. Wellington: New Zealand Institute of Economic Research.

Economic Summit Conference. 1984. *Proceedings and Conference Papers, Vol. 1*. Wellington: Economic Summit Conference Secretariat.

Epstein, Richard. 1996. *The Role of the State in Education.* Wellington: New Zealand Business Roundtable.

Evans, Lewis, Arthur Grimes, and Bryce Wilkinson, with David Teece. 1996. "Economic Reform in New Zealand 1984–95: The Pursuit of Efficiency." *Journal of Economic Literature* 34(4): 1856–1902.

Gamma Foundation. 1993. *Reshaping Social Democracy.* Wellington: Gamma Foundation.

GATT Watchdog. 1996. *Trading with Our Lives: The Human Cost of Free Trade.* Collection of papers presented to an NGO Forum on APEC, Christchurch, July 1996. Christchurch: GATT Watchdog.

Gorringe, Peter, and Peter Bushnell. 1992. "The Rhetoric of 'The Rhetoric of Treasury.'" *New Zealand Economic Papers* 26(1): 127–142.

Green, David. 1996. *From Welfare State to Civil Society.* Wellington: New Zealand Business Roundtable.

Harbridge, Raymond, ed. 1993. *Employment Contracts: New Zealand Experiences.* Wellington: Victoria University Press.

Harbridge, Reymond, and Kevin Hince. 1995. "Globalization and the Impact on the World of Work." Paper prepared as part of the program of joint investigative work of the Asian Network of Institutes of Labour Studies, 1994–1995, mimeo. Wellington: Industrial Relations Centre, Victoria University of Wellington.

Hawke, Gary. 1985. *The Making of New Zealand: An Economic History.* Cambridge, England: Cambridge University Press.

Hazledine, Tim, and Andrew Murphy. 1996. "Manufacturing Industries." In Brian Silverstone, Alan Bollard, and Ralph Lattimore, eds. *A Study of Economic Reform: The Case of New Zealand.* Amsterdam: North Holland.

Henderson, David. 1996. *Economic Reform: New Zealand in an International Perspective.* Wellington: New Zealand Business Roundtable.

Heremaia, Shane. 1996. "Free Trade and Colonisation." In *Trading with Our Lives: The Human Cost of Free Trade.* Christchurch: GATT Watchdog.

Hewison, Grant. 1995. *Reconciling Trade and the Environment: Issues for New Zealand.* Wellington: Institute of Policy Studies.

Horton, Murray. 1996. "Foreign Investment: The Recolonisation of Aotearoa." In *Trading with Our Lives: The Human Cost of Free Trade.* Christchurch: GATT Watchdog.

Hyman, Prue. 1994. *Women and Economics: A New Zealand Feminist Perspective.* Wellington: Bridget Williams.

Kelsey, Jane. 1995. "Some Reflections on Globalisation, Sovereignty and the State." *SITES* 30: 165–172.

———. 1996. *The New Zealand Experiment: A World Model for Structural Adjustment?* Auckland: Auckland University Press and Bridget Williams.

Lattimore, Ralph, and Paul Wooding. 1996. "International Trade." In Brian

Silverstone, Alan Bollard, and Ralph Lattimore, eds. *A Study of Economic Reform: The Case of New Zealand.* Amsterdam: North Holland.

Le Heron, Richard. 1993. "Internationalisation Trends, Investment and Labour: Issues and Policy Options." In Philip Morrison, ed. *Labour, Employment and Work in New Zealand: Proceedings of the Fifth Conference.* Wellington: Victoria University of Wellington.

Le Heron, Richard, and Eric Pawson, eds. 1996. *Changing Places: New Zealand in the Nineties.* Auckland: Longman Paul.

Massey, Patrick. 1995. *New Zealand: Market Liberalisation in a Developed Economy.* London: Macmillan.

McKinnon, Malcolm. 1996. *Immigrants and Citizens: New Zealanders and Asian Immigration in Historical Context.* Wellington: Institute of Policy Studies.

Mead, Aroha Te Pareake. 1994. *Maori Congress Indigenous Peoples Roundtable Meeting: Global Indigenous Strategies for Self-Determination.* Wellington: Taonga Pacific.

New Zealand Asia Institute. 1995. *Annual Report.* Auckland: New Zealand Asia Institute.

New Zealand Business Roundtable. 1994. *The Next Decade of Change.* Wellington: New Zealand Business Roundtable.

———. 1995. *Growing Pains.* Wellington: New Zealand Business Roundtable.

———. 1996a. *Moving into the Fast Lane.* Wellington: New Zealand Business Roundtable.

———. 1996b. *Why Not Simply the Best?* Wellington: New Zealand Business Roundtable.

New Zealand Council of Christian Social Services. 1996. "An Open Letter on Poverty in New Zealand Signed by Members of the Six Churches Associated with the NZCCSS." Wellington: New Zealand Council of Christian Social Services.

New Zealand Government. 1990. *Economic and Social Initiative—December 1990.* Statements by the Prime Minister, the Minister of Finance, and the Minister of Labour and State Services, December 19, 1990.

———. 1997. *Financial Statements of the Government of New Zealand for the Year Ended 30 June 1997.* Wellington: New Zealand Treasury.

O'Brien, Terence, and Frank Holmes. 1995. *New Zealand and ASEAN: The Strategic and Economic Outlook.* Wellington: Institute of Policy Studies.

Rayner, Anthony, and Ralph Lattimore. 1991. "New Zealand." In Demetris Papageorgiou, Michael Michaely, and Armeane M. Choksi, eds. *Liberalizing Foreign Trade, Vol. 6.* Oxford, England: Basil Blackwell.

Reserve Bank of New Zealand Amendment Act. 1973. *The Statutes of New Zealand 1973.* Volume 1, Act No. 16. Wellington: New Zealand Government.

Richardson, R. 1992. *Economic Strategy.* Budget Document B.6 [Pt. II], Appendices to the House of Representatives. Wellington: New Zealand Government.

Sandrey, Ron, and Russell Reynolds, eds. 1990. *Farming without Subsidies: New Zealand's Recent Experience.* Wellington: GP Books.

Silverstone, Brian, Alan Bollard, and Ralph Lattimore, eds. 1996. *A Study of Economic Reform: The Case of New Zealand.* Amsterdam: North Holland.

Small, Dennis. 1996. *The Cost of Free Trade: Aotearoa/New Zealand at Risk.* Christchurch: Campaign Against Foreign Control in Aotearoa.

State-Owned Enterprises Act. 1986. *The Statutes of New Zealand 1986.* Volume 3, Act No. 124. Wellington: New Zealand Government.

Thomson, Nicky. 1995. "Research Institutions in New Zealand." In Tadashi Yamamoto, ed. *Emerging Civil Society in the Asia Pacific Community.* Tokyo: Japan Center for International Exchange in association with the Institute of Southeast Asian Studies, Pasir Panjang, Singapore.

Treasury. 1985. "Opening 'The Books': A Reply." *New Zealand Economic Papers* 19: 95–115.

———. 1990. *Briefing to the Incoming Government 1990.* Wellington: New Zealand Treasury.

Vasil, Raj. 1995. *New Zealand and ASEAN: A Critical View of the Relationship.* Wellington: Institute of Policy Studies.

Walker, Gordon, and Marl Fox. 1996. "Globalization: An Analytical Framework." *Indiana Journal of Global Legal Studies* 3(2): 375–411.

Yamamoto Tadashi. 1995. "Preface." In *Emerging Civil Society in the Asia Pacific Community.* Tokyo: Japan Center for International Exchange in association with the Institute of Southeast Asian Studies, Pasir Panjang, Singapore.

Zanetti, G. N. 1985. "Opening 'The Books': Response to the Treasury's Reply." *New Zealand Economic Papers* 19: 123–125.

Zanetti, G. N., I. G. Bertram, P. A. Brosnan, Robert A. Buckle, M. J. Pope, R. J. Stephens, and G. M. Wells. 1984. "Opening 'The Books.'" *New Zealand Economic Papers* 18: 13–30.

6 · United States

Susan M. Collins

GROWING international economic integration has meant many things for the United States, and hence there are many dimensions to the domestic adjustment in process. However, the topic that has received the most attention in this context is whether trade—and globalization more generally—harms American workers. More specifically, has globalization made adjustment to structural change more difficult by reducing the real earnings of many American workers and increasing the incidence and costs of job loss? To examine these issues, this chapter develops three themes and highlights their interaction.

First, the United States has clearly become more integrated with the global economy. Cross-border flows of goods, services, and capital all have risen sharply since the 1970s. There has also been a significant recent increase in the number of immigrants to the United States. Importantly, increasing integration has qualitative as well as quantitative significance for Americans. The implications go beyond numeric calculations such as the effects of increased imports on demand for domestic production. Historically, the United States has been quite self-sufficient economically. As a large, wealthy country, trade with the rest of the world did not account for a major share of U.S. production or consumption. Americans saw their producers as the unquestioned technological leaders. By and large, Americans did not expect economic fortunes at home to be tied to developments abroad. In a variety of ways, this environment has changed. Other countries now compete with the United States at the technological frontier. Americans worry that, in terms of math and science, their youth lag behind those in other countries.

Second, although recent U.S. economic performance has been strong overall, the country is struggling with some difficult longer-term problems. These include slow productivity (and hence average real wage) growth and a worrisome increase in wage and income inequality. In particular, the real earnings of less educated American workers were actually falling until recently. A surprisingly large share of workers express some anxiety about their job security. In response to these developments, many have pronounced the death of the "American dream"—whereby individuals could prosper through hard work and perseverance, and could expect their children to enjoy higher living standards.

Third, rapid growth in a dynamic economy goes hand-in-hand with significant job displacement because workers are forced to move out of less efficient or contracting industries. However, by international standards, the United States does not maintain extensive support programs for displaced workers. Relatively few of those unemployed actually receive unemployment compensation. Furthermore, the United States is in the midst of rethinking its approach toward providing a safety net, as evidenced by the major overhaul of the welfare system now under way. More active policies to assist displaced workers, such as training and job search, are decentralized and fragmented.

The chapter is divided into five sections:
- The integration of the United States with the global economy.
- A summary of recent U.S. economic performance, highlighting worrisome developments in U.S. labor markets.
- An assessment of the implications of globalization for American workers, and in particular for the declining relative wage of less skilled workers.
- An overview of the experience of and policies toward displaced workers.
- Some concluding remarks.

THE UNITED STATES IN THE GLOBAL ECONOMY

The United States is becoming more integrated with the rest of the world economy. At the same time, as a large, wealthy country, the United States continues to be somewhat less "open" and more self-sufficient than most other industrial countries.

Increased Integration

Table 1 provides some indicators of economic integration. It shows that U.S. trade in goods and services (exports plus imports) more than doubled from 10.9 percent of gross domestic product (GDP) in 1970 to 25 percent in 1997. Much of this increase occurred during the 1970s.

Trade with nonindustrial countries has grown as a share of total U.S. trade. Between 1980 and 1995, trade with nonindustrial countries (excluding Eastern Europe and the Organization of Petroleum Exporting Countries) grew from 29.2 percent to 37.1 percent of total U.S. exports and from 25.4 percent to 37.5 percent of total U.S. imports. However, the increase in the share of manufactured imports coming from developing economies was somewhat smaller than this overall figure suggests, rising from roughly 30 percent in the mid-1970s to 36.0 percent in 1992. This is not primarily a reflection of developments in the United States, where trade barriers had already been reduced to low levels in all but a few sectors. Instead, the increase in trade with developing (and transition) economies reflects their dramatic and widespread shift from inward to outward orientation, combined in

Table 1. Indicators of Increased International Integration (% of GDP)

	Exports	Imports	Stock of Foreign Assets in the U.S.		Stock of U.S. Assets Abroad	
			Total	Direct Investment	Total	Direct Investment
1970	5.5	5.4				
1980	10.0	10.6	18.0	3.0	21.8	7.7
1990	9.7	10.9	41.6	9.4	37.9	12.7
1997	11.9	13.1	67.0*	16.4*	56.1*	20.1*

Sources: U.S. Council of Economic Advisers (1998, Table B-1, 280–281, and Table B-107, 401; 1989, Table B-106, 429).

GDP: Gross domestic product.
*1996.

Asia with rapid rates of economic growth. Indeed, the rise in imports from developing economies is largely a story about increased imports from the dynamic Asian economies and, more recently, of increased linkages with Mexico.

Table 1 also shows a significant increase in cross-border owner-ship of assets. In 1980, the stock of foreign assets in the United States was equivalent to 18.0 percent of domestic GDP. By 1996, this figure had risen to 67.0 percent. Strikingly, between 1980 and 1996, the stock of foreign direct investment (FDI) in the United States jumped from 3.0 percent to 16.4 percent of U.S. GDP (see Graham and Krugman 1991 for an analysis of the implications of FDI in the United States). The final two columns of the table show the rises in U.S. asset hold-ings abroad.

Savings: Investment and External Imbalances

The United States has had large and persistent trade deficits since the early 1980s. The ability to finance these deficits is related to the increased integration of international financial markets, and to for-eigners' continued willingness to expand their net holding of U.S. as-sets. Decomposing the external imbalance into savings and investment provides a useful perspective on recent developments. This decom-position emphasizes the point that globalization enables the United States to sustain investment rates that are considerably higher than national saving rates.

Net foreign investment, which is roughly equivalent to the current account, deteriorated from 0.4 percent of GDP in 1980 to minus 3.3 percent in 1987 (table 2). The deterioration reflected sharp declines in both private and government savings, with domestic investment also declining. Government savings dropped an additional 2.2 percentage points of GDP between 1987 and 1992. However, the U.S. external bal-ance improved because of an even larger decline in investment. The current account deteriorated from 1992 to 1997, but the "anatomy" of this deterioration is quite different from that during the period from 1980 to 1987. Private investment has recovered since 1992. This in-creased investment has been more than offset by higher (federal) government saving. Recent policy changes to reduce the U.S. budget deficit as well as the budgetary implications of strong economic

Table 2. Savings, Investment, and External Balance (% of GDP)

	Gross National Savings			Gross National Investment			Net Foreign Investment	Statistical Discrepancy
	Private	Govern-ment	Total	Private	Govern-ment	Total		
1980	17.6	2.0	19.6	16.7	3.5	20.2	0.4	1.0
1987	15.5	1.1	16.6	15.9	3.7	19.6	−3.3	−0.4
1992	15.6	−1.1	14.5	12.7	3.3	16.0	−0.8	0.7
1996	14.7	1.9	16.6	14.6	2.9	17.6	−1.7	−0.8

Source: U.S. Council of Economic Advisers (1998, Table B-1, 280, and Table B-32, 318–319).
GDP: Gross domestic product.

growth have both contributed to this outcome. Unfortunately, private savings have dropped from an already low level. Thus, long-awaited fiscal policy changes are helping to boost government savings. How to raise private savings remains an important but difficult issue.

Immigration

The United States has also seen a recent surge in immigration (see Borjas 1995; Friedberg and Hunt 1995). During the 1980s, the absolute numbers of new immigrants were comparable to peaks reached around the turn of the century, and accounted for roughly a quarter of U.S. population growth. In 1991, immigrants were 7.9 percent of the U.S. population (a considerably smaller proportion than in the early 1900s). In comparison, immigrants accounted for 3.1 percent, 8.2 percent, and 15.6 percent of the populations of the United Kingdom, West Germany, and Canada, respectively. Of the U.S. immigrants, 75 percent now come from Asia, Latin America, and the Caribbean. On average, recent immigrants are also somewhat less educated than previous immigrants.

Other Considerations

Increased trade, capital, and labor flows are important features of the U.S. relationship with the global economy. But there are other aspects as well. First, the United States is no longer the world's undisputed leader in terms of its technology, and its relative endowments of physical and human capital. Indeed, Edward Leamer concludes that in 1965 the United States was "on the edge of the advanced countries with abundance of both professional workers and also capital. From this uniqueness presumably came relatively great gains from trade and also insulation from competition with the most labor-abundant countries. But by 1988 the United States is only one of many. The United States is exceeded in both physical capital and human capital per worker by a collection of OECD countries. . . . [There are also] a group of low-wage countries with ratios of human and physical capital that are high enough to turn these countries into U.S. competitors" (1998, 170–171). Similarly, Collins and Bosworth (1996, 189) present estimates of the convergence between Japan and the United States. Our figures suggest that physical capital per worker in Japan grew from 31 percent of the U.S. level in 1970 to 102 percent of the U.S. level in 1994. Human capital per worker in Japan grew from 80 percent of the U.S. level to 84 percent.

Second, there appears to have been an increase in broad-based U.S. public concern about the implications of competing in a global marketplace. These concerns came to the forefront in the prolonged and heated debated over the pros and cons of further integration with low-wage Mexico through the North American Free Trade Agreement. Ross Perot's characterization of the "great sucking sound" Americans would hear as jobs moved south across the border into Mexico quickly became a household phrase.

Finally, the end of the cold war has altered the context in which the United States interacts with other countries. These changes and their implications are difficult to measure, but have clearly shifted the balance between political and economic considerations.

THE CONTEXT OF RECENT U.S. ECONOMIC PERFORMANCE

Overall, the U.S. economy is performing well and continues to look quite healthy relative to other major industrial countries. This view is strongly supported by the main economic indicators. At the same time, the U.S. economy continues to struggle with some difficult problems. The underlying causes of these problems are far from clear, and many people believe that increasing U.S. integration with the rest of the world is to blame. In particular, this has led to a large and growing literature, and to heated debates about whether globalization harms

American workers. The fact that successful remedies are not readily apparent—particularly ones that would provide "quick fixes"—may help to explain the often contentious nature of this debate.

Recent Macroeconomic Developments

Table 3 provides key indicators of recent U.S. economic performance. Real GDP growth ranged from 2.0 percent to 3.8 percent per year from 1992 to 1997. The recent economic expansion has been driven not by increased consumption but by private investment and exports.

Table 3. Recent U.S. Economic Performance (% growth rates)

	1990	1991	1992	1993	1994	1995	1996	1997
Real GDP	1.2	−0.9	2.7	2.3	3.5	2.0	2.8	3.8
Private investment*	−0.6	−6.4	1.9	7.6	8.0	9.0	9.2	9.7
Personal consumption	1.7	−0.6	2.8	2.9	3.3	2.4	2.6	3.3
Government outlays	3.0	0.6	0.5	−0.9	0.0	0.0	0.5	1.0
Federal	2.0	−0.5	−2.1	−4.2	−3.8	−3.3	−1.3	−1.4
Exports	8.5	6.3	6.0	2.9	8.2	11.1	8.3	12.5
Imports	3.9	−0.7	7.5	8.9	12.2	8.9	9.1	13.9
CPI	5.4	4.2	3.0	3.0	2.6	2.8	3.0	2.3
Unemployment rate†	5.6	6.8	7.5	6.9	6.1	5.6	5.4	4.9

Source: U.S. Council of Economic Advisers (1998, Table B-4, 285, Table B-35, 322, and Table B-63, 353).
GDP: Gross domestic product; CPI: Consumer Price Index.
*Private nonresidential fixed investment.
†Civilian unemployment rate.

Associated with the economic growth has been continued rapid job creation and persistently low rates of unemployment. In particular, unemployment fell from 7.5 percent of the civilian labor force in 1992 to just 4.9 percent in 1997. In 1998, the monthly unemployment rate dropped to 4.4 percent.

Some have claimed that the rapid job growth statistics paint an overly rosy picture of the U.S. labor market. However, the evidence does not support the claim that most of the new jobs are poor jobs with low pay and benefits. A recent Bureau of Labor Statistics study of job creation from 1989 to 1995 classifies jobs in 90 industry/employment categories as low-, middle-, or high-paying. It finds that employment in low- and high-paying jobs increased by 7 percent and 13 percent, respectively, whereas employment in middle-paying jobs decreased by 3 percent.

Table 3 also shows that U.S. consumer price inflation has remained at or below 3 percent per year since 1992. In fact, many analysts believe that actual price inflation may be even lower than these figures suggest because of difficulties in adjusting for quality changes, the introduction of new products, and the fact that consumers alter their consumption decisions in response to price changes. A recent U.S. Senate–appointed panel concluded that the likely overestimate is around 1.1 percentage points. Other economists argue that other measurement problems offset these upward biases, and that the net effect of the various measurement difficulties is unclear. However, biases in Consumer Price Index inflation rates would affect measures of U.S. productivity and real wages. Although productivity growth and real wage growth may be somewhat higher than available statistics suggest, these statistics still allow us to make inferences about whether productivity and wage growth have slowed down or sped up, and about changes in the distribution of wages.

The persistence of low inflation coupled with low unemployment is a puzzling feature of recent U.S. economic performance. A few years ago, the nonaccelerating inflation rate of unemployment (NAIRU) was widely viewed to be around 6 percent. The fact that the unemployment rate has stayed below 5.8 percent for more than 15 quarters with no apparent acceleration in the inflation rate begs an explanation. One view is that NAIRU has declined. This might have occurred as a result of demographic changes, or shifts in expected real wage gains because of the productivity slowdown or increased competition. Alternatively, special temporary features may be at work. The recent slowdown in U.S. health-care costs may explain why tight labor markets have not caused the prices of goods and services to rise. In addition, there seems to be considerable worker anxiety about job loss, which could account for slow wage growth despite relatively low rates of unemployment. Of course, it is difficult to measure such changes in attitudes, to assess their implications, and to tell whether they are temporary or likely to persist.

The sustained economic growth and low rates of unemployment and inflation are all good news about the U.S. economy. In some other areas, the news is much less positive. As a large and growing number of studies have documented, average real wages and compensation have stagnated in the United States, whereas wage and income inequality have increased.

Average Wages: Productivity and Growth

Table 4 shows what has happened to the real average compensation of the American worker during the past three decades. After growing at a rapid 2.7 percent per annum from 1960 to 1973, growth in average compensation fell sharply to just 0.6 percent from 1973 to 1995. Nearly all of this decline in earnings growth can be accounted for by the drop in U.S. labor productivity growth from 3.0 percent per annum before 1973 to just 1 percent from 1973 to 1995. Data suggest that productivity growth may have risen somewhat since 1995; however, it is too early to tell whether this higher rate will be sustained. Most of the rest of the decline can be accounted for by a deterioration in labor's terms of trade— that is, a reduction in the value of goods and services produced by U.S. workers relative to the value of goods and services consumed (Lawrence and Slaughter 1993; Bosworth and Perry 1994). Although the stagnant growth in real earnings of the average worker has not been the focus of the debate over whether globalization is harming American workers, this trend is certainly central to the underlying concerns about the U.S. labor market.

Table 4. Growth of Average Earnings and Productivity (annualized percentage growth rates)

	Real Compensation	Productivity
1960–1973	2.67	3.01
1973–1995	0.64	1.02

Source: Author's calculations from U.S. Bureau of Labor Statistics, Basic Industry Data and Industry Analytic Ratios for the Nonfarm Business Sector.

Note: The personal consumption expenditure deflator is used to calculate real compensation. Productivity refers to the nonfarm business sector.

Reasons for the well-known productivity slowdown remain unclear. Because this slowdown was experienced in most economies, the causes cannot be purely domestic. However, many analysts believe that increased U.S. capital accumulation, financed by increased national savings, would contribute to a rise in U.S. productivity growth. U.S. savings and investment remain low by international and historical standards. In this context, it is interesting to consider findings from a recent decomposition of the sources of growth in a large number of countries. These results make it possible to compare developments in the United States with those in other parts of the global economy.

Table 5. Decomposition of the Sources of Growth in Output per Worker (%)

	Growth in Output per Worker	Physical Capital per Worker	Human Capital per Worker	Total Factor Productivity
	United States			
1960–1973	1.9	0.5	0.6	0.8
1973–1994	0.6	0.3	0.2	0.1
Difference	−1.3	−0.2	−0.4	−0.7
	Other Industrial Countries			
1960–1973	4.8	2.3	0.4	2.2
1973–1994	1.7	1.0	0.4	0.4
Difference	−3.1	−1.3	0.0	−1.8
	East Asia			
1960–1973	4.2	2.3	0.5	1.3
1973–1994	4.2	2.5	0.6	1.0
Difference	0.0	0.2	0.1	−0.3
	Latin America			
1960–1973	3.4	1.3	0.3	1.8
1973–1994	0.3	0.6	0.4	−0.8
Difference	−3.1	−0.7	0.1	−2.6

Source: Collins and Bosworth (1996, Table 7, 158–159).

Table 5 shows the results of a growth-accounting exercise for the United States as well as 22 other industrial countries, 22 Latin American countries, and seven East Asian countries from 1960 to 1973 and from 1973 to 1994 (see Collins and Bosworth 1996 for details). For each country or region, the third row shows the difference between the two periods. The first column reports growth in output per worker. (Note that this definition of labor productivity differs from the one used in table 4.) Using standard growth-accounting methodology, the growth in output per worker has been decomposed into three portions in the remaining columns of the table. These are the contributions from increases in physical and human capital per worker and a residual. Typically called total factor productivity (TFP) growth, this residual indicates growth in the efficiency with which factors are used in production. Although intended as a proxy for changes in technology and "know-how" more broadly defined, the residual reflects a variety of developments, including political crises and external shocks.

Table 5 shows a 1.3 percentage point fall in the growth of output per U.S. worker between the two periods. Slightly less than half of this drop (0.6 percentage point) is accounted for by a fall in the contribution of increased physical and especially human capital per worker.

The U.S. experience has been in some ways similar and in other ways quite different from that in other regions. In 1960, the United States was the acknowledged technical leader, with an already high ratio of physical and human capital per worker. Not surprisingly, further accumulations of capital or improvements in technology contributed considerably less to U.S. economic growth from 1960 to 1973 than was true for developing countries, or for other industrial countries on average. After 1973, all regions experienced some slowdown in TFP growth. As a group, the other industrial countries are like the United States in that slower TFP growth accounts for slightly more than half of the overall reduction in growth of output per worker.

Experiences in East Asia and Latin America provide striking contrasts. The East Asian countries saw a relatively small reduction in TFP growth, which was offset by increases in both physical and human capital accumulation to maintain rapid overall growth in output per worker. In Latin America, a drop in the contribution of capital accumulation to growth (from an already low level compared with East Asia and the non-U.S. Organization for Economic Cooperation and Development, or OECD, countries) reinforced plummeting TFP growth after 1973.

Inequality and Insecurity

Another worrisome trend has been a marked increase in inequality since the late 1970s (see Burtless 1996). Increased inequality in incomes is partially attributable to a rise in wage inequality. For both men and women, low-wage workers experienced much slower increases in earnings than higher-wage workers. This trend was particularly striking for men. From 1979 to 1989, the 60 percent of men with the lowest wages (those in the bottom three quintiles of the wage distribution) saw their real earnings actually fall, whereas those in the next wage quintile saw no change in real earnings. Only the top 20 percent of male earners experienced a rise in real earnings.

Considerable attention has focused on the link between wages and skill or educational levels; more skilled workers have fared much better in U.S. labor markets than those with less skill. For example, college graduates saw their real wages rise by 18 percent relative to high school graduates between 1979 and 1993. Some (economists and noneconomists) believe that this rising skills gap is attributable to increased international integration, and specifically, to increased integration between the United States and developing economies. In the present context, it is notable that only about a third of the increase in earnings inequality can be attributed to observable differences between workers—including their skill levels.

American workers also appear to be suffering from a lingering anxiety about their labor market prospects. Opinion poll data show a decline in the share of respondents who believe their current jobs are secure. In 1995, only 51 percent believed they were "not at all likely" to lose their jobs within the next 12 months. This share was much lower than the 60 percent in 1991, when the unemployment rate was 6.8 percent, and comparable to the share in 1983, when unemployment was close to 11 percent. Similarly, quit rates are lower than would be expected from historical experience. The evidence to support the view that jobs are less secure is mixed. Some indicators suggest an increase in the rate of job loss, whereas others suggest that the rate of job loss has fallen. However, the characteristics of those losing their jobs have changed, implying that a broader cross-section of the American labor force can now expect to experience job dislocation.

INTERNATIONAL INTEGRATION AND U.S. LABOR MARKETS

Has growing integration harmed American workers? Is it to blame for the recent difficulties, particularly of less skilled workers, and will it cause even greater dislocations in the future? These questions have been the topic of an often heated debate in the United States. The debate focuses on trying to explain the causes of the increase in the premium paid to skilled relative to less skilled workers.

Circumstantial evidence suggests that globalization has played at least some role. In particular, relative wages of less skilled workers have declined over roughly the same time period as the increase in trade with developing countries. Furthermore, stories linking the two are intuitive. (It is much more difficult to explain why globalization should be associated with increased wage disparity that is not related to skill differences. Most analyses do not focus on the broader rise in wage inequality, or in other components of family income inequality, even though these trends are arguably central to recent concerns about American workers.) This section summarizes key points that have emerged from the large and complex literature about globalization and the skill premium. (For additional analysis and references, see Collins 1998 and Lawrence 1996.)

Three factors have been identified as possible causes (culprits) for the rise in the U.S. skill premium: globalization, technical change, and U.S. domestic developments. Increased economic integration, particularly with relatively low-wage economies, includes increased immigration and the prevalence of multinational corporations as well as trade in goods and services. Technological change that may be of concern includes developments that are biased toward particular types of factor inputs or toward particular sectors, or both. Factor bias could have implied a shift in relative demand away from less skilled toward more highly skilled workers. Sector bias could have shifted labor demand away from industries that are relatively intensive in their use of less skilled labor.

Finally, other relevant developments within the United States include institutional changes such as changes in the role of unions and in the relationships between workers and companies, and the decline in the real value of the minimum wage. Also included are labor supply changes, such as in the skill composition of the U.S. labor force.

The list of possible culprits makes it difficult to empirically assess the causes of the increased skill premium, because each is difficult to measure. Trade flows are often used to measure increased globalization. But many international economists have stressed that trade flows are not exogenous indicators of a "globalization change." Instead, imports and exports are endogenous variables that should reflect technological developments as well as changes in the degree of international integration. There are similar problems with changes in the prices of goods and services that are traded internationally. In particular, a large economy such as the United States is unlikely to be a price taker for many items. Explicit policy changes, such as reductions in trade barriers in the United States or its trading partners, could be considered exogenous indicators of increased integration. However, available data on tariffs and quotas are poor proxies for the underlying developments of interest, both because they do not adequately capture changes in outward orientation, and because such policy changes are only one piece of the whole picture. Other developments that should be considered important pieces of the "globalization shock" include the rapid growth of productive capacity in U.S. trading partners in Asia and elsewhere and falling transportation and communication costs.

Technical change is notoriously difficult to measure. Numerous studies estimate it using the residual, once the effects of more easily measurable contributions of factor inputs are taken into account. It is not surprising, then, that most analyses simply look at how much of the increased skill premium can be explained by measurable changes in trade and immigration and assume that the remaining unexplained portion is a measure of the importance of technology (Leamer 1998 is an exception). Relatively few studies consider a role for domestic institutional changes, and those that do tend to discuss the changes in qualitative terms.

Two main methodological approaches are used in the existing literature: the quantities or factor-content approach and the prices or Heckscher-Ohlin approach. Each is based on a model that makes simplifying assumptions about how the world works. Each therefore is subject to limitations. Disagreement among analysts about the best approach helps to explain why the debate about trade and wages has been difficult especially for nonexperts to follow and why research in this area continues to be active.

The factor-content approach is based on a simple model of labor supply and demand. The basic idea is that exports of goods and services to the rest of the world increase the derived demand for domestic factors of production, whereas imports and immigration from the rest of the world increase the effective supply of factors of production. Changes in relative supplies of factors can be related to changes in relative wages using estimates of demand elasticities. More specifically, although U.S. imports are relatively more intensive in their usage of low-skilled labor than U.S. exports, a rise in net imports should be associated with a rise in the effective supply of less skilled workers, and thus with a fall in their relative wage. A critique of this approach is that it assumes that trade flows can be treated as exogenous indicators of globalization.

A number of analysts have applied the factor-content methodology to assess the implications of globalization for relative wages, and most (though not all) conclude that trade and immigration account for at most a quarter of the recent increase in the skill premium. Borjas, Freeman, and Katz (1996) conclude that trade and immigration combined can explain 10 percent (1.6 percentage points) of the increase in the premium paid to college graduates relative to high school graduates from 1980 to 1990, with trade and immigration having similar effects. (They also conclude that trade and especially immigration may have been more important factors in the deteriorating position of high school dropouts relative to other workers.)

The other approach is based on the Heckscher-Ohlin model of international trade. In this general equilibrium model, which assumes perfect competition and constant returns to scale, there is no necessary relationship between changes in quantities of factors and changes in factor prices. Instead, the framework highlights a linkage between changes in relative prices of goods and changes in relative prices of factors. (Other implications of the Heckscher-Ohlin model have also been examined.) In the simplest case, with two factors (skilled labor and unskilled labor) and two goods (skill-intensive airplanes and unskilled-intensive apparel), the well-known Stolper-Samuelson theorem states that a fall in the price of apparel relative to airplanes will reduce the price of unskilled relative to skilled labor. The story would be that greater outward orientation in East Asia and other low-wage economies has reduced the world relative price of apparel. However, in extended versions of the model with many goods and many production factors, the relationships between goods and factor prices become somewhat more complex, making it difficult to infer the implications of goods price changes for the price of a particular type of labor.

Those basing their analysis on the Heckscher-Ohlin model stress that if globalization affected relative wages of the less skilled, the channel would be through changes in the relative price of goods that are intensive in their use of less skilled labor. Thus, many studies ask whether relative prices of goods such as apparel have declined. The maintained assumption is that changes in the prices of traded goods reflect exogenous changes in the global economy. Various studies reach somewhat different conclusions, depending in part on which sectors are included, and on how goods prices are adjusted for productivity changes. One carefully cloned analysis (Leamer 1998) concludes that the relative prices of less skill-intensive goods did not fall during the 1980s. But somewhat surprisingly, less skill-intensive goods did become relatively less expensive during the 1970s. The increase in wage disparities, and in particular in the skill premium, occurred during the past 15 years, so that this price evidence does not support the view that globalization has been the main culprit, unless it works with a significant lag.

In sum, existing evidence provides little support for the view that globalization has been at the heart of the recent problems of less skilled American workers, suggesting instead that increased integration accounts for at most a quarter of the fall in the relative wages of the less skilled. Technological change seems likely to explain the largest portion of this shift. However, the problems with existing empirical analyses make it difficult to pin down the causes conclusively. New analyses are exploring whether integration might work through channels that are poorly captured in either the factor-content or the Heckscher-Ohlin approaches.

LABOR MARKET ADJUSTMENT: EXPERIENCE AND POLICY

Any dynamic economy experiences considerable "churning." Each year, some companies (and sectors) thrive, whereas others do poorly. New jobs are created as new companies expand or are created. Jobs are eliminated as companies contract or go out of business. The extensive job creation and destruction cause employment changes for many individual Americans. In particular, some workers will be involuntarily displaced from their jobs.

Because increased integration with the rest of the world economy is associated with structural changes in the domestic economy, globalization should be expected to contribute to the natural churning of the U.S. economy. Reaping the rewards from interactions with the global economy must entail some changes at home.

As has been widely noted, employers in the United States are more likely to lay off workers (instead of adjusting hours or compensation) than employers in Western Europe or Japan. Furthermore, displaced workers in the United States receive much less assistance—they are largely on their own in preparing for and finding new jobs. Arguably, this "harsh" climate has contributed to the extent of concern over the possibility that increased international economic integration or any other structural change would harm American workers.

Experiences of Displaced Workers

The economic costs to an individual displaced from his job are substantial. The typical displaced worker suffers a large reduction in earnings (see Leigh 1995; Jacobson 1998). His income often declines in the months prior to actual job loss. Once permanently displaced, significant time is required to find a new job. (Most displaced workers are reemployed within 18 months.) The new job tends to pay lower wages—and this earnings gap (relative to earnings at the previous job) is persistent. One recent study estimated the (present value of the) total earnings loss for the average displaced worker at US$80,000 (Jacobson 1998).

The probability of being displaced appears to have been about the same in the early 1990s as it was in the early 1980s. (Among workers with at least three years on their current job, 3.8 percent were displaced in 1991 and 1992, compared with 3.9 percent in 1981 and 1982.) However, there have been some changes in the composition of displaced workers; in the early 1990s, they were more likely to be older, white collar, and well educated. (Although older workers have seen a rise in the probability of job loss, this probability continues to be lower for older rather than for younger workers.) The earnings loss associated with displacement has also increased.

Displacement is not predominantly an international trade-related phenomenon. On average, industries that face significant import competition do not tend to have higher displacement rates, and most displaced workers do not come from such industries. A recent study by Kletzer (1998) concludes that overall, workers in industries with high import penetration are no more likely to be displaced than workers in other industries. This is true even though a few highly visible sectors with high import penetration, such as apparel, do have high rates of displacement. This finding is consistent with the conclusion of the previous section that factors other than international integration per se explain most of the recent changes in U.S. labor markets.

However, the evidence on whether workers displaced from import-competing industries face greater hardships is mixed. Such workers may take longer to become reemployed, and may suffer somewhat greater earnings losses. In particular, Kletzer compares the experiences after job loss for workers who are displaced from import-sensitive industries with those displaced from other industries. The former appear to have more difficulty in finding new jobs. However, these workers are more likely to be female, and tend to be younger and less educated than workers displaced from industries that are not import sensitive. Conditional on worker characteristics, Kletzer finds no difference in reemployment probabilities between the two groups.

Americans are quite responsive to incentives. In particular, the persistent skill premium earned by more educated workers has prompted a significant rise in the percentages of those who complete high school and who go on to higher education. Over time, this labor supply response should go a long way toward alleviating what appears to be a mismatch between the high demand for skilled workers relative to the available supply.

This adjustment mechanism primarily affects new entrants into the labor force. It is much less relevant for older workers, who have been away from school for many years—an important component of those who become displaced. Moreover, not every worker can become highly skilled, or would benefit from additional schooling. Of particular concern in this regard are those who are disadvantaged and/or have weak basic skills.

Assisting Displaced Workers

A variety of U.S. government policies assist displaced workers. It is useful to distinguish between two types. Passive interventions provide general income support and/or supplement the incomes of those who are unemployed. Often also called a "social safety net," they include unemployment insurance (UI), welfare, and earned income tax credits. Active interventions are intended to shorten unemployment spells and/or to increase the earnings potential of workers seeking jobs. Included here would be various types of job search assistance, retraining, and career development programs.

Compared to many other industrial countries, the United States devotes few government resources to either passive or active labor market interventions. For example, in terms of their national incomes, Canada and Germany devote more than three times the amount devoted in the United States. Japan devotes somewhat less than the United States. However, Japan has an extensive and well-developed training system that is integrated into the general education system and that actively involves private employers.

In terms of passive interventions, concern exists about the small portion of the unemployed who receive unemployment insurance benefits. This proportion declined further during the 1980s. Leigh reports that "at present, although over 90 percent of employed workers hold jobs that are covered by the UI system, less than 30 percent of the unemployed receive UI benefits" (1995, 44).

Active interventions in the United States have been characterized as fragmented and unstable (Leigh 1995). Short-term "demonstration" projects are common, often with extensive evaluation, but little follow-up. A plethora of programs are run from different federal, state, and local agencies. The result is a maze that can be confusing, inefficient, and inequitable. However, the evaluations suggest some useful lessons about how such interventions might be improved.

Consider first job search assistance. This might include basic workshops on how to search for a job and a clearinghouse of information to help match job seekers with openings. (A problem with current participating agencies, such as the U.S. employment service, is that they have limited information about job openings.) Such programs do seem to help some displaced workers find jobs more quickly. Although the net payoffs from such schemes are relatively small, many analysts conclude that such programs are worthwhile because they are relatively inexpensive, and provide a significant "bang-for-the-buck."

Experiences in the United States and abroad suggest that, although far from a panacea, job training can help. There is, however, a widespread perception that other countries do a better job than the United States of training workers. One set of issues involves preparing young workers for the school-to-work transition. Although extremely important, job training for younger workers does not address the concerns of older workers who are more likely to be displaced by trade.

Unfortunately, the evidence about the effectiveness of training programs for older workers is mixed. In particular, it appears that classroom-based training programs are often expensive, with little payoff. Programs that seem to work best are those that are delivered on the job or in worklike settings. In addition, employer involvement is important in making sure that the skills being taught to workers in the training programs are marketable. However, it is difficult to design a program that helps all displaced workers, particularly those with weak basic skills, and such broadly targeted programs are expensive.

CONCLUDING REMARKS

A healthy, dynamic economy typically undergoes considerable structural change as some sectors expand while others contract. Although beneficial overall, this churning implies some workers are involuntarily displaced from their jobs, and these bear a disproportionate share of the costs of adjustment. Thus, experiences of displaced workers and the availability of policies to assist them are critical components of an economy's domestic adjustment.

The continued strength of the U.S. economy, with its rapid job creation and low rates of unemployment, should ease the problems of worker dislocation overall. However, other aspects of recent U.S. economic performance have been much less positive. In particular, average real wages have stagnated, whereas wage and income inequality has increased. As a result, many low-wage, and particularly low-skilled, Americans have seen their real earnings actually decline since the late 1970s. Overall, American workers are surprisingly anxious about the security of their jobs, and concerned that they may have to bear the costs of adjustment.

Increased integration with the rest of the world economy—especially nonindustrial countries—has been widely seen as the cause of recent labor market concerns. The strength of this view should be attributed not just to its intuitive nature, and to the similar timing of the two developments, but also to the fact that Americans are undergoing a profound change in how they view their economy relative to the rest of the world—the United States is no longer the clear productive and technical leader. However, extensive empirical analysis fails to find support for the view that globalization is the main culprit. Most studies conclude that trade and immigration account for at most a quarter of the fall in relative earnings of less skilled Americans, with technical change and domestic developments explaining the remainder. Furthermore, industries with high import penetration do not have a higher incidence of job displacement.

Attention to the implications of increased international economic integration has focused on the labor market. Other issues also warrant attention. For example, the United States persists in saving relatively little of its national income. The availability of foreign capital inflows enables the country to finance investment in excess of this low saving rate. A change in this environment could entail major domestic adjustments in both the short and longer run. Additional areas of interest include the implications of a global economy for design of the tax system, and for revising the regulations on the activities of U.S. financial institutions.

BIBLIOGRAPHY

Baily, Martin, Gary Burtless, and Robert Litan. 1993. *Growth with Equity.* Washington, D.C.: Brookings Institution.

Borjas, George. 1995. "The Economic Benefits from Immigration." *Journal of Economic Perspectives* 9(2): 3–22.

Borjas, George, Richard Freeman, and Lawrence Katz. 1996. "Searching for the Effect of Immigration on the Labor Market." *American Economic Review* (May): 246–251.

Bosworth, Barry, and George L. Perry. 1994. "Productivity and Real Wages: Is There a Puzzle?" *Brookings Papers on Economic Activity* 1: 317–335.

Burtless, Gary. 1996. "Widening U.S. Income Inequality and the Growth in World Trade." *Tokyo Club Papers* 9: 129–160.

Collins, Susan M. 1998. "Economic Integration and U.S. Labor Markets: An Overview and Summary." In Susan M. Collins, ed. *Imports, Exports and the American Worker.* Washington, D.C.: Brookings Institution.

Collins, Susan, and Barry Bosworth. 1996. "Economic Growth in East Asia: Accumulation versus Assimilation." *Brookings Papers on Economic Activity* 2: 135–203.

Friedberg, Rachel, and Jennifer Hunt. 1995. "The Impact of Immigrants on Host Country Wages, Employment and Growth." *Journal of Economic Perspectives* 9(2): 23–44.

Graham, Edward, and Paul Krugman. 1991. *Foreign Direct Investment in the United States.* 2nd ed. Washington, D.C.: Institute for International Economics.

Jacobson, Louis. 1998. "An Assessment of Policy Responses Aimed at Reducing the Costs to Workers of Structural Change Due to International Competition and Other Factors." In Susan M. Collins, ed. *Imports, Exports and the American Worker.* Washington, D.C.: Brookings Institution.

Kletzer, Lori. 1998. "International Trade and Job Displacement in U.S. Manufacturing: 1979–1991." In Susan M. Collins, ed. *Imports, Exports and the American Worker.* Washington, D.C.: Brookings Institution.

Lawrence, Robert. 1996. *Single World, Divided Nations? International Trade and OECD Labor Markets.* Washington, D.C.: Brookings Institution.

Lawrence, Robert, and Matthew Slaughter. 1993. "International Trade and American Wages in the 1980s: Giant Sucking Sound or Small Hiccup?" *Brookings Papers on Economic Activity: Microeconomics,* no. 2.

Leamer, Edward. 1998. "In Search of Stolper-Samuelson Effects on U.S. Wages." In Susan M. Collins, ed. *Imports, Exports and the American Worker.* Washington, D.C.: Brookings Institution.

Leigh, Duane. 1995. *Assisting Workers Displaced by Structural Change.* Kalamazoo, Mich.: Upjohn Institute.

U.S. Council of Economic Advisers. 1989. *Economic Report of the President.* Washington, D.C.: U.S. Government.

———. 1998. *Economic Report of the President.* Washington, D.C.: U.S. Government.

Developing Countries

7 · China

Ding Jingping

THROUGHOUT much of its long history, and especially in the 18th and 19th centuries, China has been closed to the rest of the world. And its first major experiences with European countries were unpleasant. After the First Opium War (1839–1842), two opposing views emerged on how to deal with foreign influences. One view was to refuse all things foreign. The other view was to be selective, accepting only what China needed. However, no consensus evolved as to what this selectivity might include. In the Qing Dynasty (1840–1911), the so-called Foreign Business Movement Supporters advocated "utilizing foreign things for China's purposes" and "Chinese theory is the base, and foreign theory is a tool." Under these principles, few foreign ideas were imported. However, foreign goods were imported, which effectively promoted Western thought and goods throughout China. Even so, the government's intent was to accept foreign things for China's purposes.

During the Cultural Revolution (1966–1976), intellectual theories from abroad were deemed antirevolutionary, and the expression of foreign ideas often resulted in severe punishment. Unlike the Foreign Business Movement in the Qing Dynasty, there were no exceptions to the ban on all things foreign during the Cultural Revolution. After the Cultural Revolution, a new group of leaders attempted to place the ideas of the Foreign Business Movement Supporters in a more positive light. However, Chinese people, generally speaking, still have difficulty dealing with foreigners.

159

China adopted its openness policies in late 1978, and the country has since undergone rapid and wrenching economic and social changes that are largely associated with globalization. These changes are so dramatic and significant as to be incomparable to any previous movement in Chinese history. They have made China a truly open and advanced society.

Since the early 1990s, the pace of globalization has accelerated owing to increased international trade, foreign investment, travel, and information flows in sum, scale, and scope. As a result, China has participated in and benefited from many aspects of globalization. Globalization has affected China's economy, culture, lifestyle, and, more important, its politics and, gradually, even its ideology.

Globalization brings both advantages and disadvantages to China. Average Chinese find it difficult to realize the advantages because of their limited scope of activities. But they can easily experience the disadvantages: enhanced competition, the availability of foreign products in the local marketplace, the income gap between those who work for foreign-funded businesses versus local businesses, and cultural influences (foreign movies, TV shows, and music). Thus, the inverse of globalization could well be nationalism.

What are the major impacts of globalization on China? How do the Chinese view globalization, and what domestic adjustments have resulted from globalization? These questions are frequently raised both inside and outside of China. This chapter approaches globalization in China primarily from an economic perspective and consists of four parts:

- The current status of globalization in China.
- The positive and negative impacts of globalization on China as evaluated by its citizenry.
- The current debate on the utilization of foreign investment.
- Domestic adjustment and the role of major Chinese research institutions in policy adjustment.

CURRENT STATUS OF GLOBALIZATION IN CHINA

The main aspects of globalization for China are foreign trade, foreign investment, international travel, and information flows between China and the rest of the world.

China's Foreign Trade since 1990

Foreign trade plays an increasingly important role in the Chinese economy. In 1980, the ratio of foreign trade to China's gross domestic product (GDP) was only 12.6 percent. In 1990, this figure reached 30.4 percent, and it advanced to 39.5 percent by 1995 (table 1). Total trade—exports and imports—rose from US$115.44 billion in 1990 to US$280.85 billion in 1995 (table 2). Exports were relatively unchanged as a percentage of total trade from 1990 to 1995 but surged

Table 1. Percentage of Foreign Trade to GDP in China (Rmb billion)

	GDP	Foreign Trade	Foreign Trade/GDP (%)
1990	1,831.95	556.01	30.4
1991	2,128.04	722.58	34.0
1992	2,586.37	911.96	35.3
1993	3,450.07	1,127.10	32.7
1994	4,644.23	2,038.19	43.9
1995	5,945.25	2,349.87	39.5

Source: China Statistical Yearbook (1996, 46, 580).

GDP: Gross domestic product.

Table 2. Total Value of Imports and Exports in China, 1990–1995 (US$ billion)

	Total	Exports	% of Total	Imports	% of Total	Balance
1990	115.44	62.09	53.8	53.35	46.2	8.74
1991	135.63	71.84	53.0	63.79	47.0	8.05
1992	165.53	84.94	51.3	80.59	48.7	4.35
1993	195.70	91.74	46.9	103.96	53.1	−12.22
1994	236.62	121.01	51.1	115.61	48.9	5.40
1995	280.85	148.77	53.0	132.08	47.0	16.69

Source: China Statistical Yearbook (1996, 580).

Note: Based on customs statistics.

by 139.6 percent by value. Imports jumped by 147.6 percent over the same period. The cumulative trade surplus has increased each year since 1990 except 1993. By the end of 1996, China's hard currency reserve exceeded US$100 billion. According to the National Statistics Bureau, China was the 10th largest trading country in the world as of 1995.

The structure of foreign trade has also changed dramatically. For

Table 3. Value of Exports and Imports by Commodity (US$ billion)

	Total	Primary Goods	% of Total	Manufactured Goods	% of Total
			Exports		
1990	62.09	15.89	25.6	46.21	74.4
1991	71.84	16.15	22.5	55.70	77.5
1992	84.94	17.00	20.0	67.94	80.0
1993	91.74	16.67	18.2	75.08	81.8
1994	121.01	19.71	16.3	101.30	83.7
1995	148.77	21.49	14.4	127.28	85.6
			Imports		
1990	53.35	9.85	18.5	43.49	81.5
1991	63.79	10.84	17.0	52.96	83.0
1992	80.59	13.26	16.5	67.33	83.5
1993	103.96	14.21	13.7	89.75	86.3
1994	115.61	16.49	14.3	99.13	85.7
1995	132.08	24.41	18.5	107.67	81.5

Source: China Statistical Yearbook (1996, 581–582).

Table 4. China's Foreign Trade (US$ billion)

	1995				1991	
	Total	Exports	Imports	Ranking	Total	Ranking
Total	280.85	148.77	132.08		135.70	
Asia	170.05	92.00	78.05		86.65	
Japan	57.47	28.46	29.00	1	20.28	2
Hong Kong	44.57	35.98	8.59	2	49.60	1
Taiwan	17.88	3.10	14.78	4	4.23	5
South Korea	16.98	6.90	10.29	5	3.24	7
Singapore	6.90	3.50	3.40	7	3.07	8
Indonesia	3.49	1.44	2.05	14	1.88	13
Thailand	3.36	1.75	1.61	15	1.27	16
Malaysia	3.35	1.28	2.07	16	1.33	14
Africa	3.92	2.49	1.42		1.66	
Europe	50.79	22.98	27.81		22.16	
Germany	13.71	5.67	8.04	6	4.97	4
Former Soviet Union	5.46	1.66	3.80	8	3.90	6
Italy	5.18	2.07	3.11	9	1.90	12
United Kingdom	4.76	2.79	1.97	10	2.02	11
France	4.49	1.84	2.65	11	2.31	9
Netherlands	4.05	3.23	0.81	13	1.31	15
Latin America	6.11	3.15	2.96			
North America	45.04	26.24	18.80		16.40	
United States	40.82	24.71	16.11	3	14.40	3
Canada	4.21	1.53	2.68	12	2.20	10
Oceania	4.92	1.90	3.02			
Australia	4.21	1.63	2.58	12	0.20	

Source: China Statistical Yearbook (1992, 623–624; 1996, 586–588).
Note: Based on customs statistics.

example, of US$62.09 billion in exports in 1990, primary goods accounted for 25.6 percent and manufactured goods 74.4 percent (table 3). This ratio changed to 14.4 percent and 85.6 percent, respectively, by 1995. However, the ratio of imported primary goods and manufactured goods did not change, at 18.5 percent and 81.5 percent, respectively, in both 1990 and 1995.

Most of China's trading partners are in Asia. Asian countries/ regions accounted for 60.5 percent of total trade by value with China in 1995, although that was down slightly from 63.9 percent in 1990 (table 4). North America's share of 1995 trade was 16.0 percent. The biggest change among China's trading partners occurred in 1995, when Japan surpassed Hong Kong as China's major trading partner.

Utilizing Foreign Investment

Foreign investment in China consists mainly of three methods: (a) foreign loans; (b) foreign direct investment (FDI), including joint ventures, foreign cooperation (arrangements in which companies combine expertise but not financial resources), and fully foreign-owned businesses; and (c) others, such as composition trade (through which foreign companies provide technology or equipment to a Chinese partner and receive products in return) and assembly or international leasing. From 1979 to 1990, foreign loans were the major source of foreign investment in China. In 1992, however, FDI become the major source. The ratio of FDI to total foreign investment was 57.3 percent in 1992, compared with 37.8 percent in 1991 (tables 5 and 6). Since 1992, this ratio has increased rapidly and reached 78.1 percent in 1994. The

Table 5. Utilization of Foreign Investment in China (US$ billion)

	Total			Foreign Loans			Foreign Direct Investment and Others		
	No. of Projects	Con-tracted Amount	Actual Amount Utilized	No. of Projects	Con-tracted Amount	Actual Amount Utilized	No. of Projects	Con-tracted Amount	Actual Amount Utilized
1990	7,371	12.09	10.29	98	5.10	6.53	7,273	6.99	3.76
1991	13,086	19.58	11.55	108	7.16	6.89	12,978	12.42	4.67
1992	48,858	69.44	19.20	94	10.70	7.91	48,764	58.74	11.29
1993	85,595	123.27	38.96	158	11.31	11.19	83,437	111.97	27.77
1994	47,646	93.76	43.21	97	10.67	9.27	47,549	83.09	33.95
1995	37,184	103.21	48.13	173	11.29	10.33	37,011	91.91	37.81

Source: A Statistical Survey of China (1996, 110).

Table 6. Structure of Actual Utilized Foreign Investment (%)

	Foreign Loans	Foreign Direct Investment	Other Foreign Investment
1990	63.5	33.9	2.6
1991	59.6	37.8	2.6
1992	41.2	57.3	1.5
1993	28.7	70.6	0.7
1994	21.5	78.1	0.4
1995	22.1	77.9	0.0

Source: China's Industrial Development Report (1996, 271).

Note: Other foreign investment refers to composition trade, assembly, and international leasing.

Table 7. Foreign Investment in China, 1979–1995 (US$ billion)

	Total Projects		Contracted Amount		Actual Amount Utilized	
	No. of Projects	%	Amount	%	Amount	%
1979–1985	6,321	2.5	16.33	4.2	4.72	3.5
1986–1990	22,728	9.1	24.04	6.3	14.26	10.7
1991–1995	220,728	88.4	344.22	89.5	114.36	85.8
1979–1995	249,777	100.0	384.58	100.0	133.34	100.0

Source: China Statistical Yearbook (1995, 1996); International Economic & Trade Information (1995).

Table 8. Foreign Direct Investment in China, 1990–1995 (US$ billion)

	No. of Projects	Contracted Amount	Actual Amount Utilized
1990	7,273	7.00	3.76
1991	12,978	12.42	4.67
1992	48,764	58.74	11.29
1993	83,437	111.97	27.77
1994	47,549	83.09	33.95
1995	37,011	91.92	37.81

Source: A Statistical Survey of China (1996).

ratio of other sources to total foreign investment fell to almost zero by 1994.

Both the number of projects and the contracted and utilized amounts have soared in the 1990s. From 1979 to 1995, overall foreign investment projects totaled 249,777 (table 7). This resulted in contracts worth US$384.58 billion and actual investment of US$133.34 billion. However, from just 1991 to 1995, 220,728 foreign-funded projects were contracted at US$344.22 billion, with actual investment of US$114.36 billion. Foreign investment peaked in 1993. From 1994, the number of projects and contractual amounts began to

Table 9. Ownership Structure of Foreign Investment (US$ billion)

	Joint Ventures			Cooperation			Fully Foreign Owned		
	No. of Projects	Con-tracted Amount	Actual Amount	No. of Projects	Con-tracted Amount	Actual Amount	No. of Projects	Con-tracted Amount	Actual Amount
					1991				
No./Amt.	24,684	21.33	11.43	11,089	18.31	6.19	6,180	9.29	2.56
%	58.8	43.6	56.6	26.5	37.4	30.7	14.7	19.0	12.7
					1992				
No./Amt.	58,910	50.77	17.81	16,831	31.58	8.27	14,969	1.90	1.27
%	64.9	47.7	57.2	18.6	29.7	26.6	16.5	22.6	16.2
					1993				
No./Amt.	113,041	105.63	32.89	27,245	57.06	13.55	33,847	55.44	11.59
%	64.9	48.4	56.7	15.7	26.2	23.3	19.4	25.4	20.0
					1994				
No./Amt.	140,931	145.82	50.82	33,879	77.36	20.63	46,854	77.39	19.63
%	63.3	48.5	55.8	15.3	25.7	22.7	21.1	25.8	21.5
					1995				
No./Amt.	161,386	39.74	19.08	38,666	17.83	7.54	58,615	33.66	10.32
%	62.4	43.6	51.7	14.9	19.5	20.4	22.7	36.9	27.9

Source: China's Foreign Economic & Trade Yearbook (1992, 1993, 1994, 1995).
Note: No. of projects is cumulative.

decline, but the amount of actual investment continued to gradually increase (table 8).

From 1979 to 1995, foreign investment projects totaled 258,667: 161,386 joint ventures (62.4 percent of the total), 58,615 fully foreign-owned businesses (22.7 percent), and 38,666 foreign cooperation (14.9 percent). Joint ventures were also the major method of foreign investment both by contract value and actual investment (table 9). The average amount invested per foreign-funded project climbed from US$960,000 in 1991 to US$2.48 million in 1995 (table 10). From

Table 10. Average Size of Foreign Direct Investment Projects

	No. of Projects	Contracted Amount (US$ billion)	Average Size (US$ million)
1991	12,978	12.42	0.96
1992	48,764	58.74	1.20
1993	83,437	111.97	1.34
1994	47,549	83.09	1.75
1995	37,011	91.92	2.48

Source: A Statistical Survey of China (1996, 110).

Table 11. Source of Foreign Investment by Country/Region (%)

	1990	1991	1992	1993	1994	1995
Hong Kong and Macao	56.4	57.0	70.0	64.9	59.9	56.4
Taiwan	6.0	10.1	9.3	11.3	10.0	9.7
Subtotal	62.4	67.1	79.3	76.2	69.9	66.1
Japan	13.9	13.1	6.6	4.9	6.2	8.1
United States	12.3	7.1	4.6	7.5	7.3	6.7
Total	88.6	87.3	90.5	88.6	83.4	80.9

Source: China Statistical Yearbook (1991, 1992, 1993, 1994, 1995).
Note: All figures are actual utilized foreign investment.

Table 12. Industrial Structure of Foreign Investment in China (%)

	1991		1992		1993		1994		1995	
	Projects	Value	Projects	Value	Projects	Value	Projects	Value	Projects	Value
Primary industries	2.5	1.8	2.1	1.2	2.0	1.1	1.2	1.2	2.4	1.3
Secondary industries	90.2	81.5	81.5	59.4	71.6	49.4	73.1	56.0	74.0	63.4
Tertiary industries	7.3	16.7	16.4	39.4	26.4	49.5	25.7	42.8	23.6	35.3

Source: China's Foreign Economic & Trade Yearbook (1992, 1993, 1994, 1995).

1990 to 1995, more than 80 percent of total FDI came from the Asia Pacific region and was dominated by Hong Kong and Taiwan (more than 60 percent of the total), followed by Japan and the United States (table 11).

In the first half of 1996, China had approved another 14,054 foreign-funded enterprises with contracted amounts totaling US$45.54 billion. The actual utilized amount reached US$19.66 billion. Next to the United States, China was the second largest recipient of foreign investment in the world from 1994 to 1996.

Foreign investment was primarily in secondary industries from 1991 to 1995, although in 1993 a large amount of foreign investment was put into the tertiary industries, mainly in real estate. After the Chinese central government curtailed real estate development in mid-1993, investment returned to the secondary industries. In fact, the secondary industries are an area in which China urgently needs improvement (table 12).

China not only is one of the largest foreign investment recipients but also is a foreign investor itself. By the end of 1995, China had set up more than 5,500 enterprises in 130 countries/regions, with total invest-ment of US$40 billion. From 1980 to 1984, China's foreign investment was only about US$50 million annually. From 1985 to 1990, such invest-ment rose to US$2.5 billion annually. From 1991 to 1995, it increased again, to US$3.5 billion annually. In the first nine months of 1996, this figure exceeded US$4 billion. Most of this investment—about US$20 billion—is in Hong Kong. Other primary recipients include North America, Japan, and Southeast Asia. China's overseas businesses are active in such fields as steel, chemicals, electronics, textiles, machinery, construction materials, petrochemicals, and pharmaceuticals.

International Travel

The third clear aspect reflecting the trend of globalization is interna-tional travel. Overseas visitors to China jumped by 68.9 percent, from 27.5 million people in 1990 to 46.4 million people in 1995. Most visitors were from Hong Kong, Macao, Taiwan, and other overseas Chinese. They accounted for 93.6 percent of total visitors from abroad in 1990 and 87.3 percent in 1995 (table 13). Among non-Chinese overseas

Table 13. Foreign Tourists by Country/Region (1,000 persons)

	1990	1995	Increase (%)
Total	27,461.8	46,386.5	68.9
Overseas Chinese	91.1	115.8	27.1
Hong Kong, Macao, and Taiwan	25,623.4	40,384.0	57.6
Non-Chinese foreigners	1,747.3	5,886.7	236.9
Japan	463.3	1,305.2	181.7
United States	233.2	514.9	120.8
Former Soviet Union	109.8	489.3	345.6
Singapore	71.7	261.5	264.7
Philippines	78.9	219.7	178.5
United Kingdom	78.9	184.9	134.3
Thailand	67.9	173.3	155.2
Germany	56.2	166.5	196.3
Australia	50.2	129.4	157.8
Canada	47.6	128.8	170.6
France	50.7	118.5	133.7
South Korea	27.9	66.4	138.0
Italy	26.3	63.7	142.2
The Netherlands	13.8	34.9	152.9
Switzerland	11.5	34.3	198.3
New Zealand	10.0	22.9	129.0

Source: *China Statistical Yearbook* (1996, 603).

Table 14. Foreign Tourists by Occupation (1,000 persons)

	1990	1995	Increase (%)
Total	1,747.3	5,886.7	236.9
Technicians	315.0	482.7	53.2
Administrators	306.6	453.3	47.8
Businesspeople	369.6	1,171.7	217.0
Office clerks		431.0	
Service clerks		468.6	
Workers and farmers	333.4	597.9	79.3
Others	232.7	1,460.8	527.8
No occupation	190.0	820.9	332.1

Source: *China Statistical Yearbook* (1996, 604).

visitors, visitors from Japan were most numerous (2.8 percent of the total in 1995), followed by those from the United States (1.1 percent) and the former Soviet Union (1.0 percent). Visitors from the former Soviet Union skyrocketed by 345.6 percent from 1990 to 1995, forming the fastest growing group. Visitors from Singapore soared by 264.7 percent and ranked second in growth for the same period, followed by visitors from Switzerland and Germany.

Foreign visitors are primarily businesspeople. Businesspeople visiting China increased by 217.0 percent from 1990 to 1995, accounting for 21.2 percent of total foreign visitors in 1990 and 19.9 percent in 1995 (table 14). Technicians accounted for 18.0 percent of total visitors in 1990 and 8.2 percent in 1995.

From 1978 to 1994, the Chinese government sponsored study abroad for about 54,000 students, of which about 23,000 had returned by the end of 1994. The number of students who went abroad to study through nongovernment channels is much higher. In addition, China has invited many foreign experts working in China to help the Chinese improve their public works. According to the Foreign Experts Bureau of the State Council, this figure exceeded 1 million persons/times in 1996. Just in Dalian, a city in Liaoning Province, more than 15,000 foreign experts from more than 30 countries were invited to provide assistance in 1995.

Information Flows

An open-door policy and modern technology have created information flows to and from China and have also strongly influenced Chinese lifestyles. Although statistics on information flows are limited, the

Table 15. Development of Telecommunications in China

	1990	1995	Increase (%)
Posts and telecommunications revenue (Rmb billion)	8.17	98.89	1,110.4
Urban switchboard capacity (million)	8.26	54.56	560.5
Rural switchboard capacity (million)	4.06	17.47	330.3
Telephones (million)	12.74	57.62	352.3
Urban telephones (million)	10.26	47.09	359.0
Rural telephones (million)	2.47	10.53	326.3
Wireless telephones (million)	0.87[a]	17.39	1,898.9
Mobile telephones	47,544[a]	3,629,416	7,533.8
Direct-dial phone calls for abroad[b] (1,000)	584	17,097	2,827.6
Internet subscribers	0	500,000[c]	

Source: China Statistical Yearbook (1996, 529).

a. 1991 figure.
b. Includes to Hong Kong and Macao.
c. Estimated figure.

development of telecommunications reflects these changes. From 1990 to 1995, the revenue of the posts and telecommunications business grew from Rmb8.17 billion to Rmb98.89 billion, an increase of 11 times. Switchboard capacity in rural and urban areas rose 5.6 times and 3.3 times, respectively, in 1995, compared with 1990. Over the same period, the number of telephones nationwide increased more than 3 times. Mobile telephones, which were rare in China in the early 1990s, have become popular and reached 3.6 million sets in 1995 (table 15). The length of optical fiber cable has reached 113,000 kilometers. Consequently, telephone calls from China to abroad expanded 75 times from 1990 to 1995. The teledensity reached 5.8 percent in 1995 from about 2 percent in 1990.

New methods of communication are also emerging in China including the public data network, electronic data interchange networks, e-mail, and the Internet. These methods broaden contacts, improve efficiency, and shorten the distance between China and the rest of the world. By the end of 1995, the public data network was used by banks and insurance companies (70.96 percent), securities and futures companies (27.29 percent), government departments (1.69 percent), and tourist and service businesses (0.06 percent).

E-mail service providers have also been established in many cities in China. By the end of 1995, China had 27,000 e-mail addresses and a network with one administration domain name and nine private domain names located all over China.

The Internet, as an international network connecting more than 150 countries, 20,000 subnetworks, and 30 million users, is also gaining popularity in China. China has set up international nodes in Beijing and Shanghai and will extend such nodes to the capitals of all the provinces in 1997. There are an estimated 500,000 subscribers in China now. The number of real users, however, is probably much greater, according to a China Telecom 1996 survey; most subscribers are in work or university settings, where each subscription is utilized by many people.

THE PEOPLE'S RESPONSE TO GLOBALIZATION

Positive Impact on China

China has accrued the benefits of foreign investment since 1978. The following aspects describe the contributions of foreign investment.

Foreign Trade Foreign trade has promoted foreign economic exchange and created a large amount of hard currency for China. The ratio of imports and exports from foreign-funded businesses to China's overall foreign trade grew from 17.4 percent in 1990 to 39.1 percent in 1995 (table 16). Within overall foreign trade, the ratio of foreign-funded exports to total exports rose from 12.6 percent in 1990 to 31.5 percent in 1995. Meanwhile, the ratio of foreign-funded imports was 47.7 percent in 1995, up from 23.1 percent in 1990.

Gross Industrial Output The contribution of foreign investment in the industrial sector can be measured by the ratio of gross output

Table 16. Exports and Imports of Foreign-Funded Businesses Relative to Total Foreign Trade of China (%)

	% of Total	Exports to Total Exports	Imports to Total Imports
1990	17.4	12.6	23.1
1991	21.4	16.8	26.5
1992	26.3	20.5	32.7
1993	34.3	27.5	40.2
1994	37.0	28.7	45.8
1995	39.1	31.5	47.7

Source: China's Foreign Economic & Trade Yearbook (1991, 1992, 1993, 1994, 1995); A Statistical Survey of China (1996).

Table 17. Gross Industrial Production (GIP) of Foreign-Funded Businesses to GIP of China (Rmb billion)

	GIP of Foreign-Funded Businesses	% of Total	GIP of China
1990	498.00	2.1	2,392.44
1991	137.00	4.8	2,824.80
1992	207.00	5.6	2,306.57
1993	579.60	11.0	5,269.20
1994	745.36	12.0	6,211.30

Source: Reference for Economist Studies (1995).

Table 18. Number of Employees of Foreign-Funded Businesses Relative to Total Employees in China (1,000 people)

	Employees in Foreign-Funded Businesses	% of Total	Total Employees in China
1990	2,000	1.4	140,570
1992	6,000	4.1	147,920
1994	12,600	8.5	148,490
1995	16,000	10.8	148,490

Source: China's Foreign Economic & Trade Yearbook (1992, 1993, 1994, 1995).

Note: Total employees in China for 1995 is an estimate.

Table 19. Tax Payments of Foreign-Funded Businesses Relative to Total Tax Payments in China (Rmb billion)

	Tax Income from Foreign-Funded Businesses	% of Total	Domestic Tax Income
1991	6.90	2.3	299.02
1992	10.70	3.2	329.69
1993	20.60	4.8	425.53
1994	39.00	7.6	512.69

Source: China Statistical Yearbook (1991, 1992, 1993, 1994, 1995).

from foreign-funded businesses relative to total gross output. This ratio was only 2.1 percent in 1990, but reached 12.0 percent in 1994 (table 17). However, in some areas, the ratio was significantly higher, for example, 20 percent in Jiangsu Province, 24 percent in Beijing, 51 percent in Shenzhen, and 70 percent in Xiamen City.

Job Opportunities   Foreign-funded businesses play an increasingly important role in creating job opportunities for the Chinese. By the end of 1990 (table 18), foreign-funded businesses employed about 2 million people. This was equivalent to 1.4 percent of total employees in China. However, these figures increased to 16 million people and 10.8 percent of total employees by 1995.

Tax Payment   In 1991, foreign-funded businesses paid Rmb6.9 billion in taxes to the Chinese government. Three years later, they paid Rmb39.0 billion. The ratio of tax income from foreign-funded businesses to the overall tax income of China increased from 2.3 percent to 7.6 percent in the same period (table 19).

Negative Impact on China

The large infusion of foreign investment has resulted in many problems and conflicts. Some of these problems are getting more and more serious. The most critical problems are "extranational treatment," property assessment, industrial and regional monopolies, pollution shifting, trade friction, and the expanding income gap between coastal and inland areas.

Stimulating Unnecessary Joint Ventures   What treatment does China provide to foreign-funded businesses and what are the consequences for China? Many Chinese believe that foreign-funded businesses receive extranational treatment—priority treatment from the Chinese government relative to local businesses. For example, before 1994 China had two taxation systems. One was for foreign-funded businesses and the other was for domestic businesses. The tax rate for domestic businesses was much higher than that for foreign-funded businesses. Local businesses in general paid a 33 percent tax rate on income. Joint ventures were tax-free for the first three years, paid half the rate the following two years, and then paid only a 15 percent tax rate after five years. Because of the different tax rates, local companies found it difficult to compete with foreign-funded businesses. In addition, foreign-funded businesses can easily hire or fire their employees, but local businesses cannot.

These preferences make local businesses feel that foreign-funded businesses have an unfair competitive edge. To obtain such priorities, many local companies want to create joint ventures with foreign investors, or even artificial joint ventures, without concern for the loss of state-owned property. The government is the big loser under such circumstances.

In fact, foreign investors do not always receive extranational treatment. They actually experience some "subnational treatment." For instance, foreigners must pay higher prices than the Chinese for their business and personal activities, such as travel tickets, advertisements, and raw materials. Foreigners complain about this unfair treatment as well.

State-Owned Property Unfairly Assessed   In the initial period of openness, the major method of foreign investment was foreign investors bringing their hard currency into China. Hard currency accounted for about 80 percent of total investment and the rest was equipment or technology. However, the proportion of equipment investment to total investment was 70 percent in 1997. In some areas, it has even reached 90 percent. Thus, the question of how to evaluate the value of bring-in equipment has become more critical. In most cases, the bring-in equipment is overvalued and exported products are undervalued because the Chinese lack adequate methods to determine the real value. Therefore, the Chinese side of joint arrangements has lost a lot: shares and profit have been less than should have been the case.

Such unfair assessments have occurred both with tangible and intangible property. Intangible property, including product brand-names, licensing, know-how, exclusive rights, and reputation, is more difficult to assess fairly. In most cases, the Chinese property was undervalued or given no value, whereas foreign assets were overvalued. Consequently, people are angry about these joint ventures, and some Chinese partners of joint ventures (for example, the Shanghai Home Chemical Company) have been called traitors.

Industrial Monopoly by Foreign Investment   In the early stages of openness, the Chinese government required the Chinese side of a joint venture to hold a majority of the shares. In the 1990s, however, foreign investors have demanded more shares and the policy has changed. Many projects today are fully owned by foreign companies. Some foreign investors have purchased an entire industry or most of the companies in an industry in certain geographic areas. Gradually, foreign companies have come to monopolize some industries. For instance, Hong Kong–based China Strategic Investment Company owns 51 percent of its joint venture with Light Industry of Dalian. In Shanghai's home chemical industrial sector, 32 local companies, or 62.7 percent of the total sector in value, are held by foreign companies. Foreign holding companies have taken one-third of total sales in the Chinese cosmetic industry. Almost all of China's detergent companies have joined with foreign companies. Foreign brands are in a dominant position for many products. In the beer industry, of 61 Chinese companies with capacity in excess of 50,000 tons annually, 50 have joined with foreign companies. In the pharmaceutical industry, 40 percent of the state-owned companies are participating in joint ventures with foreign companies. The industrial monopoly by foreign investors is quickly spreading throughout China. Many people believe that this situation will be dangerous to China over the long term.

Pollution Shifting   One motivation for developed countries to shift their industries to developing countries is to transfer polluting industries or old technology that can cause pollution. Indeed, many developing countries do not have rigorous legislation protecting the environment. Thus, the cost of pollution control is much lower than that in developed countries. These differences stimulate some foreign companies to transfer their production to developing countries such as China. This phenomenon is popular among investors from Hong Kong and Taiwan. In 1991, investment from Hong Kong and Taiwan accounted for 81.1 percent of total projects and 74.3 percent by contract value. High-pollution projects (those that cause pollution but do not have pollution-treating facilities) represented 27.6 percent of total projects by volume and 34.7 percent by value. Although the Chinese government has begun to restrict pollution-transfer investment, the existing projects have already created serious problems.

Trade Friction   Another problem shifting to China via foreign investment is trade friction. Trade friction increases when labor-intensive production transfers to China from abroad. For example, investment from Hong Kong and Taiwan into China largely reduced the trade friction between them and the United States, but severely increased friction between China and the United States. According to U.S. Customs statistics, from 1985 to 1993 the U.S. trade deficit with China expanded from only US$0.43 billion to US$22.77 billion. In comparison, the United States' combined trade deficit with Taiwan and Hong Kong decreased from US$19.3 billion to US$8.5 billion during the same period.

Products exported back to the United States by U.S. investors in China are considered Chinese exports, but, in fact, these foreign producers take most of the benefits. China receives limited benefits but bears most of the cost.

The Chinese sometimes describe relations between Hong Kong and Guangdong like a business chain. Hong Kong retails goods and mainland China manufactures them. However, when such products are sent to the United States, for example, they are considered exports from China rather than Hong Kong. This situation puts China in a difficult situation; despite reunification, Hong Kong and mainland China remain separate economic entities. China suffers the repercussions of trade friction, and foreign investors garner the real benefits from the arrangement.

Foreign investment also causes quota problems in Chinese foreign trade. The Chinese government encourages foreign-funded businesses to export those products that are not affected by quota limitations. However, severe competition exists between domestic and foreign-funded businesses to fill limited quotas. Consequently, as exports by foreign-funded businesses increase, China faces increasingly problematic trade friction and quota concerns.

Income Gap Expanding between Coastal and Inland Areas   In urban coastal China, the annual per capita income was Rmb2,289.17 in 1991 and Rmb5,391.85 in 1995, a gain of 134.9 percent (table 20). However, in urban western China, per capita income was only Rmb1,923.77 in 1991 and Rmb3,676.35 in 1995, a rise of 101.0 percent. The gap between the coastal and western urban areas was 1.19:1 in 1991 but extended to 1.47:1 in 1995. In rural coastal areas, per capita income was Rmb967.72 in 1991 and Rmb2,346.06 in 1995, an increase of 143.7 percent. In rural western areas, per capita income was Rmb551.85 in 1991 and Rmb1,051.60 in 1995, an advance of only 93.1 percent. The gap between the rural coastal and western areas was 1.8:1 in 1991 but widened to 2.2:1 in 1995.

In 1991, the ratio between the richest province and the poorest province was 7.7:1 (Rmb3,329.39 in Guangdong and Rmb430.98 in Gansu). By 1995, the gap had worsened to 8.5:1 (Rmb7,445.10 in Guangdong and Rmb880.34 in Gansu).

Impact from Multinational Companies

Globalization and internationalization cannot be separated from multinational companies (MNCs). There are an estimated 40,000 MNCs worldwide with more than 270,000 branches and subsidiaries. Annual gross output of the MNCs equals 40 percent of the GDP of the industrialized countries. They control 60 percent of foreign trade, 70 percent of direct investment, and 80 percent of research and development and technology transfers in the world. By the end of 1995, total FDI from MNCs reached US$2.7 trillion. The MNCs allocate capital, technology, highly skilled manpower, management, and raw materials in their pursuit of economic globalization.

In early 1992, Deng Xiaoping gave a speech on deepening reform

Table 20. Annual per Capita Sources of Income by Region (Rmb)

	Urban			Rural		
	1991	1995	Increase (%)	1991	1995	Increase (%)
National	1,995.87	4,288.09	114.85	686.31	1,577.74	129.9
Coastal						
Beijing	2,359.87	6,237.91	164.33	1,297.05	3,223.65	148.5
Fujian	2,139.38	4,510.53	110.83	764.41	2,048.59	168.0
Guangdong	3,329.39	7,445.10	123.62	1,043.03	2,699.24	158.8
Guangxi	2,106.09	4,809.43	128.36	639.45	1,446.14	126.2
Hainan	2,032.67	4,803.36	136.31	696.22	1,519.71	118.3
Hebei	1,959.84	3,923.15	100.18	621.67	1,668.73	168.4
Jiangsu	2,101.16	4,647.33	121.18	959.06	2,456.86	156.2
Liaoning	1,987.77	3,707.53	86.52	836.17	1,756.50	110.1
Shandong	1,929.07	4,265.35	121.11	680.18	1,715.09	152.2
Shanghai	2,925.41	7,196.42	146.00	1,907.32	4,245.61	122.6
Tianjin	2,087.38	6,931.41	232.06	1,069.04	2,406.38	125.1
Zhejiang	2,512.06	6,224.62	147.79	1,099.04	2,966.19	169.9
Mean	2,289.17	5,391.85	134.86	967.72	2,346.06	143.7
Middle						
Anhui	1,727.51	3,796.93	119.79	539.16	1,302.82	141.6
Heilongjiang	1,611.16	3,377.24	109.62	759.86	1,766.27	132.4
Henan	1,672.29	3,302.14	97.46	526.95	1,231.97	133.8
Hubei	1,906.54	4,031.90	111.48	670.80	1,511.22	125.3
Hunan	2,045.48	4,705.21	130.03	664.24	1,425.26	114.6
Inner Mongolia	1,532.08	2,873.94	87.58	607.15	1,208.38	99.0
Jiangxi	1,542.48	3,380.92	119.19	669.90	1,537.36	129.5
Jilin	1,641.14	3,176.33	93.54	803.52	1,609.60	100.3
Shanxi	1,691.53	3,306.66	95.48	603.51	1,208.30	100.2
Mean	1,707.80	3,550.14	107.13	649.45	1,422.35	119.6
Western						
Gansu	1,683.34	3,155.78	87.47	430.98	880.34	104.3
Guizhou	1,705.75	3,935.46	130.72	435.14	1,086.62	149.7
Ningxia	1,951.73	3,386.79	73.53	578.13	998.75	72.8
Qinghai	1,684.77	3,319.86	97.05	559.78	1,029.77	84.0
Shaanxi	1,764.42	3,311.11	87.66	530.80	962.89	81.4
Sichuan	2,008.35	4,004.79	99.41	557.76	1,158.29	107.7
Tibet	2,675.19	n.a.		649.71	1,200.31	84.7
Xinjiang	1,877.30	4,183.81	122.86	683.47	1,136.45	66.3
Yunnan	1,963.12	4,113.19	109.52	540.86	1,010.97	86.9
Mean	1,923.77	3,676.35	101.03	551.85	1,051.60	93.1

Source: China Statistical Yearbook (1992, 264; 1996, 288, 302).

and extending openness in southern China. It was another milestone in China's implementation of open-door policies. The new policies paved the way for the massive influx of MNCs.

Before 1992, the average size of a foreign-funded project in China was less than US$960,000 (table 10). Most investment came from Hong Kong and Taiwan and was concentrated in labor-intensive industries such as clothes, shoes, bags, toys, and simple electronic products. By and large, these investors did not threaten local businesses because (a) they had limited capability for investment, (b) their strategy was to achieve high and quick profits rather than to maximize local market share (and they had a low confidence level for staying in China anyway), and (c) they were globally oriented. Their products were mostly shipped outside China. Therefore, most local businesses did not perceive a strong threat from foreign investors, and they generally welcomed foreign businesspeople.

Since 1992, the characteristics of foreign investment have changed dramatically. More and more MNCs have entered China. Ministry of Foreign Trade and Economic Cooperation statistics reveal that more than 200 of the world's 500 largest MNCs have established a presence in China, setting up about 45,000 branches or subsidiaries there. MNCs enter China with completely different strategies than small businesses. Most come highly interested in Chinese market share and do not expect a quick profit. To extend their market share in China, they bring with them new products, new technology, and advanced management experience.

According to an Andersen Consulting survey of 53 MNCs in early 1996, total investment by MNCs had exceeded US$27.5 billion. That investment was allocated to various industrial fields, primarily in technology or capital-intensive industries such as machinery, electronics, telecommunications, food processing, automobiles and parts, and chemicals. So far, most of this investment has been in operations.

The average size per MNC project in 1995 was nearly US$20 million, whereas the average size of all foreign-funded projects was only US$2.48 million. MNCs typically make a series investment in China, including the production of final products, the production of parts and components, and the creation of sales channels. Because of their strong capability and broad diversification of investment, they are a serious threat to local businesses.

In high-technology production fields or fields in which China is not yet strong enough, MNCs introduce new products to the local market. For example, foreign companies, especially U.S. companies, dominate computers and computer accessories in China. Almost all of the world-class computer giants are now in China: IBM, DEC, Compaq, AST, Microsoft, NEC, and Fujitsu. In telecommunications, Motorola started its pager and mobile phone production in China in early 1990. Now it controls 80 percent of the pager product market and 30 percent of the mobile phone market. The balance of the market share in these two categories is dominated by such MNCs as Ericsson, Norkia, Nortel, and NEC.

Many service areas in China are still young or not yet developed. Some MNCs have exploited these opportunities and quickly taken dominant market positions. For instance, DHL and UPS now dominate door-to-door delivery service. McDonald's and Kentucky Fried Chicken have developed extremely rapidly. In just three years, McDonald's has set up more than 20 restaurants in Beijing. The American International Insurance Group opened its life insurance business in Shanghai in 1995 and now has 80 percent of the market there. The three major state-owned insurance companies share the balance of Shanghai's life insurance market.

Foreign brands are rapidly spreading throughout China. The more popular a local brand, the higher the interest from a foreign company. However, many foreign companies have purchased a local brand and then replaced it with their own brand. For example, after Maxam, a popular Shanghai toothpaste and cosmetic brand, was acquired by a joint venture, the brand-name disappeared from the Chinese market. Many other popular Chinese brand-names have suffered the same fate.

FOREIGN INVESTMENT
AND DOMESTIC ADJUSTMENT

In early 1996, debate surfaced on China's foreign economic relations. Unlike previous policy debates, this one began at a grass-roots level. In economic terms, the debate focused on Chinese branding. Critics contend that China's national industries are endangered by the onslaught of foreign brands. The Chinese now drink Coca-Cola and Pepsi, eat McDonald's hamburgers, wear Pierre Cardin clothes and

Nike shoes, drive the Santana (a Volkswagen-designed car), and fly Boeing aircraft. Some have asked: Where are the Chinese brands? What is the purpose of openness? Should China continue to be open, or close again?

The Chinese have a wide spectrum of views regarding these questions. Some people believe that these problems are too serious to ignore, and that China should not open its doors so wide to foreign investment. Others believe that the Chinese market should open further and allow more joint ventures with foreign investors. Still others support a compromise; they believe that China should insist on openness, but adjust existing policies to address the needs of a changing situation. A sampling of opinions from the July 18, 1996, edition of the Chinese newspaper *Economic Daily* follows:

> Looking at all of the products in the domestic market, almost all of the Chinese producers have joint arrangements with foreign businesses. Some of these arrangements are good for the Chinese producers but others are not. Openness must not mean that China will give up its domestic market to foreigners. Rather, it must allow access under certain conditions. Like industrial protection in the United States, Japan, and South Korea, some areas must necessarily be opened. Other areas should not be opened or joint participation with foreigners allowed.
>
> —Tong Limin, Marketing Company of Sino-Petrochemical Co.

> Our products do have some problems that fail to meet the needs of customers—even some prominent brand-names. This is the reason why we have to participate in joint ventures. However, the cost of joint venture participation is too high if we must give up our own brands. The economic strength of a country and even the reputation of a country are demonstrated by its world-class enterprises and their products. As a big country with 1.2 billion people, how can we show our reputation and economic strength if we do not have our own brands?
>
> —Zhou Yunwu, *Hunan Daily*

> How to treat joint ventures and how to protect national industries? I have three points of view:
>
> Protecting national industries does not contradict joint venture participation. However, the relationship between the partners

of a joint venture must be fair. The long-term national interest must not be sacrificed, especially in large and influential projects. Regardless of the conditions required by foreign investors, the Chinese parties must maintain a majority share and insist on the use of Chinese brands. The government must restrict joint ventures in some ways.

The government needs to support the development of national industries. On the one hand, the smuggling and dumping of foreign goods must be heavily punished. On the other hand, Chinese pillar industries and good brands must be protected. National industries need the understanding and the support of local communities. The masses should be aroused to protect our national industries.

—Li Wei, Business Bank, Dachaong County, Hebei Province

Because there are now many joint ventures, some have raised the question of how to protect our national industries. But I want to ask these people: Will our national industries develop successfully without joint ventures? Before reform and openness, we had 100 percent national industries. But what single product from these industries could compete in the world market? Reform and openness are the best ways to make our country rich and strong. Today, we do not have enough money and advanced technology. But we can attract money and technology through joint ventures. Once we are rich and strong, we can buy back the shares. Factories are built on Chinese land, taxes are paid to the Chinese government, and salaries are paid to Chinese employees. The national industries will not go bankrupt. Why should we worry so much? I believe it will be better for China to have more joint ventures.

—Zhen Bin, Capital Steel Co.

For some reasons, many of our state-owned enterprises have heavy debt. Because of the commercialization of state banks, these enterprises have no way to get new capital investment from banks to improve their current situation except to join with foreign investors. The state has no capability with which to care for its own enterprises. The enterprises actually have no choice. It is not fair to criticize only the enterprises. We should not blame enterprises for joining with foreign investors, even though some of the arrangements are not good ones.

—Hui Yang, Beijing No. 1 Consumer Chemical Factory

The debate has forced the authorities to make some adjustments. Domestic adjustments have been made in response to the perceived disadvantages of globalization, especially the influence of MNCs in Chinese society. Some reactions from Chinese enterprises and the government follow.

Adjustments by Chinese Enterprises

Chinese enterprises have undertaken several countermeasures in response to the challenges created by foreign investors. The first is forming large-scale business groups. MNCs brought both a threat and new ideas to China. They threaten local businesses because of their size. At the same time, local businesses have come to realize that to compete against MNCs in both domestic and international markets they must form large-scale business groupings themselves. Otherwise, they will not survive. Existing companies are increasingly forming larger companies through asset restructuring. The government has eased restrictions on mergers and now even promotes mergers across regions. The government encouraged the recent mergers between First Auto-works in Changchun and Golden Cup Auto-works in Shenyang, and between the Changling Group and Huanghe Electronics in Xian.

In the 1990s, China has emphasized two principles in the reform of state-owned enterprises: (a) maintaining large companies and losing small companies and (b) maintaining key companies within industries. Following these principles, the government has decided to support the country's 1,000 largest companies by providing them priority treatment in such areas as bank loans, taxes, and import tariffs. These companies accounted for only 0.33 percent of all state-owned enterprises, but totaled 48 percent of overall assets, 46 percent of total sales, and 71 percent of net profit. Since 1992, the government has supported 57 key companies in 21 industries, most of which are heavy industry or infrastructure related.

Local governments are also promoting the consolidation—mergers and industry groupings—of large companies. For example, Shanghai has formed 38 business groups representing one-quarter of its state-owned enterprises, which accounted for one-half of the fixed assets and two-thirds of the sales of all locally based state-owned enterprises. By June 1995, more than 20,000 business groups had registered in China. Of course, their average size in assets is still small compared with the MNCs. However, these companies anticipate growing to compete with the MNCs both domestically and internationally.

Second, Chinese companies are implementing a strategy of trying to maximize their market shares, especially in the domestic market. This trend is most obvious in the so-called mature markets, such as home electrical appliances and consumer electronic products. For example, in mid-1996, Changhong TV Company reduced the prices of its TV sets, especially wide-screen TVs, up to 20 percent in an effort to extend its domestic market share. This action forced other competitors to cut prices, including importers of TV sets such as Hitachi, Sony, Toshiba, and Samsung. Some small domestic producers were pressured by the move and nearly went bankrupt. However, Changhong's market share in TV sets grew from 15.3 percent to 27.4 percent.

A third countermeasure is maximizing brand equity. In many cases, the foreign partner in a joint venture prefers its foreign brand to the local one. Many popular Chinese brand-names have disappeared as a result of joint venture arrangements. However, many local brands had good reputations and occupied large market shares. In many cases, the local brands were eliminated because the foreign investor wanted to market their own brand. In some situations, the Chinese partners had to accept this condition when negotiating with foreign investors for a variety of reasons: some needed investment capital, others lacked knowledge of intangible assets and the value of their own brand-names, and still others had less confidence in their own brands than in the foreign investor's.

As foreign brands proliferate, Chinese enterprises are better understanding the value of their own brand-names. Some have begun to negotiate to keep their own brands, at least in the domestic market, when setting up a joint venture. For example, an air-conditioning joint venture between Hire Electric Co. and a Mitsubishi group company in Qingdao was structured such that the original brand-name would be used domestically but the Mitsubishi brand-name would be used overseas. This was the first such arrangement between Mitsubishi and a Chinese company; the benefits thus accrue to both sides.

Shanghai Home Chemical Company lost one of its famous brand-names when it became a partner with Watson's several years ago. The company received a commission of Rmb12 million per year for having given up the brand-name. In 1996, the company abandoned the commission strategy and reintroduced its brand-name, Maxam, and made a profit of Rmb200 million from the original brand-name.

Fourth, Chinese enterprises are speeding up the product innovation process. Faced with increased competition, Chinese enterprises have enhanced their R&D and innovation capabilities. According to a State Science and Technology Commission survey in 1994, from 1991 to 1994 the number of R&D departments increased from 8,792 to 12,499 in 20,000 state-owned enterprises. The number of staff employed in R&D activities expanded from 820,000 to 1,170,000. R&D expenses rose from Rmb16.6 billion to Rmb32.1 billion over the same period. Technology import expenses grew from Rmb9.02 billion to Rmb27.57 billion, and expenses related to the utilization of imported technology climbed from Rmb406 million to Rmb970 million (*China Statistical Yearbook for Science & Technology* 1995).

A fifth countermeasure is shifting to high-value-added production. In the early 1980s, Guangdong Province was the first open region. Its booming economy was fueled by investment from Hong Kong and other countries/regions. However, most of the investment was in labor-intensive industries offering low-value-added products. Since the early 1990s, some inland areas have improved their infrastructure and therefore their attractiveness to foreign investors. To maintain a competitive advantage, coastal areas such as Guangdong have up-graded their industrial structure and switched from labor-intensive to technology-intensive industries. As a result, the production of high-tech products has increased dramatically in coastal areas. From 1990 to 1995, the gross output of high-tech products in Guangdong increased 12 times, a rise of 60 percent annually. By the end of 1995, the total output of high-tech products in Guangdong reached Rmb67.3 billion (US$8.4 billion), or 7.2 percent of the gross output of all industries. Exports of Guangdong's high-tech products totaled US$5.3 billion and represented 52.9 percent of China's total high-tech exports.

Guangdong produces 1,700 kinds of high-tech products, which accounts for 27 percent of all varieties of high-tech products produced in China. Many of Guangdong's products hold domestic market shares in excess of 50 percent, including program control telephone switching devices, 3-D cameras, and multichannel cordless telephones (Dai 1996).

The Shenzhen Special Economic Zone in Guangdong annually produces 450,000 personal computers (PCs), or 35 percent of the national output; 6 million motherboards (70 percent); 4.5 million PC power switches (75 percent); 1.5 million monitors (50 percent); 200,000 printers (80 percent); and 250 million floppy disks (80 percent of the national output and 10 percent of worldwide production) (Dai 1996).

Adjustments by the Chinese Government

In an effort to end the debate over the extent of Chinese openness, the *People's Daily,* the newspaper of the Chinese Central Communist Party, published an article titled "Insistently Utilizing Foreign Investment" on August 12, 1996. The article stated that openness will always be an important economic policy for China, and that China should insist on using foreign investment. However, the government also initiated policy revisions designed to improve the quality of foreign investment and to further promote foreign economic relations.

Creating New Policies for Further Openness   The Chinese government has emphasized its openness by implementing new policies. For instance, to help implement the Osaka Action Agenda, an initiative of the Asia-Pacific Economic Cooperation (APEC) forum, China has (a) reduced tariffs on more than 4,000 items by at least 30 percent, (b) moved to lift tariff quotas and import control measures on more than 170 products, (c) opened certain cities such as Shanghai for trial operations of Sino-foreign joint venture trade enterprises, and (d) extended trial operations of Sino-foreign joint venture retailing enterprises.

On December 1, 1996, China made its currency convertible. Thus, with authentic trading vouchers, businesses or individuals can exchange renminbi (yuan) for foreign currencies from banks to pay for trade, services, transportation, tourism, and nontrade purposes such as international donations. These new policies have escalated the engagement between China and rest of the world (*China Daily*, 20 November 1995 and 29 November 1996).

Creating Guidelines for Foreign Investment   In June 1995, the Chinese government released two sets of guidelines for foreign investment: Regulations for Governing Foreign Financial Investment and the Guidelines for Foreign Investing Industries. The new guidelines have made the foreign investment policies more transparent than was previously the case. The government divides foreign investment projects into four categories: promoted projects, allowed projects, restricted projects, and prohibited projects. Promoted (and allowed) projects consist of development of new agricultural technology; development of new technology for the conservation of energy and raw materials; promotion of exports or development of new markets; recycling of natural resources or protection of the environment; development in western China; and other projects promoted by national laws or government regulations. Projects categorized as restricted are technology that China possesses or for which it has the capacity to meet the needs of the domestic market; projects in testing industries for foreign investment or exclusive industries; projects in rare material industries; projects in industries governed by a state plan; and other projects restricted by national laws or government regulations. Prohibited projects refer to projects that harm national security or the public interest; projects that pollute or damage natural resources and human health; projects that occupy large portions of land or harm military facilities; projects in which China has exclusively owned technology; other projects prohibited by national laws or government regulations.

Providing "National Treatment"   In January 1994, China began further reforms in finance, investment, foreign trade, and enterprises. The issue of national treatment (equivalent regulations in areas such as taxes, bank loans, raw material supply, and import tariffs) for foreign-funded businesses was also raised. In fact, no country provides foreign investors with full national treatment. In other countries, some types of foreign investment are restricted or prohibited; China is not the exception. However, as to what extent each area should be given national treatment, different countries have differing policies. China needs to adjust its priorities while the situation is changing.

Shenzhen was given the authority to test the provision of national treatment for foreign investors in January 1997. The experiment further opens the local market and implements single pricing systems for both local and foreign-funded businesses. Any foreign-funded business that produces products in the promoted projects category will face no restrictions in selling to the domestic market. If the municipal government identifies a foreign-funded enterprise as an "advanced technology" company, then 100 percent of the company's products can be sold to the domestic market without tariffs. Any foreign-funded project that invests in improving the quality and production of agriculture can also sell its products to the domestic market without restrictions.

Furthermore, there are no longer to be no price differences between foreign-funded businesses and Chinese businesses regarding highway tolls, electrical fees, medical expenses, tour costs, and housing rent. All of these expenses are to be charged at the domestic standard (*Wuhan Evening Newspaper,* 24 August 1996). These new policies have been extended throughout China.

Promoting Foreign Investment in Middle and Western China The economic gap between the coastal areas—which first opened to globalization—and the middle and western areas has widened considerably. This disparity has the potential to cause domestic strife if it proceeds unabated. To narrow the gap, the Chinese government implemented its Ninth Five-Year Plan (1995–2000) to promote economic development in middle and western China. The new policies promote foreign-funded projects for the development of natural resources. Some projects, such as those in low-tech industries, that are restricted in coastal areas are allowed in the middle and western areas. Local governments in these areas also have greater authority to approve foreign-funded projects, particularly those up to US$30 million per project. The central government intends to raise the proportion of foreign investment utilization in these areas to 60 percent of total foreign investment from only 30 percent at present (*People's Daily,* 2 November 1996).

Setting Up New Industrial Policies   The State Council of China has approved new industrial policies in machinery, electronics, and housing construction. These industries and the automobile industry are considered the pillar industries for China's next stage of development. The new policies were revised to conform to World Trade Organization (WTO) standards. Although specific export and localization requirements and equity limits for foreign investors were deleted from the plan, government officials suggest that such requirements will remain in force. Each ministry will continue to develop more detailed plans for directing foreign investment; most have already designated companies and the types of companies that will require majority Chinese holdings.

Other industrial policies under consideration include those in telecommunications and residential housing, including the mortgage market. The telecommunications policies will separate regulation of telecommunications from operations and clarify bureaucratic authority over the Internet, mobile telecommunications, and other technologies. Foreign companies are not currently permitted to participate in the mortgage market.

In the meantime, foreign investors will have greater access to some fields, such as agriculture and infrastructure-related development. From 1979 to 1994, the ratio of foreign investment to total investment by contract value was only 1.4 percent in agriculture, 1.8 percent in transportation, and 2.9 percent in construction. To promote foreign investment in these fields, the State Planning Commission has published regulations to provide exclusive rights to foreign investors to protect their interest in a particular area for a specified period.

THE ROLE OF RESEARCH INSTITUTIONS IN POLICY ADJUSTMENT

Research institutes help provide a full and clearer picture of reform and openness. China has 310 research institutes in the social sciences and humanities that are sponsored by central and local governments. These institutes employ 18,000 people, of which about 70 percent are professional researchers in various fields. The balance of the staff works in data collection, publications, and administration. Institutes sponsored by central and local governments focus on issues that directly affect them. Many companies also have their own research institutes. University institutes have a greater degree of flexibility because their primary task is teaching. However, university institutes do not have good access to updated information and materials and have limited influence on decision makers.

Among these institutes, there is lots of cooperation. The level of cooperation depends on the nature and budget of a project. The project leader decides how many people can join the project and who should be invited to participate from other institutes.

Two major think tanks exist at the national level: the Chinese Academy of Social Sciences (CASS) and the Development Research Center (DRC). Both are under the State Council. CASS has a theoretical and long-term issue orientation, whereas the DRC is more practical and oriented toward current issues. Furthermore, each ministry in the central government has its own research institute. Although the size of these institutes differs radically, all of them exist to serve their respective ministries. At the local level, each provincial government has a research institute. The Shanghai Academy of Social Sciences is the largest of these.

The Role of the Chinese Academy of Social Sciences

CASS was part of the Chinese Academy of Sciences before 1978. At that time, CASS was separated from the Chinese Academy of Sciences and became an independent professional research academy so that it could concentrate on social science research and play a more active role in China's reforms and development. CASS has 31 research institutes, three publishing houses, one information center, and one graduate school, with overall staffing of 4,500 people. Two-thirds of the staff are professional researchers.

Study topics typically come from three sources: the government, nongovernment sectors, and self-selections. The government usually asks CASS to study basic issues. Some funding will also be provided to support these studies. Topics from nongovernment sectors—the majority of the academy's research—vary widely. These topics come from Chinese foundations, international foundations, and business. Finally, CASS funds young scholars and new theories for which other funding is unavailable.

Each of the academy's institutes plays a different role in Chinese society. For instance, the Institute of Law has contributed to updating the Chinese legal system in laws related to foreign investment and openness. The Institute of Contemporary History provides reports, data, and results to the government on matters related to U.K.-Hong Kong issues and Portugal-Macao issues. Since 1990, the institute has published several books on the history of Hong Kong and Macao. This institute helps the government to understand international issues from an historical perspective such that proper countermeasures can be adopted.

The academy's international relations sector consists of eight institutes. They form the largest sector in the academy. They are equally important to other government departments in dealing with international issues. Unlike historical studies, their studies are mostly current and urgent. For example, the Institute of America Studies provided suggestions and analysis to both the government and the public as China-U.S. relations entered a difficult stage. The Institute of World Economic and Politic Studies analyzes the status of and trends in the global economy. This institute also has a center for Multi-National Company Studies, through which experts are organized throughout China to study MNCs. The center provides information and suggestions to policymakers on preventing the disadvantages that MNCs could cause in China. The center suggestion that MNCs be given national treatment was accepted by the government.

The academy's second largest sector—economics—consists of six institutes. They play an important role in economic reform and development, especially in domestic adjustment policies. The Institute of Industrial Economics is strong in enterprise reform, especially in the reform of state-owned enterprises (SOEs). Because of the institute's strength in this field, the central government invites input from experts at this institute on such enterprise issues as foreign companies, SOEs, and private enterprises. In 1996, the institute studied the formation of large business groups to make domestic companies more competitive with MNCs. The institute supports openness but urges enterprises to protect their brand-names and the government to protect the national industries through antitrust and antidumping legislation.

The Institute of Finance and Trade assists in financial and monetary reform. This institute spearheads most important issues in these areas. Experts at this institute led the effort to make China's currency convertible. Other recent topics include the commercialization of banks and the liberalization of stocks, bonds, and securities.

A major mission of the Institute of Quantitative and Technological Economics is to annually forecast the Chinese national economy. It forecasts short-term development and provides a report to the State Planning Commission and the State Council for their macroeconomic adjustment. The State Council supports this continuous project.

The Institute of Rural Development mainly focuses on agricultural issues such as food and other agriculture products. It also provides ideas on preventing competition from abroad in this area and deals directly with the Ministry of Agriculture and the State Council.

The Institute of Economics, the oldest economic research institute in China, still plays a comprehensive role in economics, basically from a theoretical perspective. In general, it has only indirect contact with current issues.

The Role of the Shanghai Academy of Social Sciences

The Shanghai Academy of Social Sciences (SASS) was founded in 1958. It features 16 research institutes in such fields as philosophy, economics, industrial economics, world economics, Asia Pacific studies, law, peace, and development. The academy employs 900 people, of which 670 are professional researchers. SASS is the second largest professional research institution in China. Unlike other local academies, SASS receives much attention from the central government because of its strength in a number of fields, including foreign trade, finance, monetary affairs, urban development, and technology development. From 1990 to 1995, it focused on such topics as the general design of China's modernization, China's regional development, SOE reform, the history of Shanghai's reform, Pudong's openness and the development of the Yangtze River, the securities market, and a comparative study between SOEs and FDI business.

CONCLUSION

Globalization presents both benefits and risks for a nation. The extent of those benefits or risks depends on domestic policy. By and large,

China has experienced more benefits than risks because its policies are generally appropriate. Of course, China could not benefit from globalization without giving up something. To maximize benefits and minimize risks, policies must be adjusted according to the needs of the changing environment. In the past 18 years, the Chinese government has done much to maximize the benefits of China's openness. Although the policy of openness has been much debated, it will continue. However, the government will move to make its domestic policies more appropriate for both China and the rest of the world. Bringing China into an open and globalized society is a long-term task for the Chinese government.

The speed of globalization in China will also depend on the efforts of both the Chinese and foreigners. China's engagement with globalization will be eased if those outside China provide China with a mutually beneficial environment in which to operate. But the process of globalization will not be stopped. However, globalization should not mean that China will eliminate its own culture and traditions. Companies operating in China should maintain those traditions in conjunction with the advanced knowledge obtained from globalization. Local culture and tradition will not contradict globalization if there is a good balance between them. In this case, Japan and South Korea are good examples.

BIBLIOGRAPHY

China Statistical Yearbook for Science & Technology—1994. 1995. Beijing: State Science and Technology Commission.

China Statistical Yearbook. 1991. Beijing: China Statistical Press.

———. 1992. Beijing: China Statistical Press.

———. 1993. Beijing: China Statistical Press.

———. 1994. Beijing: China Statistical Press.

———. 1995. Beijing: China Statistical Press.

———. 1996. Beijing: China Statistical Press.

China's Foreign Economic & Trade Yearbook. 1991. Beijing: National Statistics Bureau.

———. 1992. Beijing: National Statistics Bureau.

———. 1993. Beijing: National Statistics Bureau.

———. 1994. Beijing: National Statistics Bureau.

———. 1995. Beijing: National Statistics Bureau.

China's Industrial Development Report. 1996. Beijing: Economic Management Press.

Dai Zhigeng. 1996. "High-Tech Industries Booming in Guangdong." *Xinhua Daily Telegraph* (23 October).

International Economic & Trade Information. 1995 (21 December). Beijing: Ministry of Foreign Trade and Economic Cooperation.

Reference for Economist Studies. 1995. Beijing.

Statistical Survey of China, A. 1996. Beijing: China Statistical Press.

Wang Peng. 1996. "Foreign Purchasing: Wolves Coming." *Economic Watch* (9).

8 · Indonesia

Sukardi Rinakit
Hadi Soesastro

I N Indonesia, the issue of globalization is pretty much a matter of rhetoric. It is almost a matter of faith. Those that believe in globalization argue that it opens up new opportunities that are largely beneficial. Those that distrust globalization emphasize its dark side. Between these two extreme views exists a wide range of opinions, perceptions, and attitudes on the nature and inevitability of globalization. Nonetheless, all seem to agree that globalization is inevitable and that nations cannot seal themselves off from this process. Thus, there is no alternative other than to try to cope with it or, in the words of Juwono Sudarsono (1996), Indonesia's foremost political scientist, to "survive" globalization.

Attempts to clarify what globalization means and what its possible implications are for the Indonesian society, nation, and state dominate the domestic literature on globalization. The literature identifies a long list of what the nation must do to survive the globalization process and a similarly long list of complaints directed mostly at the government for failing to formulate the necessary responses to the challenges of globalization. Sudarsono notes that in the case of Indonesia, "intense globalization and regionalization have heightened the dangers of fragmentation. . . : ethnic animosity, racial antagonism, narrow provincialism, linguistic assertiveness and religious fanaticism" (1996, 60). Therefore, the nation's agenda should focus on (a) the perennial problems of defining the relationships of central authority with the periphery, (b) the widening gap in terms of productivity and access to factors of production between the modern and the traditional sectors, (c) the fate of low-skilled and poorly educated workers and their lack of a social safety net, (d) the rise of an emergent middle class that will increasingly lead to more assertive political demands for participation, and (e) the ability of political and administrative institutions (the bureaucracy in particular) to bear the twin burdens of good governance and timely delivery of public goods.

Empirical research on the impact of globalization in Indonesia is lacking, hence the dominance of rhetoric. The government itself has not gone beyond rhetoric in defining its responses to the challenge of globalization. Its attitude toward globalization has been largely influenced by that of the top leadership. In October 1994, just prior to hosting the annual Asia-Pacific Economic Cooperation (APEC) forum leaders' meetings, President Suharto stated that the nation should not oppose globalization. Rather, it should make use of the positive aspects of globalization while keeping itself on guard against its negative aspects (*Suara Karya*, 29 October 1994). As chair of APEC, President Suharto crafted and mobilized support for the so-called APEC Bogor Declaration for free and open trade and investment in the Asia Pacific region. This declaration has been widely hailed in the region as a milestone in regional and international economic integration through the sustained opening of regional economies. At home, responding to questions about Indonesia's involvement in this regional initiative, President Suharto claimed that globalization is a reality that the nation has to face, whether it likes it or not, whether it is willing or not, and whether it is ready or not.

The past 15 years or so saw a significant opening of the Indonesian economy. With the opening up of trade and investment, liberal policies have been introduced with regard to the flow of people (e.g., expatriates), ideas, and information. The government has enacted these policies for various reasons.

The Indonesian government embarked on unilateral liberalization in the mid-1980s to quickly restructure the economy away from an overdependence on oil. The economic reform program began with a readjustment of the exchange rate and was followed by various measures to promote exports and liberalize trade, investment, industry, and the financial sector. The economy quickly began to develop international competitiveness in a few sectors of production outside oil and primary commodities. This enabled the government to proceed with liberalization. However, the process has been far from smooth. Resistance to change has developed from sectors or groups in the economy that feel threatened by liberalization. Big business and powerful political groups have a greater influence in dictating the pace of liberalization than small entrepreneurs.

In the process of regional liberalization under the ASEAN Free Trade Area (AFTA), the government has shown increased concern about the interests of small entrepreneurs and farmers. Agriculture and a number of manufacturing activities that are believed to have a significant effect on the livelihood of these groups are being excluded from the arrangement or the changes applicable to them are being deferred until the final phase of liberalization. The government's policy response to globalization is manifested in a timetable of tariff reductions and other economic liberalization measures. Little attention and few policy measures have focused on strengthening society—especially the weaker groups—in facing the challenge of globalization. The efforts thus far seem to be confined mostly to the so-called first-order adjustments, which deal with the restructuring and liberalization of the economy. The second-order adjustments resulting from the economic, social, and political impacts of the first-order adjustments have been reactive rather than proactive.

THE POLICY AND PROCESS OF GLOBALIZATION

The Indonesian government initiated the country's globalization policy and process. Globalization is an extension of the government's policy of economic reform, which encompasses deregulation, liberalization, and privatization, and is supplemented by a policy of promoting regional cooperation and community building. To understand the context in which the policy and process of globalization and the discussion about them are shaped, it is instructive to review the policy and process of economic reform in Indonesia.

In undertaking economic reform, the government has never formulated any grand design to guide the process. The process has been driven by pragmatism and necessity. As such, the question of how far the process should go has never been made explicit. Indeed, the government does not want to initiate a debate on which policy measures and reforms are in accordance with or are in violation of Article 33 of the 1945 Constitution, which stipulates a dominant state role in the economy. It might be difficult to reconcile the reforms with the state-controlled economic system that is widely interpreted as being the system that is stipulated by the Constitution. An open debate on this matter could necessitate an amendment to the Constitution. This would risk creating precedence for amending other articles of the Constitution, which could have serious ramifications for national cohesion and political stability. Therefore, the liberalization policy has been kept at the level of "low politics" (Soesastro 1989). Since the mid-1980s, the preferred label for the liberalization agenda has been "deregulation."

The process of liberalization began in the mid-1960s as a response to the economic policies of the previous government; it signified the change from the "old order" to the "new order." Packaged as a total correction of the policies of the previous government, the new government had no difficulty justifying the policies and programs adopted during the first period of liberalization (1966–1972). To rehabilitate the economy, the new government moved decisively to restore macroeconomic stability and introduce market-oriented reforms. Market-oriented reforms were originally introduced to change the trade and incentive regime. A significant step was the dismantling of the import licensing system. The government also removed most domestic price controls. The open-door investment policy was strengthened with the adoption of the Foreign Investment Law in 1967, which removed restrictions on foreign equity and employment of expatriates and allowed 100 percent foreign ownership. The public supported these policies and programs with some enthusiasm because the results were immediate.

However, a number of these policies and programs were subsequently reversed. The sudden upsurge of foreign direct investment (FDI) aroused nationalist reactions. In response, investment regulations were made more restrictive. There was also a shift back toward an increased role of the public sector in the economy. The oil booms of 1973–1974 and 1979–1980 enabled the public sector to expand. Public enterprises began to play a dominant role in a number of sectors, and public investments were increasingly directed into heavy industries, petrochemicals, and mining. The civil service also expanded rapidly, and bureaucratic interventions became rampant. Moreover, the incentive system was made progressively more inward oriented. With the oil booms, the economy became heavily dependent on oil revenues. The country also experienced an erosion in the competitiveness of the non-oil economy due to the rise in the real exchange rate. Eventually, this led to a recognition of the need to totally overhaul the economy, which opened the way for the second period of liberalization (1982–1990).

Owing to political feasibility, the liberalization process in the 1980s was undertaken in a gradual and pragmatic fashion. Ali Wardhana (1989), one of the architects of economic liberalization, argued for gradualism rather than a "big bang" approach because the former has the advantage of progressively winning over a new constituency for further reform. Proponents of the big bang argued that their alternative would be more effective in preventing vested interests from rallying forces to oppose further opening up. Also, a big bang has more credibility in that it would send strong signals regarding the government's commitment to the reforms. Yet, in the Indonesian policy environment, where considerable doubt existed about the benefits of liberalization, even within the government itself, gradualism appeared to be the only viable option. A gradual approach could be made credible by introducing a major reform in the beginning and following up with a clear action agenda and timetable for further liberalization.

The second liberalization period was undertaken in response to the significant drop in oil revenues. This process began with some difficulties. The first half of this period was characterized by ambivalence (Pangestu 1991) and partial reforms (Hill 1997). Substantial reforms were undertaken only in the second half of this period. The dramatic drop in oil prices in 1986 created a sense of economic crisis that resulted in more dramatic measures being implemented. These included the first serious attack on the import licensing system that created opportunities for rent-seeking activities and was a major source of the "high-cost" economy. Also, the plastic and steel import monopolies were dismantled; these were seen as a symbol of the then newly emerging cronyism.

The financial reforms introduced in 1988 were widely regarded as the most sweeping reforms during this period. They aimed to increase competition within the financial sector by removing some of the barriers to entry. This liberalization resulted in dramatic growth of the financial system. It significantly altered the market structure and competitive situation facing the banking sector. Concerns were expressed in the early 1990s about the possibility that the resulting rapid expansion of bank credits could lead to financial distress and instability. The economic crisis that hit the country in 1997 shows that those concerns were justified. The crisis led to serious questioning of the government's policy and process of globalization. In fact, although the process of liberalization in the 1980s was widely supported, there were increasing concerns over who gains and who loses in the process (Anwar and Aziz 1988).

In 1991, the country began to experience "reform fatigue." This changed in mid-1994 with the issuance of liberalization measures in the investment field. These measures marked the beginning of a process that was driven by the need to compete with other countries in the region. Indeed, competitive liberalization has increased throughout East Asia since the early 1990s. The investment measures permitted 100 percent foreign ownership of companies as a way to enhance the attractiveness of Indonesia's investment regulation in the face of increased competition from China, Vietnam, and other countries in the region. In May 1995, the government for the first time issued a timetable for reducing tariffs on most applicable items by 2010. This unilateral liberalization measure was issued in response to the competitive liberalization environment in the region. In addition, it signaled the government's determination to implement its liberalization commitments under AFTA, APEC, and the World Trade Organization.

The issue of who gains and who loses from liberalization and globalization in Indonesia has become important because the future of the process depends on such a critical assessment by the body politic and the public at large. It is no longer sufficient for the government to show the overall favorable impact of the process in terms of economic growth rates or export expansion. An urgent need exists to study the issue in some depth to respond to the growing popular beliefs about the negative impacts of liberalization and globalization. Some have argued that the liberalization and globalization process has been responsible for the proliferation of monopolies, increased inequality and poverty, the demise of small companies, and a widening of regional disparities. Hill (1997) assessed each of these propositions based on available empirical evidence and suggested that simplistic conclusions are faulty.

Perceptions are powerful and they must be considered in formulating effective responses to the challenges of globalization. The questions of whether liberalization and globalization have gone too far or have been too fast cannot be addressed and answered simply by studying their differential impacts on various sectors or segments in the society. There will always be a difference in impact, and there will always be winners and losers. But identifying them would help devise the necessary policy instruments and the required institutions to deal with the negative effects of liberalization and globalization.

ADJUSTMENTS TO GLOBALIZATION

Indonesians see the globalization process mainly as an economic phenomenon. The process is characterized by the widening and deepening of market integration in goods and services. Thus, the immediate responses have been couched in terms of enhancing the international competitiveness of companies. For instance, Finance Minister Mari'e Muhammad believes that the focus of Indonesia's agenda should be international competition. Cooperation between the private sector and the government could help transform Indonesian companies into global players. Muhammad observes that Indonesian companies are weak in trading and ideas. These deficiencies can be rectified by developing access to global business (*Media Indonesia*, 4 March 1996). Radius Prawiro (1996), former governor of the Central Bank, points to the importance of raising the level of education and other efforts to develop the country's human resources. He further suggests that the government should assist weak and small enterprises. In addition, large companies should develop partnerships with weaker ones to strengthen the latter. A similar proposal was previously made by Soemitro (1994). The chairman of the Indonesian Chamber of Commerce and Industry (Kadin Indonesia), Aburizal Bakrie, believes that Indonesian enterprises are far from ready to participate in the globalization process. He points to the large inflows of FDI, technology, and expatriates as well as the high import penetration in many sectors of the economy. He suggests the need to reintroduce the principle of self-reliance in national development and underlines the importance of human resource development (*Kompas,* 7 November 1996).

There is a strong perception that liberalization and globalization have resulted in increased domination by foreign enterprises in the economy and a weakening of small and medium-sized domestic enterprises. A study by Farrukh Iqbal (1995) examined the effects of liberalization on companies of different sizes and concluded that during the 1980s both large and small companies appeared to benefit from the reforms. Frida Rustiani (1996) is concerned that globalization only benefits those who are ready and that the so-called people's economy tends to be left behind. Her view represents the sentiments of many nongovernmental organizations (NGOs) that are active in development programs. Indonesian sociologist Loekman Soetrisno blames the increasing incidence of poverty on globalization and calls for efforts to empower poor people, both economically and politically (*Merdeka,* 11 October 1997).

Globalization is also seen as a cause of greater inequalities within and among nations. Such views have been expressed by Budi Permana from the National Council for Defense and Security (*Media Indonesia,* 1 December 1997) and by the commander-in-chief of the Navy, Admiral Arief Kushariadi (*Suara Karya,* 8 January 1998). Such strong views from within the defense establishment appear to have been influenced by the current economic crisis. Catholic priest J. B. Mangunwidjaja (1998) regards globalization as a form of economic and cultural neocolonialism.

Makmur Keliat (1997) observes that many high-ranking Indonesian officials blame globalization for the current economic crisis, although they had supported reform. To the person on the street, Keliat argues, globalization has always been viewed with skepticism. The term "*gombal*ization" has long been used for globalization. *Gombal* refers to a piece of old cloth that is no longer used except to dust shoes or clean kitchen utensils. The wide usage of this term can be seen as an act of silent protest by the people. Indeed, Djauhari Oratmangun (1998) worries that silent protests could turn into social upheaval and fragmentation and a political backlash against globalization.

Therefore, it seems necessary, according to Sayuti Hasibuan (1997), director of the Institute of National Development Studies, for

Indonesia's development strategy to incorporate noneconomic factors. Hilman Adil (1997a and 1997b) makes the same plea. Sarbini Sumawinata (1995), a retired economics professor, underlines the importance of social and political development by stating that globalization has exposed Indonesia's underdevelopment and weaknesses in the political and social fields.

Global integration is seen by some as a cause for national disintegration (*Suara Karya,* 12 March 1997). Thus, regional and international integration must go hand-in-hand with efforts to strengthen national integration (Soesastro 1991 and 1996b). National integration is a major challenge for a society as culturally and ethnically diverse and as geographically dispersed as Indonesia. In addition to concerns about the ability to compete internationally, there are equally strong concerns about the integrity of the nation as a cultural entity. Such concerns were expressed by a police officer, Anton Tabah (1996), as well as Vice President Try Sutrisno (*Bisnis Indonesia,* 15 August 1996). They are concerned with the intensive cross-border flows of information and the resulting rapid penetration of ideas and values (Muis 1995; Prasetyantoko 1995). Yet, there have not been strong suggestions from either the public or the government to control the flows of information. Instead, responses to this development have been directed at efforts in human resource development and education, which are clearly seen as priorities in dealing with globalization (Mardiatmadja 1995; Prasetyantoko 1995; Sarwono 1995; Tabah 1996; Mulyani 1997; Tono 1997).

The increase in the number of expatriates is seen as a major indicator of the weakness of the Indonesian education system (Arisanto 1996). In 1990, there were less than 30,000 expatriates, but that increased to 75,000 in 1996. Many believe that a serious mismatch exists between the output of the educational system and the demand for skills in the rapidly growing and changing economy. Since 1990, an average of 135,000–150,000 high school graduates entered the labor force annually, but only 40,000–65,000 found employment.

To rectify this situation, the government has introduced three policies: the nine-year universal (compulsory) education program, an increased share of private-sector-organized education, and a dual system of education. The nine-year universal education program is intended to raise the educational level of the work force; only about

40 percent of the work force has a six-year education (elementary schooling) or more. The greater involvement of the private sector in providing educational services is meant to both raise the quality of education and to enable the government to reallocate its scarce resources to financing the nine-year universal education program. The private sector has begun to develop partnerships with foreign institutions to provide education and training relevant to the business community. Yet, the challenges in the field of education remain huge. The general view is that the government needs to have the political will to allocate a larger share of public resources to education and human resource development. Among countries in the ASEAN region in the early 1990s, Indonesia allocated the lowest share of public expenditures for education, at 1.3 percent of gross domestic product, compared with 2.4 percent in the Philippines, 3.8 percent in Thailand, and 5.3 percent in Malaysia (United Nations Development Programme 1997).

The second priority area that this literature survey has identified in the area of governance involves a redefinition of the role of government, reform of the bureaucracy, and reform of the judicial system. Ginandjar Kartasasmita, chairman of the National Planning Board (Bappenas), also identified these areas as a priority for Indonesia in responding to the challenges of globalization (*Suara Karya,* 25 July 1997).

Sudarsono has rightly stated that in the era of globalization, "market authority has challenged state power for the high ground to determine public policy" (1996, 51). Political economist Dorodjatun Kuntjoro-Jakti (1995) sees a continuing strong role for the government because globalization tends to produce greater inequalities. The government is important because it (a) can ensure continuity and consistency of national development, (b) can rectify social dislocations, (c) has accumulated the knowledge to anticipate and detect problems, and (d) possesses information that is not readily available to the public or the private sector. This is, perhaps, too optimistic a view of what governments can perform. However, as yet there is no substitute for governments. The government's role is essentially as a facilitator (Widoatmodjo 1996). The task, therefore, is to continuously improve the functioning of the government through restructuring, reform, and reengineering of the bureaucracy (Kristiadi 1998).

The importance of good governance has been recognized by the chairman of the National Planning Board, Ginandjar Kartasasmita

(*Suara Karya,* 25 July 1997); the former minister of justice, Ismail Saleh (*Suara Pembaruan,* 13 November 1997); and by students (Wahyuni and Suwito 1996). The era of globalization makes it more urgent for governments and their bureaucracies to become more transparent and accountable.

CONCLUSION

When B. J. Habibie was still minister of research and technology, he proposed that the government establish a team to deal with the impact of globalization. This team, known as "Tim Globalisasi," was to be composed of experts from various disciplines. The main task of this team was to "manipulate globalization to produce a synergy" with the national interest that is positive, compatible, and mutually reinforcing (*Republika,* 21 March 1997). The team was to be proactive rather than reactive and would work in a systematic and integrated fashion.

The basic idea for establishing this team was sound. Such institutional innovation is necessary for the country to address and undertake second-order adjustments. However, internal developments since Habibie made the statement have not been conducive to establishing the team. The country was hit first by an economic crisis that led to a political crisis. A new Suharto government was installed in March 1998 with Habibie as vice president, which lasted for only two months. In May 1998, President Suharto was forced to resign, and Habibie became the new president. As president, he may reintroduce and implement his proposal. Even if the present government is a transition government, it would be desirable to have such a team feed directly into the government's policy-making process. However, the introduction of such institutional innovation may not loom large in Habibie's current agenda because of more pressing issues.

BIBLIOGRAPHY

Adil, Hilman. 1997a. "Globalization: A Homogenization." *Jakarta Post* (24 November).

———. 1997b. "Globalization Could Complement Diversity." *Jakarta Post* (25 November).

Anwar, M. Arsjad, and Iwan Jaya Aziz. 1988. "Perkembangan ekonomi

Indonesia 1987 dan proyeksi 1988" (Indonesia's economic developments in 1987 and projections for 1988). In M. Arsjad Anwar et al., eds. *Ekonomi Indonesia: masalah dan prospek 1988/1989* (The Indonesian economy: problems and prospects 1988/1989). Jakarta: UI Press.

Arisanto. 1996. "Peluangan dan tantangan dunia kerja dalam era globalisasi" (Opportunities of and challenges to the workplace in the era of globalization). *Business News*, no. 441: ix.

Hasibuan, Sayuti. 1997. "Kita dan globalisasi" (We and globalization). *Media Indonesia* (26 February).

Hill, Hal. 1997. "Myths About Tigers: Indonesian Development Policy Debates." *Pacific Review* 10(2): 256–273.

Iqbal, Farrukh. 1995. *Deregulation and Development in Indonesia.* Paper presented at a conference on Building on Success: Maximizing the Gains from Deregulation, organized by the Indonesian Economists Association (ISEI), the World Bank, the Faculty of Economics at the University of Indonesia, and the Magister Management Program of the University of Indonesia, Jakarta, 26–28 April.

Keliat, Makmur. 1997. "Globalization and Economics." *Jakarta Post* (10 November).

Kristiadi, J. B. 1998. "Globalisasi dan pergeseran peran birokrasi" (Globalization and the shift in the role of the bureaucracy). *Media Indonesia* (12 January).

Kuntjoro-Jakti, Dorodjatun. 1995. *Perencanaan ekonomi nasional menghadapi tantangan globalisasi* (National economic planning in the face of globalization). Inaugural address as professor of economics, Faculty of Economics, University of Indonesia, 17 June.

Mangunwidjaja, J. B. 1998. "Globalisasi adalah neokolonialisme ekonomi dan budaya" (Globalization is economic and cultural neocolonialism). *Kompas* (24 January).

Mardiatmadja, B. S. 1995. "Globalisasi: madu beracun" (Globalization: poisoned honey). *Kompas* (8 August).

Muis, A. 1995. "Tempat globalisasi dalam sistim national" (The role of globalization in the national system). *Kompas* (8 August).

Mulyani, Sri. 1997. "Bisnis dan globalisasi" (Business and globalization). *Media Indonesia* (30 July).

Oratmangun, Djauhari. 1998. "New Policies a Must for Globalization." *Jakarta Post* (12 and 13 January).

Pangestu, Mari. 1991. "Managing Economic Policy Reforms in Indonesia." In Sylvia Ostry, ed. *Authority and Academic Scribblers: The Role of Research in East Asian Policy Reform.* San Francisco: International Center for Economic Growth.

Pangestu, Mari, and Ira Setiati. 1996. *Mencari paradigma baru pembangunan*

Indonesia (In search of a development paradigm for Indonesia). Jakarta: Centre for Strategic and International Studies.

Permana, Budi. 1997. "Globalisasi mendorong kesenjangan" (Globalization creates gaps). *Media Indonesia* (1 December).

Prasetyantoko, A. 1995. "Posisi Indonesia dalam arus informasi dan globali-sasi" (Indonesia's position in information flows and globalization). *Bisnis Indonesia* (16 October).

Prawiro, Radius. 1996. "Persaingan di era globalisasi" (Competition in the era of globalization). *Media Indonesia* (17 June).

Rustiani, Frida. 1996. "Globalisasi: Masihkah ekonomi rakyat boleh berha-rap?" (Globalization: does the people's economy still have hope?). In Frida Rustiani, ed. *Pengembangan ekonomi rakyat dalam era globalisasi* (The development of the people's economy in the era of globalization). Jakarta: Yayasan AKATIGA and YAPIKA.

Saleh, Ismail. 1997. "Globalisasi, liberalisasi dan transparansi" (Globalization, liberalization and transparency). *Suara Pembaruan* (13 November).

Sarwono, Sarlito Wirawan. 1995. "Era globalisasi dan generasi muda" (The era of globalization and the young generation). *Suara Pembaruan* (28 October).

Soemitro. 1994. "Globalisasi, tantangan negara berkembang" (Globalization, challenges of developing nations). *Kompas* (26 August).

Soesastro, Hadi. 1989. "The Political Economy of Deregulation in Indonesia." *Asian Survey* 24(9): 853–869.

———. 1991. "Integrasi ekonomi internasional, regional dan nasional" (In-ternational, regional, and national economic integration). In Hadi Soe-sastro, ed. *Untuk kelangsungan hidup bangsa* (For the continuity of the nation). Jakarta: Centre for Strategic and International Studies.

———. 1996a. "Globalization and the Threat to the National Economy." *Telstra* 39(March–April): 17–23.

———. 1996b. "Liberalisasi ekonomi dalam proses globalisasi" (Economic liberalization and the process of globalization). In Kajat Hartojo, Harry Tjan Silalahi, and Hadi Soesastro, eds. *Nalar dan naluri* (Reason and instinct). Jakarta: Centre for Strategic and International Studies.

Sudarsono, Juwono. 1996. *Surviving Globalization—Indonesia and the World.* Jakarta: Jakarta Post.

Sumawinata, Sarbini. 1995. "Globalisasi dan kita—sebuah catatan reflektif memasuki 1995" (Globalization and us—a note of reflection entering the year 1995). *Media Indonesia* (2 January).

Tabah, Anton. 1996. "Globalisasi dan kita" (Globalization and us). *Media Indonesia* (29 August).

Tono, Suwidi. 1997. "Agenda Indonesia menjelang globalisasi" (Indonesia's agenda in the face of globalization). *Bisnis Indonesia* (29 July).

United Nations Development Programme. 1997. *Human Development Report 1997*. New York: United Nations Development Programme.

Wahyuni, Budi, and Atmo Suwito, R. S. 1996. "Globalisasi, reformasi biro-karsi dan ekonomi" (Globalization, reform of the bureaucracy and the economy). *Bisnis Indonesia* (18 September).

Wardhana, Ali. 1989. *Structural Adjustment in Indonesia: Export and the "High-Cost" Economy*. Keynote address, 24th Conference of Southeast Asian Central Bank Governors, Bangkok, 25 January.

Widoatmodjo, Sawidji. 1996. "Paradigma baru peran pemerintah di era glob-alisasi" (A new paradigm on the role of government in the era of globali-zation). *Bisnis Indonesia* (29 August).

9 · Philippines

Maria Socorro Gochoco-Bautista

FOR the Philippines, the path to economic growth and stability has been a long and tortuous one. Despite enviable growth rates in the 1950s and 1960s among countries in the region, the oil shocks of the 1970s exposed the vulnerability of the economy's long experience with import substitution. The massive foreign borrowing in the halcyon days of the petrodollar, which fueled debt-driven growth in the 1970s, turned into a nightmare as recession swept the major export markets of developing countries. The Philippines found itself mired in debt for which heavy interest payments absorbed a large portion of its export earnings. The Philippines experienced its first negative rates of growth in the postwar era in 1984 and 1985, and policymakers responded with orthodox stabilization measures—tight fiscal and monetary policies—to rein in the balance-of-payment (BOP) deficits and prevent the depletion of international reserves.

In an effort to quell demand by containing inflation and the BOP deficits, these orthodox methods of stabilization engendered a painful and unpopular domestic recession. That this program was undertaken under pressure from the World Bank/International Monetary Fund (IMF) made it worse and unacceptable to many, who viewed it as an imposition from without and an infringement on national sovereignty.

Structural adjustment, the natural sequel to stabilization programs, entails measures aimed at making the economy work more efficiently.

207

The Philippines has used various structural adjustment loans (SALs) from the World Bank/IMF to liberalize its economy. Economic liberalization is the pillar of orthodox structural adjustment programs. The Philippines has made many attempts at trade liberalization and financial liberalization. Initially, these attempts were modest: the lifting of import controls on selected products and the removal of interest rate ceilings.

Although the Philippines undertook these structural adjustment measures with its back against the wall, the experience of dealing with such externally induced shocks to the economy conveyed several important lessons. First, an import substitution industrialization policy, or protection via high tariff walls, had failed to make the economy resilient to adverse external shocks and did not produce the type of sustained economic growth desired. In other words, inward-looking policies did not hold the key to industrialization and prosperity. The successful experience of the East Asian newly industrializing economies (NIEs), based on export-led growth, further underlined this. Second, although domestic policies were important, the economic fate of the country did not lie solely in its hands. Rather, with international economic interdependence, external events and the policies of other countries were important determinants as well. Third, the success and acceptability of reform programs were dependent on when they were undertaken and whether they were perceived to be internally generated rather than imposed from without. When such measures are not well understood by the public or are perceived to be imposed from without, opposition to such measures combines with bureaucratic politics to produce inconsistent and reversible policies.

Today, the Philippines is no longer the "sick patient of Asia." Although the growth rate of real gross domestic product (GDP) is fairly modest in comparison with other countries in the region, it was a respectable 5.5 percent in 1996. The sustainability of this growth, however, depends on many factors, including how the Philippines seizes the new opportunities provided by globalization, defined loosely as the openness of countries to the greater movement of factors of production, goods, and information through market-based mechanisms such as trade. The rhetoric from the government, at least, seems to understand this. The current buzzwords are "globalization," "global competitiveness," and "economic diplomacy." "Philippines 2000" is not just another catch phrase, but rather an ambitious policy aimed at making the Philippines an NIE by the year 2000. It is ambitious in part because the Philippines is a late industrializer, having abandoned import substitution fairly late relative to other countries in the region. It is also ambitious because the country does not have a first-mover advantage in adjusting to globalization. Indeed, almost all countries, including the former communist ones, are trying to become part of the global production network.

This chapter examines the economic reform and liberalization experience of the Philippines and how these relate to the ongoing worldwide globalization process. Additional discussion addresses the following:

- The global context as seen from the Philippines and the features of the current world order.
- Economic reform and adjustment measures in the Philippines.
- The social reactions to globalization.
- Future research directions.

GLOBAL CONTEXT AS SEEN FROM THE PHILIPPINES

Several features of the existing world order are relevant in designing appropriate domestic responses to globalization.

Creating a Level Playing Field

The establishment of the World Trade Organization (WTO) represents the desire of nations to level the playing field in the conduct of trade by adhering to certain rules of the game. It is unclear how developing countries will fare under these rules. Nevertheless, the mad scramble by developing countries to join in part reflects their awareness that the Uruguay Round of the General Agreement on Tariffs and Trade (GATT) brought down the average tariffs on less developed country (LDC) exports to developed countries to 3.9 percent from 6.3 percent, and included some important sectors and export products of developing countries, such as agriculture and garments. The WTO also makes certain allowances for developing countries, for example, a longer adjustment period. In any case, developing countries can look for ways to make the WTO work to their advantage.

Regional Economic Groupings

The emergence of regional economic groupings such as the ASEAN Free Trade Area (AFTA) and the North American Free Trade Agreement (NAFTA), and the strengthening of the European Union, is likewise relevant to globalization and domestic adjustment. First, there is concern that these regional groupings do not contravene multilateralism. Second, the inclusion of Mexico in NAFTA enhances its position in the U.S. market, the dominant export market of the Philippines and a major market of Association of Southeast Asian Nations (ASEAN) countries. Third, the creation of AFTA, in part as a response to the emergence of regional economic groupings elsewhere, was used domestically to push for unilateral trade liberalization (see Gochoco-Bautista and Faustino 1994). Fourth, welfare-reducing effects, such as trade diversion, will occur if more efficient third-country producers are displaced by member country producers simply because of the zero or lower tariff rates accorded member countries. Fifth, although regional economic groupings, such as AFTA, make ASEAN more attractive as a production base, country differences tend to become obscured. There is no necessary reason why foreign direct investment (FDI) into ASEAN should necessarily come to the Philippines, or for that matter, why a company wishing to sell in the Philippine market must necessarily produce in the Philippine market. Finally, it remains unclear how the country's unilateral and various external commitments will dovetail with its WTO commitments.

The Globalization of Capital

The globalization of capital came to the Philippines by way of the return of private capital in the 1990s. Some of this has been in the form of FDI. However, in the early 1990s private capital also came in huge amounts to the so-called emerging markets in part because of the low U.S. interest rates. In 1991, for example, FDI flows to the Philippines amounted to US$881.30 million, whereas portfolio investment totaled US$3.23 billion (see Fabella 1996, 8). That portfolio flows were coming in even though domestic interest rates had fallen, largely as a result of the resolution of the debt problem, was all the more confounding to the authorities. Suddenly, not being the pariah in the international creditor community did not seem to be all that desirable. The Central Bank was faced with a policy dilemma of either sterilizing the inflows and incurring huge costs—the interest rate on the domestic liability used for sterilization was higher than that earned on foreign assets (see Kletzer and Spiegel 1996)—or not sterilizing the inflows and de-railing monetary and inflation targets. In fact, the monetary authority had earlier liberalized the capital account, which allowed the problem to emerge.

Evidently, the earlier lessons of the Southern Cone countries had not been learned. This policy exposed the Philippines to something like a Mexican tequila effect. When the capital flows were reversed, the stock market took a nose dive and the domestic currency came under heavy pressure to depreciate. The portfolio inflows were basi-cally short term, and, hence, easily reversible, as indeed happened. Furthermore, the inflows went largely to the stock market and non-tradables such as real estate, further exacerbating the bias against the tradable goods sector relative to nontradables. This latter problem is fundamentally due to the noncompetitive exchange rate.

Regional Competitors

The emergence of China and Vietnam as important regional econo-mies is also of great concern to the Philippines. China is the largest re-cipient of FDI, mostly from the NIEs, whose middle-level technology is suitable to the level of labor skills in China. Similarly, as the NIEs pursue cross-border division of labor, the Philippines also receives much of its FDI from these countries. China itself has become an in-vestor in the Philippines, mostly in the areas of utilities and power generation. China's rice purchases in the world market are so large that the world price of rice is affected to the detriment of rice-importing countries such as the Philippines. In terms of export markets, most of China's manufactured exports go to the United States, as do the manu-factured exports of ASEAN. Already, Philippine garment exports have declined owing to greater competition from Chinese producers as well as producers in other countries such as Bangladesh. Chinese goods have likewise flooded the domestic market. Vietnam also has become a favorite destination of FDI, despite its lack of a physical and legal infrastructure.

The Greening of International Trade

The "greening" of international trade, brought about by increasingly green consumer expectations in developed countries, could both be a source of conflict in international trade, especially in view of the over 150 international environmental agreements in place, and a means by which businesses can compete in the emerging world order. The adoption of ISO 14000, an international standard of product quality, is expected to have a negative effect on the costs of producing and exporting goods. Intal (1996) points out that if there is a negative externality in the production process, reducing tariffs and nontariff barriers will increase environmental stress if the good being produced is exportable.

From 1975 to 1990, the pollution intensity index of Philippine exports declined. This was largely the result of a decline in primary exports. However, exports of manufactured goods, particularly electronics and garments, which are both relatively labor intensive, increased (Intal 1996).

Maintaining Global Competitiveness

The notion of the competitiveness of a nation's industries takes on new meaning with the increasing mobility of factors of production and cross-border division of labor. The phenomenon of the cross-border division of labor is based on shifting comparative advantage. There is much current debate among economists on whether, in this era of globalization or global production networks, the theory of comparative advantage is passé. Indeed, the law of comparative advantage itself has nothing to do with factor mobility. The law states that a country should specialize in the production of those goods in which it has the greatest relative cost advantage, even if it has an absolute cost advantage in the production of all goods. If factors of production are mobile, it is possible that the greatest relative cost advantage may be found in another set of goods, and, hence, following the law of comparative advantage, the country should specialize in the production of these (see Fabella 1996, 18, for a fuller discussion). Cross-border division of labor based on changing comparative advantage is in fact what underlay the massive wave of Japanese outward investments following the Plaza Accord, which saw the revaluation of the yen. With the rise in the yen, and, thus, of the cost of immobile factors of production such as labor, Japanese companies exported labor-intensive manufacturing processes to countries in Asia, including the Philippines, in which labor was cheaper.

The characteristics of post-1980 FDI differ from that prior to 1980. In the 1970s, much of the Japanese and U.S. FDI that came to the Philippines sought to establish a domestic market and earn rents based on the import substitution policy, in which high tariff barriers protected domestic producers from competition. Japanese investments into the United States in the first half of the 1980s were meant to maintain market access in view of protectionist moves in the United States, which was undergoing a recession at that time.

That FDI based on tariff jumping tends toward welfare reduction is not surprising. Under the two-country, two-good model of trade called the Heckscher-Ohlin model, a country tends to export the goods that intensively use its relatively abundant factor, under several strong assumptions. Under this theory, trade in factors substitutes for trade in goods. The old type of FDI was welfare reducing because FDI tended to substitute for exports from home countries, reinforce the distortions under import substitution, and raise their welfare costs (Fabella 1996, 19).

In contrast, a large portion of the new FDI is export-oriented. Whereas the old type of FDI reinforced the distortions under import substitution, the new FDI is based on host country comparative advantages. Capital mobility has reinforced this. Given less rent-seeking FDI, chances are that FDI will improve welfare for the host country. Capital mobility reinforces trade in goods. This is the dominant pattern of world trade today.

Curiously, however, it is not the mobility factors that have a bearing on the attractiveness of a particular country as a destination of FDI. Fabella (1996) cites the lessons of location theory à la Johann Heinrich von Thunen. Rather, the burden of attracting mobile factors of production lies with immobile factors at some distance from the center. For the periphery to be attractive, it must offer a combination of immobile factors that make mobile factors productive. Competition, therefore, lies in improving the set of immobile factors. The implication of this for the Philippines is that both its "hard" and "soft" infrastructure must be developed because it is the quality of these permanent resources that will ultimately bring in the more mobile factors of production and FDI (see also "Catching the Next Wave" [1996, F1], a study commissioned by the Department of Foreign Affairs). This is how the competitiveness of a nation's industries can be enhanced.

Evidently, cross-border division of labor has yet to have a significant impact on the Philippine economy (Fabella 1996, 28). The industrial structure has not changed much over time. Industry's share of GDP went from 24.6 percent in 1986 to 34.8 percent in 1995, even as the share of agriculture in GDP dropped somewhat from 24.6 percent in 1985 to 22.9 percent in 1989. Manufacturing has remained virtually stagnant at 34.8 percent in 1995 relative to 34.7 percent in 1986. Although manufactured exports increased in the same period, the growth in exports came from a few sectors such as electrical equipment/parts and telecommunications, and garments. As FDI increased, so did imports of capital goods.

Part of the reason for the inability to take fuller advantage of the cross-border division of labor is the perception that the Philippines is deficient in both hard and soft infrastructure (Fabella 1996, 24–25). A 1992 survey of the World Competitiveness Report ranked the Philippines 33rd out of 41 countries. A Japan External Trade Organization (JETRO) survey done in 1995 showed that the Philippines had higher wages than other countries in East Asia, the highest power costs, the highest truck freight costs after Japan, and the highest marine freight costs after Japan and South Korea.

ECONOMIC REFORM AND ADJUSTMENT

The Aquino administration that succeeded the Marcos dictatorship began an import liberalization program that called for the lifting of import controls on many goods. However, because of the political difficulties and the period of political consolidation that followed two decades of dictatorship, the Aquino government did not get far with its goals of economic reform.

Politically, of course, the easiest measures to take were those that broke up the coconut and sugar monopolies controlled by Marcos. Trade liberalization was tougher. Executive Order (EO) 470, signed in 1990, was a unilateral program providing for a gradual reduction in tariffs over five years. The previously protected big business sector strongly opposed this, coming as it did on the heels of the AFTA proposal. Specifically, they objected on the grounds that EO 470 was injurious to the manufacturing sector in that it imposed deep tariff cuts on finished products, whereas tariff rates on raw materials and intermediate inputs were not similarly reduced because of government revenue considerations (subsequently, this was shown to be the exception rather than the rule); that the tariff rate schedules under EO 470 were lower than those set under the Common Effective Preferential Tariff program of AFTA; and that EO 470 granted tariff discounts for imported finished products from ASEAN countries that are produced domestically by sensitive industries (Gochoco-Bautista and Faustino 1994).

Because of the political fluidity under Aquino, liberalization sometimes took strange and contradictory turns, as in the imposition of a temporary 9 percent surcharge on imports despite ongoing trade liberalization, when government revenues fell short. Unfortunately, because reforms were derailed, postponed, or not deep enough, the economy went through another recession in 1991.

In 1992, Fidel Ramos was elected president. With greater political stability arising from the orderly transition of power, it was now possible to implement the needed reforms.

Privatization and Deregulation

Several prominent public institutions were subsequently privatized. Among these were the oil company, Petron, and the Philippine National Bank. Portions of Fort Bonifacio, located in Makati, were sold by public bidding. Camp John Hay, a favorite vacation spot, was also privatized. The telecommunications industry was deregulated, which opened the door to potential competitors of the Philippine Long Distance Company, the dominant phone company. The water distribution system was also recently bid out to the private sector.

Republic Act (RA) 7721 allows foreign banks to operate in the Philippines under modes of entry such as acquiring, purchasing, or owning up to 60 percent of the voting stock of an existing bank, and by establishing branches with full banking authority. Ten foreign banks have been allowed entry.

In March 1996, Congress passed RA 8180, known as the Downstream Oil Deregulation Law. This lifted all the restrictions previously imposed on the oil industry, and subjects the sector to open competition. Price controls over petroleum products were removed, and there is freer entry of oil companies into the industry. The Energy Regulatory Board adopted the Automatic Pricing Mechanism, which sets local oil prices based on the movement of Singapore posted prices and the exchange rate. Full deregulation of the industry will occur in mid-1998. Critics of the oil deregulation policy charge that it is antipoor because it will mean higher transport fares and, hence, higher prices of goods.

Trade Liberalization

The Ramos administration put in place a tariff reduction and import liberalization program by way of EO 264, the successor to EO 470. Under EO 264 (and EO 288), a uniform tariff of 5 percent on industrial and nonsensitive agricultural products will be in place by the year 2004. Critics of this program charge that the government is opening the domestic market to foreign multinationals to the detriment of local manufacturers, and, more important, that the government is giving up more than it should as 2004 is earlier than the 2020 date required for compliance under the Asia-Pacific Economic Cooperation (APEC) forum.

RA 8179 amends the Foreign Investment Act by deleting the negative "c" list, which is an investment category that prohibits any amount of foreign equity in certain industries, and reducing the equity requirements for domestic and export-oriented foreign-owned companies. Critics charge that the government is amending "nationalist" laws because of globalization.

In agriculture, the government has designed a program to increase investments in rural infrastructure as well as increase spending on research and development. In addition, RA 8178 removes quantitative restrictions (QRs) on agricultural products and replaces them with tariffs. Because the Philippines is not rich enough to provide large farm subsidies for inputs or agricultural exports, liberalization in the agricultural sector takes the form of the removal of QRs and a commitment to increased market access under the WTO. This will hit hard crops such as rice, corn, sugar, livestock, meat products, coffee, cabbage, onions, and garlic, which had been protected by QRs (Mendoza 1996, 23). There is great fear about the loss of employment in agriculture.

Fiscal Reform

Reform of the tax structure will broaden the tax base and reduce tax rates to induce compliance. The expanded version of the value-added tax, or E-VAT, replaced a variety of sales and percentage taxes and reduced the average indirect tax even as it increased coverage. Nevertheless, the E-VAT generated much protest as being antipoor.

While tax reform proceeds, there remain glaring cases of inequity, which, if addressed, would probably generate more revenue than the taxes introduced so far. For example, real property taxes, which affect the rich, easily can be used to generate revenue by adopting a more realistic land assessment. This will also correct the bias in favor of nontradables such as land.

The government has also attempted to streamline the bureaucracy. It continues to implement aspects of the so-called Attrition Law to reduce spending for personnel services. However, official statistics show that public-sector employment has continued to grow in cost and size. As a percentage of the national budget net of debt service, personnel services grew from 22.5 percent in 1982 to 40.9 percent in 1996, whereas as a percentage of gross national product (GNP), the government's total wage bill increased from 3.4 percent in 1982 to 6.0 percent in 1996, with the latter largely due to the Salary Standardization Law of 1989 (Diokno 1996). The devolution of some activities in the health, social services, agriculture, and public works to local governments under the Local Government Code has meant substantial savings for the national government.

The government has also come up with an innovative scheme called Build, Operate, and Transfer, or BOT. In this scheme, the private sector participates in the provision of infrastructure.

Monetary and Exchange Rate Policy

A new central bank was created in 1992 to ensure the institutional independence of the monetary authority and to reduce or eliminate its inflation bias. However, more profound changes in policy have yet to become apparent. With increasing liberalization in many areas, the authorities liberalized the capital account and foreign exchange transactions. The peso was allowed to float, with supposedly only minor interventions from the monetary authority when movements became excessive. Exporters were allowed to retain all their foreign exchange earnings, banks were allowed to lend against their foreign currency deposits, and ceilings on foreign equity investments were relaxed.

The challenge of pursuing an independent monetary policy becomes daunting in a world where capital is freely mobile and the domestic currency adjusts. Given the greater interdependence of countries in the region, it might be asked why any country would want to have an independent monetary policy. This, in turn, is related to the questions of whether the shocks that affect the economy are common to those that affect other countries in the region, and, if so, whether a country would want to have a different response from those of other countries. These are the kinds of profound questions that have yet to be considered in the debate on the appropriate conduct of monetary policy.

The exchange rate policy, although essentially allowing the peso to float, in fact attempts to prevent the peso from appreciating as a result of capital inflows, for example, because this is disadvantageous to export growth. Unfortunately, such a policy also raises the inflation rate because of the resulting undervaluation of the peso in real terms.

However, the most relevant issue regarding trade liberalization is that an uncompetitive exchange rate policy will leave domestic producers without any ammunition or protection as tariffs are reduced. Indeed, many small exporters who went under when the liberalization measures were instituted complained loudly about the flawed exchange rate policy. This is also an area of great concern to the biggest group of exporters, PHILEXPORT (Philippine Exporters Confederation).

In addition to the above programs and measures, other measures being considered are as follows (see Cueto 1996, 6):

- an amendment to the Condominium Law that would allow foreigners to own factories and residences in industrial estates;
- the repeal of the Retail Trade Nationalization Act, which would initially allow foreign ownership of up to 40 percent and after three years up to 100 percent;

- an amendment to RA 7721 that would allow more than the initial 10 foreign banks to operate in the country;
- an amendment to the Financing Company Act that would allow 100 percent foreign ownership of financing companies;
- the liberalization of provisions on foreign equity participation in investment banks and equity houses; and
- an amendment to the Investment Company Act that would allow membership of foreign investors on the boards of investment companies and allow foreign investors in the mutual funds industry.

Critics of economic liberalization view such measures as further evidence of the parcelization of the economy to foreigners.

SOCIAL REACTIONS TO GLOBALIZATION

The phenomenon of globalization represents, on the one hand, market-oriented reforms based on economic considerations of efficiency and welfare gains. However, it also has greater political dimensions, including increasing demands for democratization. The demise of socialism and the breakup of the Soviet Union, the fall of the Berlin Wall, and the attempts by China to introduce market reforms all have significantly contributed to the push for globalization.

In the Philippines, the Marcos dictatorship ended with the People Power revolution in 1986. Following two years of negative rates of GNP growth, the economy grew at close to 1 percent in 1986. Unfortunately, the Aquino government, which succeeded the dictatorship, could not implement its economic programs much beyond the initial pump-priming measures because it had to deal with numerous coup attempts. Under these circumstances, it was preoccupied with efforts to maintain sufficient political support. Accommodating various domestic interests resulted in inconsistent policies and meant the government was in no position to take on an economically painful reform process.

Under the Ramos administration, many of the reform programs started by the Aquino government moved forward. The adjustments to globalization have taken place in an economy that is more stable and growing respectably. Furthermore, popular empowerment has been reflected in the decentralization of power and the devolution of government services to local government units, as well as in the freer expression of opposition to government policies perceived to be anti-poor. Unilateral moves for economic liberalization have occurred almost contemporaneously with the formation of regional economic groupings such as AFTA, the APEC forum, growth polygons, and the formulation of global trading rules via WTO, each of which entails commitments on the part of the Philippines.

The November 1996 hosting of the 4th APEC Economic Leaders' Meeting revealed the range of public views on economic liberalization and globalization. Alternative forums were sponsored by various groups with differing stances on APEC (see Sarmiento and Herrera 1996, 1 and 6). These included the following.

The Asia Pacific Sustainable Development Initiative (Apsud), which is made up of the Caucus of Development NGO networks (Code NGO), Green Forum Philippines, the Philippine Sustainable Agriculture Coalition, the Center for Development Initiatives, the Women Action Network for Development, the Asian NGO Coalition, and the National Peace Conference, cosponsored the "International Conference on Confronting the Challenge of Liberalization: Sustainable Development and APEC." Apsud is perhaps the most pro-APEC of the various interest groups; the group advocates a critical collaboration with the government on APEC.

The Manila People's Forum on APEC (MPFA) is composed of such groups as the Philippine Rural Reconstruction Movement; the Philippine Peasant Institute; Demokratikong Magbubukid ng Pilipinas (Democratic Peasants of the Philippines); Siglo ng Paglaya (Century of Liberation); Bisig (Union for Socialist Thought and Action); the Institute for Popular Democracy; Urban Poor Associates; the Philippine Alliance of Human Rights Activists; the Freedom from Debt Coalition; and the Center for Agrarian Reform, Empowerment and Transformation. They held a conference titled "Fair Trade and Sustainable Development: Agenda for Regional Cooperation." This group offers itself as an alternative to the split Communist Party of the Philippines, and, although not anti-APEC, the group is critical of certain aspects of it. For example, the MPFA opposes the binding commitments an APEC member has to make because this limits the member's ability to formulate trade and investment policies consistent with its national interest. In fact, however, commitments made through APEC are politically, not legally, binding; APEC is a consensual process involving voluntary and unilateral actions. The MPFA also believes that people's concerns with respect to other issues, such as human rights, gender and social equity, and environmental sustainability, should be reflected in the APEC agenda. The group is also critical of the APEC process because it does not have room for nongovernmental organizations (NGOs) to participate.

The "People's Conference Against Imperialist Globalization" was held by the so-called Reaffirmist faction of the split Communist Party of the Philippines and the National Democratic Front. Groups affiliated with this conference include Bagong Alyansang Makabayan (New Nationalist Alliance), Kilusang Mayo Uno (May 1st Movement), Kilusang Magbubukid ng Pilipinas (Peasant Movement of the Philippines), Gabriela, Karapatan (Right), the League of Filipino Students, the League of Urban Poor Alliance, Promotion of Church People's Response, and Kapatirang Simbahan para sa Bayan (Kasimbayan) (Ecclesiastical Brotherhood for the People). They reject APEC because they see it as a ploy by imperialist countries such as the United States to exploit countries with weak economies. They foresee the displacement of millions of workers and farmers as a result of the liberalization of the economy.

Another conference was sponsored by Solidarity of Labor Against APEC, or SLAM, which identifies with the other breakaway faction of the Communist Party of the Philippines called the Rejectionists. Groups affiliated with SLAM include Sanlakas (United Force), Bukluran ng Manggagawang Pilipino (Union of Filipino Workers), Bukluran ng Progresibong Magbubukid ng Pilipinas (Union of Progressive Peasants of the Philippines), the National Confederation of Labor, Kapatiran ng mga Pangulo ng Unyon sa Pilipinas (Brotherhood of Union Presidents in the Philippines), and the National Federation of Student Councils. They warn that economic liberalization will lead to the loss of millions of jobs as multinational corporations replace labor with machines.

Finally, there was a conference titled "International Conference on Subic: The Social Cost of Globalization." Among the groups represented at this conference were Preda, the Asian Women's Human

Rights Council, the National Council of Churches of the Philippines, Bayan-Central Luzon, Solidaridad Foundation, and IBON Philippines. These groups simply reject APEC and globalization.

Several interesting observations can be made. First is the wider range of views currently available on the issues of economic reforms and liberalization. In the past, only the so-called left and the powerful protected interests were organized enough to have antireform stances. The left's opposition is based on the long-running themes of imperialist domination by foreign monopolists and exploitation, an antinationalist policy of opening up the economy for the benefit of foreigners, and the massive unemployment that reforms would bring about. That the two divided factions of the Communist Party of the Philippines still use this kind of ideological rhetoric is, therefore, not new. The other most common criticism of reform programs is that the burden of adjustment is not equally shared by everyone in society and falls heavily or solely on the poor.

Other objections relate to the possible destruction of societal values as a result of liberalization, and the fear that historical claims by certain social groups will be forgotten as a result of globalization. Another criticism relates to the perceived inflexibility of multilateral commitments, in which measures can only be reversed at the pain of incurring trade sanctions or diplomatic censure.

Many groups have emerged that offer a middle-of-the-road stance, including critical collaboration with the government in developing policy approaches toward APEC. The views expressed by these middle-of-the road groups are not entirely ideologically based, although they still sometimes play the nationalist card. Rather, they have suggestions dealing specifically with issues that they want included in the APEC agenda, or opposing views based on the technical merits of certain matters, for example, how fast Philippine tariffs decline relative to those of other countries and the implications of liberalization in terms of the competitiveness of domestic industries.

There is the danger, however, that the momentum for active participation from the private sector on APEC and broader liberalization issues generated by the summit will be dissipated. Six months prior to the hosting of the Economic Leaders' Meeting at Subic, an ad hoc task force was formed under the Presidential Advisory Commission on the WTO to dialogue with the various people's organizations and solicit their views. The Secretary of Agrarian Reform convened the social reform agenda. Initially, the task force dealt primarily with the MPFA. This was unable to continue due to internal ideological differences within the MPFA. Subsequently, the task force dealt with Apsud and incorporated its idea of sustainable development into the Individual Action Plan of the Philippines.

Since Subic, however, the lack of a formal institutional mechanism to link the activities of these people's organizations with government policymakers is apparent. The task force no longer exists, and a subcommission under the Presidential Commission on the WTO that is to continue the work of the task force has yet to be created. The Presidential Commission had funded the task force's activities. The current thrust of the government is to have particular departments in government coordinate directly with people's organizations in their sector. Hence, the person assigned to do this at the Department of Agrarian Reform, for example, coordinates with the Philippine National Peasant Caucus, whereas their counterpart at the Department of Labor and Employment coordinates with various labor sector groups. Currently, there is an almost deafening silence about ongoing activities.

RESEARCH DIRECTIONS

Countries are faced with many challenges because of globalization. These challenges suggest several directions for useful research.

First, the most important area of research is the appropriate national growth strategy for a country because nearly all the economic and political parameters are changing. A sound justification must be made for the choice of strategy. The reform program to implement this strategy must have a holistic approach rather than reacting piecemeal to external events, and it must be internally consistent. Although the Philippines has a medium-term development program, it is not well understood or detailed. Furthermore, the program is mostly a collection of inputs from different government agencies. The design and elements of economic reforms should be understood and publicly debated. The technical difficulties of designing appropriate monetary and exchange rate policies, for example, should not be used as an excuse to exempt them from public scrutiny and debate. It is equally important to develop institutions that allow meaningful participation from the private sector, given the fact that globalization emphasizes market-based mechanisms.

Second, it is important in designing such a strategy to examine the domestic economic, social, and political context in which globalization is occurring. The success of economic reform programs depends to a large extent on public support for them and the timing and sequencing of reforms. It is important to know how different sectors in society will likely be affected, their perceptions of the likely effects of the reforms, where opposition will come from, and how this can be dealt with. For example, research should identify which groups of the poor might be affected by policies perceived to be antipoor, their margins of poverty, and their ability to adjust and benefit given appropriate government programs. The likely impact depends on which group of poor people is considered, what they do, where they get their incomes, and whether they have access to land. Similarly, the impact of reforms on companies depends on such factors as their relative position in the economy and whether they are primarily exporters. Safety nets, adjustment and training programs, and other coping mechanisms are important in selling the reforms by lowering adjustment costs. These must target the right groups.

Third, the role of the state must also be redefined. For market-based mechanisms to work, the state must provide the necessary hard and soft infrastructure, and enabling measures that allow ordinary citizens to participate in the market process. This is difficult in practice because the state is oftentimes the source of market failure itself. The state must also find ways to work creatively with the private sector to provide public goods without jeopardizing its fiscal position.

Fourth, like many countries, the Philippines has embarked on a unilateral trade liberalization program, but it is also engaged in regional and multilateral undertakings. Little work has been done on how consistent all of these commitments are to each other. For example, the ASEAN countries agreed to adopt a common tariff vis-à-vis each other under AFTA by a certain date. However, there was evidently a lack of appreciation for the importance of discussing the nature of the transition period. As a result of this lack of regional focus, for some important export products such as electronics, the Philippine tariff rates are currently low relative to those in Indonesia and Thailand. This means that in the interim period, Indonesian and Thai companies can potentially enter the Philippine market whereas the converse is not necessarily true. In effect, some existing anti-intra-ASEAN trade biases are reinforced. It is also important to study what strategic policies or stances, if any, a small country or groups of countries can take in WTO negotiations.

BIBLIOGRAPHY

Alburo, Florian A. 1996. "An Overview of the Emerging World Economic Environment." Paper presented at the Conference on the Emerging World Economic Order/Arrangement, February 29–March 1.

———. 1997. "Effects of Globalization on Growth and Equity in the Philippines: An Overview." Paper presented at the Third Human Development Forum, Shangrila-EDSA Plaza Hotel, April 4.

Bello, Walden. 1992. *Revisioning Philippine Industrialization.* Quezon City: Freedom from Debt Coalition.

———. 1995a. *APEC 1995: The Other Side.* Bangkok: Focus on the Global South, Chulalongkorn University.

———. 1995b. *Competing Visions of Regional Integration in the Asia Pacific Region.* Bangkok: Focus on the Global South, Chulalongkorn University.

———. 1997. "Reflections on the Effects of Globalization on Equity in the Third World." Paper presented at the Third Human Development Forum, Shangrila-EDSA Plaza Hotel, April 4.

Canlas, Dante B. 1996. "Institutional Challenges of the Emerging World Economic Arrangements." Paper presented at the Conference on the Emerging World Economic Order/Arrangement, February 29–March 1.

Cantos-Reyes, Jessica. 1996. "Globalization: Threats and Opportunities for Management and Labor-Chemical Industry." Unpublished paper by the Philippine Center for Policy Studies—Industry Studies.

"Catching the Next Wave." 1996. *Philippine Daily Inquirer* (21 November).

Cueto, Donna S. 1996. "Three Views in Search of a Strategy: Problem without a Name." *Philippine Daily Inquirer* (20 November).

Diokno, Benjamin E. 1996. "Philippines: Public Sector Employment: Pattern, Priorities and Policies." Paper presented at the Symposium on Economic Adjustment and the Philippine Labor Market, December 13.

Doyo, Maria Ceres. 1996. "Three Views in Search of a Strategy for the 21st Century: Neither Pro nor Anti." *Philippine Daily Inquirer* (20 November).

Durano, Marina Fe B. 1996. "Garments Industry of the Philippines—Responding to the Global Challenge." Unpublished paper by the Philippine Center for Policy Studies—Industry Studies.

Fabella, Raul V. 1996. "Features of the Emerging World Economic Order:

Implications on Growth Strategies." Paper presented at the Conference on the Emerging World Economic Order/Arrangement, February 29–March 1.

Fukuda-Parr, Sakiko. 1997. "Sustainable Human Development in a Globalizing World: The Scope for Managing the Process in the Interests of the People." Paper presented at the Third Human Development Forum, Shangrila-EDSA Hotel, April 4.

Glick, Reuven, and Ramon Moreno. 1994. "Capital Flows and Monetary Policy in East Asia." Federal Reserve Bank of San Francisco Center for Pacific Basin Monetary and Economic Studies Working Paper No. 94-08, November.

Gochoco-Bautista, Maria Socorro, and Jaime M. Faustino. 1994. *AFTA and the Philippines: National Economic Policy-Making and Regional Economic Cooperation.* Quezon City: Institute for Strategic and Development Studies.

Gonzales, Eduardo T. 1996a. "Has Globalization Left Its Mark on Governance Structures and Institutions in Employer-Employee Relations in the Philippines?" Unpublished paper by the Philippine Center for Policy Studies.

———. 1996b. "Equity and Exclusion: The Impact of Liberalization on the Philippine Working Class." Unpublished manuscript.

Institute for Labor Studies. 1996. *Efficacy of Selected Labor Market Reforms in Promoting Globalization with Equity: The Philippine Case.* Manila: Department of Labor and Employment.

Intal, Ponciano S., Jr. 1996. "The Emerging World/Economic/Trading Arrangements: Trade and Environment Linkages." Paper presented at the Conference on the Emerging World Economic Order/Arrangement, February 29–March 1.

Jones, Ronald. 1967. "International Capital Movements and the Theory of Tariffs and Trade." *Quarterly Journal of Economics* 81(1): 1–38.

Kemp, Murray. 1966. "The Gain from International Trade and Investment: A Neo-Heckscher-Ohlin Approach." *American Economic Review* 56(4): 788–809.

Kletzer, Kenneth, and Mark Spiegel. 1996. "Speculative Capital Inflows and Exchange Rate Targeting in the Pacific Basin: Theory and Evidence." Paper presented at the Conference on Managing Capital Flows and Exchange Rates: Lessons from the Pacific Basin, Federal Reserve Bank of San Francisco, September 26–27.

Manila People's Forum on APEC. 1996. "Manila Declaration and Plan of Action." Paper presented at the Conference on Fair Trade and Sustainable Development: Agenda for Regional Cooperation, Manila Midtown Hotel, November 21–24.

Mendoza, Amado M., Jr. 1996. "Socio-Potential Challenges of the New Trade Regime: The Impact of GATT-Uruguay Round on the Informal and Marginal Sectors of the Philippines." Paper presented at the Conference on the Emerging World Economic Order/Arrangement, February 29–March 1.

Mundell, Robert. 1967. "International Trade and Factor Mobility." *American Economic Review* 47: 321–335.

Ofrenco, Rene E., and Ina A. Ortiz. 1996. "Emerging IR/HR Responses to Globalization-Implications on Unionism." Unpublished paper by the Philippine Center for Policy Studies—Industry Studies.

Sarmiento, Juan V., and Christine Herrera. 1996. "Guide to the Other Forums." *Philippine Daily Inquirer* (19 November).

10 · South Korea

Sung Hee Jwa
In-Gyu Kim

NOW that South Korea has joined the Organization for Economic Cooperation and Development (OECD), it must rise to the challenges of globalization. In the current wave of globalization, national economies are increasingly integrated into a global economy, having moved from shallow integration under the General Agreement on Tariffs and Trade (GATT) system to deeper policy integration under the new World Trade Organization (WTO) system.[1] Moreover, the private-sector initiative for globalizing economic activities is an even more important force driving economic integration than the efforts of cooperative international groupings. Thus, the political and geographical borders of national economies no longer effectively hinder the international flow of economic activities.

Defining globalization is not easy because there are no systematic theories on it. Roughly speaking, however, globalization implies the expansion of economic activities across politically defined national and regional boundaries through the increased movement of goods and services, including labor, capital, technology, and information, via trade and investment. The spread of new information technologies has accelerated globalization. What then does globalization imply for national economic policy making? Most important, any preferential or discriminatory policy becomes increasingly ineffective under the globalized economic environment owing to the increased mobility of economic goods and services, factors, and agents, and due to the resulting inability of the national economic authority to hold these elements within the national boundary.

This chapter elucidates economic policy issues concerning the effects of globalization on the South Korean economy and then details policy suggestions in response to globalization. In the coming decades, as globalization expands, domestic economic liberalization and reform will gain new momentum. As a result, economic management based on direct regulation in macro- and microeconomic policies will tend to lose effectiveness and become inconsistent with the general philosophy of economic liberalization. Therefore, a globalized South Korean economy implies that to ensure healthy and stable economic growth, economic policy making and implementation must follow internationally compatible rules and the market mechanism.

The chapter breaks down as follows:

- *A brief review of South Korea's economic performance over the past three decades.* South Korea's economic development has been one of the most rapid and sustained in the world. Yet it is difficult to ascertain the secret of South Korea's success. Most researchers agree, however, that the success has been based on a government-led, export-oriented development strategy, under which companies have been encouraged to adapt to the opportunities of the world market. Still, the South Korean economy must be further globalized.

- *Macroeconomic policy issues such as capital flow liberalization, monetary and fiscal policy, and exchange rate policy.* During the past three decades, and especially in the 1970s, these macroeconomic policies in South Korea were employed to support economic development, thereby losing the macroeconomic stabilization role. Low interest rates, base money creation, and tax and expenditure instruments supported policy loans for important industries (as selected by the government). Furthermore, the exchange rate policy was constrained by the concern for export promotion. The restoration of these policy tools as a macroeconomic management system will enhance compatibility with the general trend of globalization, including the swift evolution of global financial markets.

- *The issue of institutional stability against the political business cycle.* Some authors, such as Amsden (1989), argue that South Korea's authoritarian governments in the past were effective in enhancing economic performance with a long-term policy horizon. In contrast, the Kim Young Sam government, when in an early phase of democratization, had to deal with the possibility of the political business cycle and of political pressure from interest groups. Thus, South Korea had to devise some institutional safety nets to prevent political forces from destabilizing the economy. Three primary issues of stability are the independence of the central banking system, rule-based policy making, and the economic policy horizon.
- *Microeconomic policy issues.* During the past three decades, South Korean industrial policy has taken an interventionist approach in its efforts to promote, restructure, or protect domestic industries. Government intervention and regulation, which were once so effective in developing the South Korean economy, are no longer appropriate in an era of globalization. Thus, the government must lift all entry barriers and deregulate the economy. This would promote competition such that the private sector could freely make rational choices on optimal business strategies, including the organizational structure of companies and how to produce for the global market environment of the 21st century. Here, the focus is on deregulation, privatization, and structural adjustments.
- *Concluding remarks.* The struggle over labor law in 1996 has implications for South Korea's preparedness in meeting the challenges of globalization.

ECONOMIC PERFORMANCE

South Korea's successful economic development has been held up as a model for other developing countries to emulate. The World Bank (1993) does not hesitate to call it a "miracle." This is because, even some 35 years ago, South Korea was one of the poorest countries in Asia, with a low industrial base and few natural resources. Per capita income in 1963 was US$100 (table 1). In 1995, however, the World

Table 1. Major Indicators of South Korean Economic Growth, 1963–1995 (%)

	Export Growth	GNP Growth	Wholesale Price Index	Per Capita GNP (US$)
1963	9.0	9.1	19.4	100
1964	23.5	9.6	34.9	103
1965	35.9	5.8	10.3	105
1966	42.4	12.7	8.6	125
1967	32.7	6.6	6.5	142
1968	39.5	11.3	8.1	169
1969	36.1	13.8	6.9	210
1970	19.6	7.6	9.4	252
1971	20.9	8.8	8.6	288
1972	36.6	5.7	13.8	318
1973	55.3	14.1	6.9	395
1974	−2.8	7.7	42.1	540
1975	15.9	6.9	26.5	590
1976	41.6	14.1	12.2	797
1977	22.6	12.7	9.0	1,008
1978	19.9	9.7	11.6	1,392
1979	−3.8	6.5	18.8	1,640
1980	9.7	−5.2	38.9	1,589
1981	17.3	6.2	20.4	1,719
1982	6.2	5.6	4.7	1,773
1983	13.8	9.5	0.2	1,914
1984	8.1	7.5	0.7	2,044
1985	2.1	5.4	0.9	2,242
1986	26.6	12.5	−1.5	2,568
1987	36.2	12.3	0.5	3,218
1988	12.8	12.0	2.7	4,295
1989	16.3	6.9	1.5	5,210
1990	14.4	9.6	4.2	5,883
1991	17.5	9.1	5.4	6,757
1992	2.9	5.0	2.2	7,007
1993	3.4	5.8	1.5	7,446
1994	13.8	8.4	2.7	8,483
1995	30.3	8.7	4.7	10,076

Source: Bank of Korea, *Economic Statistics Yearbook*, various issues.

GNP: Gross national product.

Bank classified South Korea as an upper-middle-income country, with per capita income of US$10,076. South Korea's rapid economic growth has been accompanied by a big transformation in industrial structure. In 1960, only 1.8 percent of all workers were engaged in mining and manufacturing, whereas 68.3 percent were in the agriculture, forestry, and fishery sector (table 2). In 1995, however, employment

Table 2. Changes in South Korea's Industrial Structure (%)

	Agriculture, Forestry, and Fishery		Mining		Manufacturing		Other	
	GDP	Employment	GDP	Employment	GDP	Employment	GDP	Employment
1960	36.9	68.3	2.1	0.3	13.6	1.5	47.4	29.9
1965	38.7	58.6	1.8	0.9	17.7	9.4	41.8	31.1
1970	25.8	50.4	1.3	1.1	21.0	13.1	51.9	35.4
1975	24.9	45.7	1.4	0.5	26.6	18.6	47.1	35.2
1980	15.1	34.0	1.4	0.9	30.6	21.6	52.9	43.5
1985	13.9	24.9	1.5	1.0	29.2	23.4	55.3	50.7
1990	9.1	18.3	0.5	0.4	29.2	26.9	61.2	54.4
1995	7.3	12.5	0.4	0.1	29.9	23.4	62.4	64.0

Sources: Economic Planning Board, *Major Statistics of Korean Economy,* various issues; Bank of Korea, *Economic Statistics Yearbook,* various issues.

GDP: Gross domestic product.

in mining and manufacturing soared to 23.5 percent of total national employment, whereas that in the agriculture, forestry, and fishery sector decreased to 12.5 percent.

In 1961, General Park Chung-hee came to power, first as leader of a military junta and after the election of 1964 as president, displacing the democratic but ineffectual government of Chang Myon. This shift of regime was accompanied by dramatic changes in economic policies. The Park government adopted an outer-oriented trade and development strategy and discarded the policies of import substitution that had been followed during the 1950s. Though continuously adopting an outer-oriented trade and development strategy to the present, South Korea has undergone three distinct phases since 1961: (a) export-led growth (1961–1972); (b) heavy and chemical industry promotion (1973–1979); and (c) stabilization, liberalization, and renewed growth (1980–1995).

Export-Led Growth: 1961–1972

In this phase of growth, the Park government initiated major policy reforms and established institutions to promote export-oriented industrialization. Resources from both within and outside of South Korea were mobilized to achieve this goal. The emphasis in South Korea's first five-year plan (1962–1966) was primarily on export promotion.[2] Among a series of reforms, the reforms of 1964 reflected those characteristics succinctly: (a) an intensification of export financing,

(b) a reduction in the fiscal deficit and in inflationary pressures by reforming the budgetary process, (c) a large devaluation of the South Korean won and a shift to a unified and floating exchange rate system in early 1965, and (d) a doubling of interest rates on bank deposits and loans (which, with reduced inflation, resulted in a shift to positive real interest rates).

The reforms of 1964 are a typical example of how heavily the government tried to influence the private sector. During the 1960s, the government even nationalized all commercial banks and established many state-owned banks. This nationalization enabled the government to fully control the creation and supply of credit. Thus, the government could provide export-oriented companies with greater access to credit. However, the novelty of the reforms was that the government made good use of the market mechanism to allocate resources. For instance, export financing or preferential loans to exporters provided uniform incentives to induce increased exportable production, with individual producers left to decide which industries and products were most promising in a fairly competitive market environment. In this way, the government could reduce possible distortion in resource allocation from an interventionist approach. The reforms also provided many other incentives for exporters, such as various tax exemptions and export subsidies.[3]

During the 1960s, most of the protectionist measures of the 1950s were still in place, although import liberalization began in 1967. Westphal and Kim (1982) assert, however, that the antiexport bias of the protectionist measures was largely offset by the export promotion policies during the 1960s. They argue that companies were substantially indifferent to either selling their products in the domestic market or exporting them. In other words, South Korean exporters operated in a free-trade-like market environment.

The reforms were followed by a dramatic increase in the rate of economic and export growth (table 1). The annual growth rate of the gross national product (GNP) from 1963 to 1971 reached 9.5 percent with strong annual export growth. The share of manufacturing output to gross domestic product (GDP) surged from 13.6 percent in 1960 to 21.0 percent in 1970, whereas the share of agriculture, forestry, and fishery output declined from 36.9 percent to 25.8 percent during the same period (table 2). Over this period, however, inflation was relatively mild, at a 13.7 percent annual rate, largely due to a much less expansionary fiscal policy after the reforms of 1964.

The Heavy and Chemical Industry Drive: 1973–1979

In the early 1970s, the Park government believed that the South Korean economy had really taken off and needed industrial upgrading from labor-intensive to capital-intensive industry. With the success in the 1960s, the government was confident that it could successfully replace the market mechanism. In 1973, this belief took concrete shape as the heavy and chemical industry (HCI) promotion policy. The HCI drive was also supported by the noneconomic consideration of improving self-defense capability through heavy industries such as steel and machinery.

The HCI drive aimed to promote the development of key industries such as steel products, nonferrous metal, shipbuilding, automobiles, general machinery, petrochemicals, and electronics. Such key industries were expected to reduce costs and induce employment in other linked industries. However, the private sector was reluctant to invest in these key industries because the investment appeared risky in terms of profitability. Moreover, the private sector could not afford a large amount of product-specific capital with a lengthy pay-back period. To promote the HCI drive, therefore, the government had to mobilize all possible policy tools at its disposal, including tax exemptions, tax holidays, and investment tax credits.

Among these various policy tools, the most important one was policy loans, through which the government directed all feasible funds to the development of the key industries. The central bank's base money and the commercial banks' credit supply were geared to support the key industries in addition to the export industries in general. The amount of funds supplied to the key industries reached 70.6 percent of the banking sector's total equipment loans at the end of 1978. Because the key industries required huge amounts of capital, the government had to mobilize foreign capital as well as domestic savings. With private companies' limited abilities to secure foreign loans, the government had to guarantee the reimbursement of all foreign loans. All foreign loans, as with domestic credit, were allocated according to companies' importance to the key industries.

The effects of the HCI drive on the economy remain controversial.

As intended, the HCI initiative upgraded the industry structure from labor intensive to capital intensive. The share of HCI output to GDP rose substantially, from 11.9 percent in 1970 to 26.3 percent in 1980, exceeding that of light industry. Yoo (1990) found, however, that from the inception of the HCI drive to the late 1980s, the rate of return on capital for the heavy and chemical industry group was lower than that for the entire group of light industries.

The HCI drive represented a significant shift away from the relative uniformity of incentives for exporters in the 1960s, under which entrepreneurs could freely decide which and how many products they had to produce in the presence of market competition. With the HCI drive, the government became directly involved in resource allocation at the industry and even company levels. Market tests or market competition could make businesspeople avoid unwise investments, whereas bureaucratic judgments could lead to serious mistakes in investment decisions.[4] Moreover, the government produced innumerable interventionist regulations, many of which were hard to remove even when deregulation became necessary. The HCI drive was essentially the same as the import substitution policy in the heavy and chemical industry sector, although the government expected to export such products eventually and never intended to displace the export-oriented policies. As a result of the import substitution, the growth rate of exports slowed from 1973 to 1979.

The active government role resulted in excessive money creation, which, in turn, produced high inflation with various signs of macroeconomic imbalances. Two oil price shocks experienced in this decade, one in 1973 and the other in 1979, also contributed to the inflationary situation. In this period, South Korea achieved economic growth at an 8.5 percent annual rate, but experienced relatively high inflation, at a 15.2 percent annual rate, generating a concern that the growth could not be sustained without some strong corrective measures to curb the inflationary pressure.

Stabilization, Liberalization, and Renewed Growth: 1980–1995

South Korea began the 1980s with strong anti-inflationary policy measures. Monetary growth was decelerated and fiscal expenditures were tightened. The HCI drive was toned down. In addition, efforts were made to change the degree of government intervention in re-source allocation. Kim describes the shift in policy regime as follows: "In 1979, the government began to shift not only its policy emphasis from growth to stability, but also its industrial policy focus from the previous, industry specific policies toward a functional approach. The new government that came into power in 1980 reorganized the system of incentives and financial support to research and development activities and the training of technical manpower, irrespective of industrial branch. In other words, the government began to reduce its role in industrial planning and targetting, and attempted to undertake policy reforms to promote competition in domestic markets" (1994, 350). Along with the stabilization program, the government slackened the reign of credit control, which was tightened in the process of the HCI drive. Hoping to spur the development of the domestic financial market, the government sold most of the commercial banks to the private sector. Deregulation and market opening were also adopted as a part of the general economic policy stance, but not in full force.

For the first half of the 1980s, South Korea succeeded in curbing inflationary pressures as the stabilization program was firmly maintained at the cost of low growth performance. The Wholesale Price Index fell from 38.9 percent in 1980 to 20.4 percent in 1981, 4.7 percent in 1982, and 0.2 percent and 0.7 percent, respectively, in the subsequent two years (table 1).

From 1986 to 1988, South Korea experienced a strong economic boom thanks to favorable external conditions, namely the so-called three lows: (a) the low dollar and won vis-à-vis the yen, (b) the low international interest rate, and (c) the low oil price. South Korea enjoyed this opportunity with a sizable current account surplus, a double-digit growth rate, and low single-digit inflation. Being intoxicated with success, however, the government as well as the private sector failed to take serious efforts toward structural adjustment and in response to the shift in policy regime. It was quite well known, for instance, that the strict government regulations had retarded the development of the financial sector. To develop the financial sector, therefore, a full-scale deregulation of the financial industry and market was necessary, but it was not even attempted.

Due to the trade surpluses in the late 1980s, South Korea could no longer seek special and differential treatment in the international market. The government had to open its domestic market further. The number of imported items subject to automatic approval of import soared from 68.6 percent of the total in 1980 to 96.3 percent in 1990. The average rate of tariffs fell, from 24.9 percent in 1980 to 11.4 percent in 1990.

The downturn in 1989, due to the deterioration in external economic conditions, and the subsequent economic ups and downs, again brought back the typical interventionist role of the government in economic management, although for different purposes this time. The so-called balanced industrial structure between *chaebol* (South Korea's big business conglomerates) and small and medium-sized companies was thought to be the important element for industrial competitiveness. Thus, financial institutions shifted their priority in the distribution of policy loans to small and medium-sized companies.

Efforts to upgrade industrial competitiveness by encouraging more investment through easy financial credits in a short time, in addition to financial support for small and medium-sized companies, inevitably created an expansionary economic situation. The inflation rate again approached double digits in 1990 and 1991, but was arguably much higher because the measured inflation rate underestimates the true rate owing to the price index management of widespread price regulation.

Since 1992, inflationary pressure seems to have subsided in the index number but various regulations on individual prices are still ubiquitous. The government's propensity to favor maximum growth even with some inflation and the rapid political democratization that will activate various interest groups' voice for governmental favor could result in an ever-expansionary economic situation. It seems that there are still plenty of reasons to watch for a resurgence of inflationary pressure in the future.

The government of Kim Young Sam, inaugurated in 1993, placed its top policy priority on structural reform of the South Korean economy to deal with the rapidly changing world economic environment. In doing so, the government emphasized the importance of deregulation, privatization, competition policies, and financial reform, in the belief that intervention and regulation are not appropriate in an era of globalization and heightened competition.[5]

MACROECONOMIC ADJUSTMENTS

Under the globalized economic environment, management of private investment, consumption, and imports by regulatory measures will not be available as instruments for macroeconomic stabilization policy. Price regulations will be lifted, and price index management will also be unavailable. Thus, macroeconomic management must rely on traditional macroeconomic stabilization policies based on indirect control methods through the market system.

One important condition under which the macroeconomic stabilization function becomes beneficial to economic development is that macroeconomic management does not distort relative price structures and, thus, resource allocation. Put differently, macroeconomic management should stabilize the aggregate economy and inflationary pressures, but should not disturb the microeconomic resource allocation.

However, South Korea's macroeconomic management has relied on direct price and quantity regulations, thereby distorting the relative price structures; money and credit supply and tax and fiscal expenditure measures have usually been geared to support the targeted industry. As a result, the effectiveness of macroeconomic stabilization policy has increasingly worsened, and actual inflationary pressure has always been more severe than the managed and officially announced price index suggests. At the same time, the distortive impacts on the relative price structure must have been getting larger.

Jwa (1997a) suggests three remedies to correct these distortions. First, the most urgent reform is the active development and utilization of traditional macroeconomic policy instruments and the establishment of indirect macroeconomic management systems. Second, all regulated prices should be liberalized, not only major service prices, including public utilities prices, but also major industrial product prices. Through this reform, South Korea could discard the so-called price index management practices and pave the way for a genuine macroeconomic policy system. Finally, South Korea should then try

Table 3. Capital Flow Liberalization Schedule, 1995–1999

Type of Investment	Prior to 1995	Changes in 1995	1996–1997	1998–1999
Overseas direct investment	Subject to approval	Partially liberalized	Liberalized	
Stock investment by nonresidents	12% per issue	15% per issue	20% per issue as of October 1996; ceiling raised	Liberalized
Overseas portfolio investment by South Korean companies	Limits	Broader limits	Liberalized as of April 1996	
Overseas deposits by:				
• South Korean companies	Limits	Partially liberalized		Liberalized (1998)
• Institutional investors	Limits	Partially liberalized	Liberalized (1996)	
• Individuals	Not permitted	Very strict limits		Liberalized (1998)
Domestic bond issuance by nonresidents	Not permitted	Partially liberalized	Won-denominated bonds liberalized	Liberalized
Overseas bond issuance by residents	Partially permitted	Restrictions eased	Equity-linked bonds liberalized	Liberalized
Commercial loans	Not permitted	Within limits for small and medium-sized companies and foreign investors	Liberalized for small and medium-sized companies, and partial limits for others	Liberalized

Source: Constructed using various policy announcements from the Ministry of Finance and Economy.

to avoid a macroeconomic management system that relies heavily on various regulatory measures purported to encourage or discourage the economic activities of specific sectors.

Capital Flow Liberalization and Its Implications

South Korea has continuously opened aspects of its banking and capital markets since the early 1990s. Foreign banks and securities firms are expanding their branch networks in South Korea. The stock market was opened to foreign involvement in 1992 and is expected to open further. As a new member of the OECD, South Korea's capital flow liberalization policy will enter a new stage (table 3).

Toward the beginning of the 21st century, South Korea's capital account is expected to be fully opened to a level comparable with the advanced OECD countries. In addition, the foreign exchange market will be comparably deregulated and the exchange rate of the South Korean won will be freely floated. The South Korean economy will integrate more fully with world economies and strengthen its macroeconomic linkages with the major economies.

The immediate implication of these changes on macroeconomic policy making is that domestic policy cannot be concerned only with domestic issues but must give careful consideration to the possible repercussions to and from the major foreign economies. In addition, the autonomy of monetary and exchange rate policies cannot be simultaneously guaranteed in an open economy. Furthermore, South Korea has to consider the international political economy in macroeconomic policy making and must prepare for its active participation in international macroeconomic policy coordination, if necessary.

Reform of Monetary Policy Practices

The introduction of an indirect monetary control system will be the most urgent step in establishing an indirect macroeconomic management system. The operation of an open market should be given the highest priority as a monetary policy instrument, instead of relying on credit control by commercial banks, direct manipulation of interest rates, frequent changes of the required reserve ratio, and nonmarket allocation of government bonds to private-sector financial institutions.

Moreover, interest rate regulation in the short-term securities market should be liberalized to help in the development of an open short-term money market. With these reforms, monetary policy can operate indirectly through the central bank's base money control without causing distortions in financial resource allocation.

Reform of Fiscal Policy Practices

Unlike in developed countries, the use of fiscal policy as a macroeconomic tool has been virtually nonexistent in South Korea. Fiscal policy in South Korea has played an important role in supporting industries. To have fiscal policy as an active tool of macroeconomic stabilization, therefore, the government should de-emphasize its role of industrial support, except for necessary cases of government involvement such as social infrastructure investment and R&D support. It is also necessary to improve the flexibility of fiscal expenditures by lengthening

Table 4. Foreign Exchange Market Liberalization Schedule, 1995–1999

Category	Prior to 1995	Changes in 1995	1996–1997	1998–1999
Exchange rate system	Rule band ±1.5 percent	Enlarging the band to ±2.25 percent	Review a free-floating system	
Position system	Restrictions	Ceiling on spot O/S raised	Ceiling on overall O/S, O/B, and spot O/S raised	Further raised or liberalized
Foreign exchange concentration system	Partially liberalized	Liberalized		
External credit collection requirement	Limits (US$20,000)	Limits (US$30,000)	Ceiling raised	Ceiling raised

Source: Constructed using various policy announcements from the Ministry of Finance and Economy.

O/S: over-sold (position); O/B: over-bought (position).

the expenditure planning horizon beyond the yearly span but without succumbing to political pressure for fiscal expansion.

In addition, to improve the capability to monitor fiscal stance correctly and to take proper policy actions, South Korea should prepare a consolidated account of central government and public sector data on a quarterly basis with the least time lag possible. Local government accounts should also be included in the public sector data.

Reform of Exchange Rate Policy

South Korea's exchange rate determination system was liberalized in March 1990. The central value of the South Korean won/U.S. dollar exchange rate is determined as an average of individual exchange rates weighted with respective foreign exchange volumes of all exchange transactions executed during a previous market day. Initially, the band around the central value within which the market rate was allowed to fluctuate was plus or minus 0.4 percent, but it has gradually been expanded to 2.25 percent (table 4). The government plans to expand the band further and will eventually adopt a free-floating exchange rate system.

However, South Korea does not yet seem fully prepared to use the exchange rate as a tool of macroeconomic policy. The exchange rate was often used and regarded as an instrument for export promotion. The major concern in exchange rate management was on maintaining export competitiveness. A typical example was the reluctance to appreciate the won from 1986 to 1988, when the economy was rapidly expanding due to the sharp real depreciation caused by the strong yen. South Korea paid a high price for mismanagement through a loss in international competitiveness from a belated exchange rate response and domestic inflation. However, the concern for achieving current account surpluses still looms larger than the concern for macroeconomic stabilization, although since the early 1990s the importance of the exchange rate as a macroeconomic variable has been reevaluated.

As South Korea's economy gets more open and further integrated with the world economy, exchange rate policy cannot be confined to the role of export promoter but should also promote macroeconomic stabilization and act as a buffer against foreign shocks. Therefore, the exchange rate of the won should be given more flexibility, and further deregulation of the foreign exchange market is necessary. Table 4 summarizes the government's plan for deregulation of the foreign exchange market through 1999.

INSTITUTIONAL REFORM WITH DEMOCRATIZATION

The political system and the economic system do not always work in unison. Until recently, South Korea's political system was rather authoritarian. The authoritarian government could see merit in improving the economic performance with a much longer policy horizon than a democratic government. As argued in Amsden (1989), this observation seems to reflect South Korea's experience since the beginning of a more democratic system in 1987.

The current political situation, with presidential elections every five years, national assembly elections every four years, and the newly begun local elections every four years, could generate a good environment for the political business cycle in the future. As political pluralism and the democratic political system further develop in South Korea, the possibility of a political business cycle will increase. As a result, economic policy may become contaminated by political manipulation from the ruling political party as well as from lobbying by interest groups. Thus, the stability of the institutional and legal system can help to avoid, or at least minimize, problems caused by the political business cycle. Unfortunately, South Korea has a relatively short history with which to structure such stability, whereas most OECD countries have a long and successful history. Without such stability, a populist government could easily revert globalized South Korea to the old days of government intervention in accordance with whimsical popular discontent.

Certain safety devices will be necessary in the macroeconomic management system to prevent political factors from distorting the macroeconomic policy stance. During the past 30 years, South Korea has achieved a relatively stable macroeconomic environment even with enthusiastic support for industrial development through the central bank's base money and the commercial banks' policy loans. However, the degree of central bank autonomy in South Korea has been relatively low in terms of legal independence and the governor's turnover rate.[6]

Despite the relatively low central bank independence, the South Korean government's inflation consciousness has helped achieve relatively low inflation even with the rapid economic growth. In this sense, the South Korean government seems to have prioritized national economic considerations over any other political concerns. Both the Bank of Korea and the Ministry of Finance (now merged into the Ministry of Finance and Economy) have functioned just like any other staunch inflation-fighting central bank to some extent, even if the independence of the Bank of Korea was relatively low.

However, the political environment has already changed toward further democratization such that interest groups and political parties now seek their own interests more actively. Interest groups such as national federations of big business as well as small and medium-sized companies and labor unions will lobby the political parties, which, in turn, will pressure the government to change the macroeconomic policy stance to appease the interest groups. Furthermore, the political parties, concerned with reelection and staying in power, will try to manipulate macroeconomic policy to increase their chances of reelection. As a result, the so-called political business cycle might be more than a remote possibility.

To prepare for the worst possible case of politically directed macroeconomic management, South Korea has to introduce some institutional safety nets to prevent political forces from influencing the macroeconomic policy stance. Three possible directions are (a) reform of the central banking system toward more independence from political influences, (b) emphasis on rule-based policy making, and (c) lengthening the policy horizon.

Reform of the Central Banking System

Currently, South Korea's central banking system consists of the Monetary Board and the Bank of Korea. The Monetary Board is the nation's supreme committee on monetary and credit policy and is supposed to function, in spirit, like the Federal Reserve Board in the United States.

However, the Monetary Board is not fully integrated with the Bank of Korea, which is supposed to be the nation's central bank. The chairperson of the board is the finance and economy minister, who is also the deputy prime minister and the chief economic policymaker of the government. The governor of the Bank of Korea is the deputy chairperson of the board and is appointed by the nation's president through the recommendation of the finance and economy minister. Therefore, because the board is statutorily the supreme committee for monetary matters, the central banking system cannot be an independent identity from the administrative body of the government. Furthermore, the relationship between the board and the Bank of Korea is not well defined.

Taking these aspects into consideration, the basic principles of central banking reform should be as follows: First, the board and the Bank of Korea should be fully integrated in a real sense. Second, the independence of the central banking system from the administrative body and also from other political bodies should be improved. However, some degree of dependence between the central banking system and the administrative body may be kept if it is necessary to maintain the strong leadership of the nation's president in economic policy making. Third, the nation's president should have access to various independent sources of information on economic policy not only from the Ministry of Finance and Economy but also from the central bank.

Based on these understandings, the chairperson of the board should be the governor of the Bank of Korea, or vice versa. The governor of the bank should be appointed directly by the nation's president without the involvement of the finance and economy minister, and the rank of the governor should be elevated at least to that of deputy prime minister. In this case, the governor plays a role as an additional and independent advisor to the president. Also, the members of the board, including the chairperson, should be given more independence in the process of being appointed and in terms of their tenure. In the process of appointment, the national assembly could intervene, and the tenures of board members could be lengthened to longer than that of the president and should also be protected from political considerations. Currently, the governor of the bank has a four-year term, but the members of the board have two-year terms. Their terms should overlap to maintain the continuity of the board's activities.

Emphasis on Rule-Based Economic Policy Making

Interest groups lobby the government directly or through political parties when they perceive the possibility that a policy stance can be changed. Therefore, the surest way to protect economic policy making from political influences is to convince the public that policy stances cannot be changed except for special and rare cases.

The issue of rule versus discretion in economic policy making has been raised in the context of how to maintain time consistency in economic policy making and implementation after experiencing high inflation under the discretionary macroeconomic policy regime.[7] A rule-based policy is recommended as a substitute for a fine-tuning, discretionary policy. The underlying reason why a fine-tuning, discretionary policy regime tends to become time inconsistent is the economic agents' conception that government policy making is endogenous or can be made to become endogenous. Therefore, the issue of maintaining time consistency in policy making is exactly the same as protecting economic policy from interest group politics. In this sense, the government should make itself less free in policy change not only to improve the time consistency of macroeconomic policy but also to avoid distortions in macroeconomic policy stance due to lobbying by interest groups, thereby signaling to the public the government's commitment to a given policy stance. Once the public is convinced that the government will stick to a given stance under any circumstances, then the leadership role of government policy can be improved.

For this purpose, it will be necessary to introduce some characteristics of a rule-based policy in macroeconomic management. To protect the monetary policy stance from political pressure, it is important to have an independent central bank, but it is even more important to emphasize rule-based policy in monetary policy making. In the past, the government announced a monetary growth target annually, but, often, the target was not kept or was changed. Therefore, the growth target of money supply has not constrained central bank behavior in the usual sense.

Lengthening the Economic Policy Horizon

Rule-based policy making is an important step toward the improvement of the macroeconomic policy environment, but may not be enough to achieve its intended purposes unless the horizon of rule making is set long enough. South Korea previously used a series of five-year economic development plans, but the horizon of economic policy making has now been altered to periods as short as a quarter. The tradition of making five-year plans was discontinued when the Kim Young Sam government launched the so-called New Economy Plan to replace the then existing seventh five-year economic plan, and the Kim government then seemed to have no intention of returning to the practice of making five-year plans. With the loss of its long-term policy horizon, the government was perceived as less stalwart about its policy stances.

Under this situation, there is no room for even a rule-based policy to be beneficial if it is adopted on a quarterly basis. If a monetary growth target is adopted as a strict rule but can be easily and regularly changed in a quarter, the rule cannot be an effective protection against the political economic forces. Therefore, it will be beneficial to incorporate a policy horizon of longer than a quarter or even a year into the nation's economic policy making. For this purpose, it may be more useful to have a flexible long-term development strategy rather than a typical five-year economic plan.

MICROECONOMIC ADJUSTMENTS

According to Oman, there have been three waves of globalization, including the current one, in this century. He argues that the microeconomic dimension differentiates the current wave of globalization from the two previous waves: "Globalisation resembles and builds on earlier periods of globalisation; but globalisation today also differs crucially from earlier periods. Policies to deal with globalisation must come to grips with the specificity of the process today, especially at the microeconomic level, relative to globalisation in the 1950s and 1960s, in particular" (1996, 6). The actions of individual economic actors such as firms, banks, and people drive the growth of economic activity, usually in the pursuit of profit, often spurred by the pressures of competition. A government can facilitate such actions in the microeconomic dimension by establishing a competitive environment.

The microeconomic dimension involves broad policy issues, ranging from policy loans to South Korea–specific chaebol policy. At this point, it would be better to clarify the characteristics of the chaebol policy. The big-business-oriented growth strategy, coupled with entry regulations and protection from foreign competition, was criticized for having resulted in chaebol problems. As argued in Jwa (1997b), the chaebol problems include most microeconomic policy issues, including entry regulations, credit control, investment regulations, and protection of small and medium-sized companies. He summarizes the major focus of the anti-chaebol policy as follows: (a) industrial policy instruments such as entry regulations (including the license and permit system, and ownership regulations) and business area regulations; (b) regulations based upon the credit control system, including prior approval requirements for investments, regulations on the purchase of land, and entry restrictions into a new line of business; (c) investment regulations to rationalize industries and to curb excessive or duplicative investments in many and the same industries; (d) designation and protection of small and medium-sized companies; (e) regulations on total ceilings, such as basket control of credit supply (credit control system) and equity investment regulations (Fair Trade Act); and (f) industrial area specialization policy (introduced in 1991 and reinforced in 1993), that is, the 30 largest chaebol are advised to select their "core industries" and "core firms," which then are allowed exemptions or preferential treatment in regulations such as the credit control system and equity investment regulations. Because the chaebol problems involve most microeconomic issues as well as macroeconomic issues, the analysis herein naturally touches certain aspects of the problems associated with the chaebol.

Some microeconomic issues are intimately related to macroeconomic management issues. To support policy loans for the key industries, for instance, the government controlled the financial resource allocation with regulations on interest rates and the lending activities of financial institutions. Here, the scope is limited to deregulation, privatization, and structural adjustments.[8] Both deregulation and privatization bear great significance for competition policy because government intervention takes the form of various regulations, mostly under the name of industrial policy, and the form of public ownership or public enterprises. As suggested in Jwa (1997b), structural adjustments are also needed to overcome the problems resulting from industrial policy.

Deregulation Policies

Together with the law and institutions, government regulations are essential for the proper functioning of a market economy. Although the government touches almost everything, its intervention falls into three categories according to its objectives and effects: economic, social, and administrative/procedural regulations. But the distinction is sometimes hard to make. Economic regulations are restrictions on rates and on business entry, and, thus, they are sometimes called price and entry control regulations. Social regulations (or environmental and risk-reduction regulations) are mandates aimed at lessening pollution and other social risks. Administrative and/or procedural regulations are compliance procedures and paperwork requirements, which do not have any clear-cut economic or social objectives.

In pursuit of its economic and social goals, a government produces lots of regulations. The trouble is, however, that in many cases, the economic costs of implementing regulations exceed the benefits they offer. Economic and administrative/procedural regulations have been the primary concern of deregulation in South Korea, because they either severely restrained competition by protecting established businesses or undermined the efficiency of private-sector companies by hindering swift and timely decision making in business activities. Moreover, these regulations impose burdens on the private sector, such as expenses for compliance, lobbying, and bribery. The government in the 1970s believed that it could successfully replace the market mechanism. The HCI drive of the 1970s, however, led many people to question the government's ability to appropriately allocate resources, although such efforts in the 1970s obviously contributed to laying the foundation for today's industrial structure.

Yoo examines the origin of South Korea's deregulation policy as follows: "In sum, economic and administrative regulations, which once worked as a driving force in achieving industrial policy objectives, began to work as a hindrance to the efficiency and competitiveness of industries and firms, and also caused serious side effects. Under these circumstances, deregulation was expected to be an attractive cure for the apparent problems associated with economic and administrative regulations. However, it was not until the late 1980s when the Korean government actually embarked upon serious deregulation efforts" (1994, 4).

Since the beginning of the Sixth Republic in 1988, the government has embarked on a program of full-scale deregulation, which aims to cope with the changing economic environment reflected in the accelerated opening of the domestic market and in the progress toward economic freedom. In March 1993, the newly elected government of Kim Young Sam announced its 100-Day Program for a New Economy, which was followed by the broader Five-Year Plan for a New Economy. Deregulation was the catchword in these plans. The government organized a number of agencies to implement deregulation policy. For example, the Ministry of Finance and Economy (formerly the Economic Planning Board) established the Committee for Administrative and Economic Deregulation. The committee, in turn, formed the Working Committee for Economic Deregulation, headed by the deputy minister of finance and economy.

Compared with the previous administration, the deregulation performance under the Kim government improved considerably in terms of the number of deregulation measures taken and their effectiveness. However, the main emphasis of deregulation was on simple administrative/procedural regulations instead of economic regulations. Thus, the Kim government's deregulation policy was regarded as an attempt to relieve the difficulties that businesses may face, and was criticized for leaving untouched many price and entry control regulations.

Kim Iljoong (1995) makes several suggestions aimed at greater rationality in South Korea's deregulation policy: (a) deregulation must be subject to the rule of law; (b) deregulation must be designed to promote competition; (c) the priority order of deregulation policy should be based on the cost/benefit analysis; and (d) it is necessary to establish a central bureau, headed by the president, which is able to merge or integrate the works of the presently decentralized commission.

Privatization Policies

Public ownership or public enterprises are an extreme form of government intervention in a market economy. During the 1960s and 1970s, the South Korean government nationalized or established many public enterprises to implement its government-led development strategy, believing its relative superiority over the market mechanism in allocating resources. The growth of the public sector, both in its absolute size and in its share in the economy, was accelerated due to the government policy of promoting public enterprises in many sectors of the economy, such as electric power, communications, gas, steel, railroads, and banks. Since the early 1980s, however, privatization has been an important issue. Indeed, the government has lost its relative superiority over the private sector.

The history of privatization in South Korea dates back to the late 1960s, when the government privatized some public enterprises, including the airline, trucking, maritime shipping, shipbuilding, and steel sectors. This first privatization, carried out from 1968 to 1973, was primarily the disposal of public companies that were proven unproductive. The second round of privatization took place in the early 1980s and was mainly aimed at developing the domestic financial market. Though most of the commercial banks were privatized during this period, their top managers continued to be appointed by the government. The third round of privatization, announced in 1987, was characterized by a so-called people's share program, under which lower and middle-class people had the opportunity to buy shares of money-making public enterprises. The true purpose behind the third privatization was to gain the electoral support of these classes. The proposed privatization programs were interrupted due to the stock market breakdown in 1990.

The fourth large-scale privatization program, introduced in December 1993 by the Kim Young Sam government, selected 61 public enterprises (out of 133 considered) as candidates for privatization from 1994 to 1998. This privatization also included the restructuring of 10 more public enterprises. The 61 public enterprises were selected on the grounds that they no longer needed to be publicly owned and managed and also that their privatization would enhance their efficiency.

Yoo states that the fourth privatization is based upon a few essential principles that exhibit a striking difference from the previous privatization programs: "First, the objective of privatization has been clearly identified as the enhancement of efficiency in the public enterprises included in the program. Second, all government ownership shares are to be sold out to the private sector and the government is to cease exercise of control over the management. Thus, the privatization of both ownership and management is to be pursued. Third, the level of ownership shares that enables a stable management is to be sold to the largest shareholder, who will be selected via an open competitive bidding process, while the remaining portion of ownership shares is to be distributed in many other ways" (1994, 12).

Kim Jaehong (1995) makes several suggestions aimed at greater rationality in South Korea's privatization policy: (a) the government should trust the market mechanism, (b) the consideration for long-term economic benefits of privatization must precede that for short-term political interests, (c) the concern over the concentration of economic power by chaebol should not be a serious obstacle to the privatization plan, and (d) the government must consider policy consistency and the establishment of a legal base for privatization.

Structural Adjustments

In the past decade or so, it has been popular for governments to implement one form or another of an industrial policy similar to the ones adopted by the successful East Asian economies such as Japan, Taiwan, and South Korea.[9] This tendency becomes even more conspicuous as a possible policy response to the so-called unlimited competition forced by globalization. An increasingly common view seems to be that the government should help businesses successfully compete in the international market. The government should intervene, to a large extent, in adjusting the industrial structure under globalized competitive environments.

However, the basic stance concerning the role of government taken in this chapter suggests the following implications that are diametrically opposite to this new trend of industrial policy. As pointed out in Oman (1996), above all, globalization is basically a diversified and sometimes conflicting phenomenon that has different economic implications depending on the context. It is especially difficult for a government to design a particular industrial structure that is supposed to be optimal for its economy. In this sense, the economists' search for an alternative industrial organization among the so-called American Fordist, German Craft, and even the lean and flexible production systems will not likely yield any definitive, single optimal structure of industrial organization.[10] Therefore, instead of adopting an active interventionist industrial policy that requires a tremendous volume of information and does not easily produce the right solutions, an efficient response to globalization might be to let the market order prevail in discovering an optimal business structure and, for this to occur, to let the private sector freely compete and thereby discover optimal solutions and make appropriate structural adjustments.

If this logic is applied to the case of South Korea, a search for an alternative to the existing mass production system should not be the responsibility of the government. Instead, the South Korean government should lift all entry barriers, domestic and otherwise, and deregulate the South Korean economy. Moreover, a search for or a discovery of a new optimal industrial organization should be the responsibility of the private sector given the undistorted market incentive structure provided by a rational government policy.

CONCLUSION

During the past three decades, South Korea has achieved remarkably high economic growth with a government-led export promotion strategy. The government has been actively involved in almost every important aspect of an economywide decision-making process, and the private sector has largely followed the signals given by the government. In other words, government-led order has dominated the spontaneous market order. However, South Korea's economic policy environment has undergone a drastic change since the mid-1990s, forcing the reform of the government-led development strategy. South Korea can no longer rely on direct regulations and interventions, as the South

Korean economy is becoming increasingly open and integrated with the global economy. Moreover, globalization and an increasingly borderless economy will tend to limit the feasibility of the government's control of the domestic economy and will force the adaptation of economic management based on the market mechanism and internationally compatible rules.

The recent struggle over labor law may show that in some areas, South Korean society has not yet prepared for the challenges of globalization. Most South Koreans, including some union leaders, believe that there should be sufficient flexibility in the labor market for companies to compete successfully in the international market. At the same time, however, they are afraid of losing long-term employment security if labor laws are amended to accommodate the rapid pace of structural change in industry. The government withdrew an amendment of 1996 to the labor laws because the revision failed to ease public fears.

It may be too early to assess the effect of globalization on the South Korean economy. It is quite certain, however, that the current wave of globalization will affect the prospects of the South Korean economy in various ways. A complete analysis of globalization should include social issues as well as economic issues. Unfortunately, this chapter does not include the analysis of social issues such as education, immigration, and cultural and information policies. But interested readers may refer to Yeon (1995) for a discussion of such social issues.

The interaction between globalization and regionalism is another important issue that this chapter has not touched upon. The global economy is now driven by the two parallel trends of globalization and regionalism: Regionalism is being strengthened, whereas the current wave of globalization has provided a turning point for the world economy to converge toward the market economy mostly along the lines of the United States (see Oman 1996 for additional discussion of this issue).

NOTES

1. See Lawrence, Bressand, and Ito (1994) for a detailed discussion on the possibility and the necessity of deeper policy integration under the new world economic order.

2. The first five-year plan was followed by six more five-year plans.

3. President Park urged senior government officials and businesspeople to promote exports by presiding himself at a monthly meeting of the Export Promotion Council, which was organized to provide solutions to domestic economic problems and information on international market trends. The government also established the Korea Trade Promotion Corporation to assist exporters with information on foreign markets.

4. Yoo argues that "in retrospect it is fair to say that the economic policies in the 1960s worked much better than the policies in the 1970s" (1996, 15).

5. In January 1997, President Kim formed the Presidential Commission on Financial Reform, which had three months to decide whether reform should take the so-called big bang approach or be liberalized gradually. But the reform effort turned out to be a flash in the pan. Its failure was blamed as an underlying cause of the current currency and financial crisis in South Korea.

6. See Cukierman (1992) for an international comparison of central bank independence.

7. Kydland and Prescott (1977) have initiated a series of discussions on this issue.

8. There remain a few other important issues of microeconomic policy concern such as labor, industrial, trade, and competition policy. Interested readers may refer to Lee Ju-Ho (1996) for labor policy, Seong (1996) for industrial policy, Lee Honggue (1996) for trade policy, and Yoo (1994) for competition policy in South Korea.

9. The World Bank (1993) emphasizes that although government intervention was helpful in certain periods and conditions, the most important factors for the East Asian miracle are macroeconomic stability and market-conforming economic policies.

10. Jwa (1996) analyzes the implications of globalization on the optimal industrial structure and arrives at the identical conclusion.

BIBLIOGRAPHY

Amsden, Alice II. 1989. *Asia's Next Giant.* Oxford, England: Oxford University Press.

Bank of Korea. *Economic Statistics Yearbook* (various issues; in Korean).

Cukierman, Alex. 1992. *Central Bank Strategy, Credibility, and Independence: Theory and Evidence.* Boston: MIT Press.

Economic Planning Board. *Major Statistics of Korean Economy* (various issues; in Korean).

Jwa Sung Hee. 1996. "Globalization and New Industrial Organization: Implications for Structural Adjustment Policies." In T. Ito and A. Krueger, eds. *Regionalism vs. Multilateral Trade Arrangement*. Cambridge, Mass.: National Bureau of Economic Research.

———. 1997a. "Reorganization of Korea's Macroeconomic Management." Mimeo. Seoul: Korea Development Institute.

———. 1997b. "Role of the Government in Economic Management." Mimeo. Seoul: Korea Development Institute.

Kim Iljoong. 1995. "The Results and Future Course of Korea's Deregulation Policy." In I. Kim, ed. *The Role of the Three Branches of Government for the Rule of Law and the Free Market in Korea*. Seoul: Korea Economic Research Institute.

Kim Jaehong. 1995. "Privatization in Korea: Political Motivation and Economic Results." In I. Kim, ed. *The Role of the Three Branches of Government for the Rule of Law and the Free Market in Korea*. Seoul: Korea Economic Research Institute.

Kim Kwang Suk. 1994. "Trade and Industrialization Policies in Korea." In G. K. Helleiner, ed. *Trade Policy and Industrialization in Turbulent Times*. London: Routledge.

Kydland, Finn E., and E. C. Prescott. 1977. "Rules Rather than Discretion: The Inconsistency of Optimal Plant." *Journal of Political Economy* 85: 473–491.

Lawrence, Robert Z., Albert Bressand, and Takatoshi Ito. 1994. *A New Vision for the World Economy*. Washington, D.C.: Brookings Project on Integrating National Economies, Brookings Institution.

Lee Honggue. 1996. *Challenges and Responses in the New Trading Environment: A Korean Perspective*. Seoul: Korea Development Institute.

Lee Ju-Ho. 1996. "Trade and Labor Standards: A Korean Perspective." KDI Working Paper No. 9605. Seoul: Korea Development Institute.

Oman, Charles. 1996. *The Policy Challenges of Globalization and Regionalization*. Paris: Organization for Economic Cooperation and Development.

Seong Somi. 1996. "Competition and Cooperation among Asian Countries and the Future Prospect of Korea Industrial Policy." KDI Working Paper No. 9601. Seoul: Korea Development Institute.

Westphal, Larry E., and Kwang Suk Kim. 1982. "Korea." In Bela Balassa, ed. *Development Strategies in Semi-Industrial Countries*. Baltimore: Johns Hopkins University Press.

World Bank. 1993. *The East Asian Miracle*. Oxford, England: Oxford University Press.

Yeon Hachung. 1995. "Social Development in Korea: An Overview." Working Paper No. 95-01. Seoul: Korea Institute for Health and Social Affairs.

Yoo Jungho. 1990. "The Industrial Policy of the 1970s and the Evolution of the Manufacturing Sector in Korea." KDI Working Paper No. 9017. Seoul: Korea Development Institute.

————. 1996. "Challenges to the Newly Industrialized Countries: A Reinterpretation of Korea's Growth Experience." KDI Working Paper No. 9608. Seoul: Korea Development Institute.

Yoo Seong Min. 1994. "Deregulation and Privatization: The Korean Experience and Lessons for Competition Policy." Paper presented at the 5th Conference on Competition Policies among Asian and Oceanian Countries, Tokyo.

11 · Thailand

Chantana Banpasirichote

G LOBALIZATION is not really new to Thailand. Since the middle of the 19th century, Thailand has had to adjust to an international capitalist economy. It did so successfully enough to retain its independence throughout the colonial period and to lay the basis for a modernizing economy after World War II. In more recent years, with the growth of integrative economic forces, the foreign impact on Thailand has intensified. External pressure produced Thailand's first economic development plan in the 1960s, and foreigners have been prominent in each subsequent Thai reconsideration of its development program.

By the late 1980s, Thailand was poised to become a full-fledged newly industrializing economy (NIE) on the level of Singapore, Taiwan, Hong Kong, and South Korea. The appreciation of the yen following the Plaza Accord of 1985 brought new foreign investment on a massive scale and provided new opportunities for Thailand's export-oriented economy. In the following decade, Thai manufacturing industries and exports boomed.

Despite this history of accelerating foreign-Thai economic interaction and investment-induced growth from the mid-1980s, it was only in the early 1990s that the Thai began to use the term *globalization.* Today, the term is widely used by columnists, social critics, scholars, and even the public. Commentary on globalization tends toward the topical rather than the conceptual.

257

This chapter deals with four aspects of contemporary globalization in Thailand:
- The forces of globalization as they affect Thailand.
- Thai government policy and its results.
- The views of various interest groups concerning globalization.
- The macroeconomic areas of research interest in Thailand.

FORCES OF GLOBALIZATION

A number of phenomena have stimulated interest in globalization. Most significant among these are economic liberalization, modern communications and transportation technologies, and the spread of global human rights and labor standards. Most Thai observe globalization in their everyday life. Increasingly, in the urban centers, Thai buy more foreign goods, drive more foreign automobiles, see more foreign-language signs, use more automated machines, work in foreign or joint venture factories, and communicate via mobile telephones and the Internet. Their livelihood frequently depends on markets in North America, Northeast Asia, or Europe. The business community pays handsomely to hear famous international speakers talk of reengineering, competitiveness, the information highway, and even globalization. Foreign-style radio and television talk shows on politics and social issues have become popular overnight. Similarly, globalization has spread Thai influences to neighboring countries, where people can now read Thai magazines, listen to Thai radio, view Thai television, and even use the baht to buy goods.

Labor migration is also obvious to the average Thai. Since the 1970s, poorer Thai have migrated to Japan, Taiwan, and the Middle East in search of better-paying jobs to support a more affluent lifestyle. More recently, Thailand has become a host country—and a transit point—for foreign workers from Myanmar, Indochina, and South Asia.

Trade and investment liberalization has generated considerable attention among educated Thai. The media closely tracks such developments as the Uruguay Round of the General Agreement on Tariffs and Trade (GATT), the establishment of the ASEAN Free Trade Area (AFTA), and the Asia-Pacific Economic Cooperation (APEC) forum's vision of free trade and investment in the region by 2020.

Government agencies, scholars, and even the media study the impact of such schemes.

Finally, Thailand's openness to the world of ideas has affected many aspects of Thai life. The introduction from abroad of new concepts of democracy, human rights, and fair labor practices has changed Thai expectations of their government, the rights of individuals, and civil society. However, the infusion of global cultural influences has also raised concerns over the erosion of traditional Thai culture and values.

The use of the term *globalization* itself has generated controversy over how this English word should be best translated into Thai. The various terms suggested reveal much about the connotation that the Thai elite places on globalization. Chai-Anan Samudavanija was the first to introduce a Thai word, suggesting *lokanuwat,* which means "to act according to the world." Other scholars and social critics, including Saneh Chamarik (1993) and Kasian Techapeera (1995), support this term because it implies that Thailand eventually will be dominated by the world economy. The supporters of lokanuwat believe that Thailand will be on the defensive as globalization proceeds.

In October 1994, however, the Thai Royal Academy officially adopted another word, *lokapiwat,* which means "expanding globally," "conquering the world," or "globally accessible." This term has a more physical connotation and suggests that the Thai can be active in the globalization process. However, the academy's decision did not end the debate. Other suggestions include *lokanuwok,* meaning "the world coming on to us" (Niti 1996), and *lokawibat,* or "global disaster" (*Tid Tang Thai* 1994; Charnvit 1996). Both of these terms express skepticism and reservations about the impact of globalization.

The language debate unintentionally reveals the different positions attached to globalization. Kasian (1995) detects two opposing views: those of globalizers and those of communitarians who want to protect the Thai community from the negative aspects of globalization. This analysis may overstate the distinction as the pros and cons of globalization are not always clear. However, the dichotomy has provoked considerable debate on how policy should balance economic nationalism with international liberalization.

THAI ECONOMIC POLICIES

Structural Adjustment

Since the late 1980s, when the speed of growth accelerated, the Thai economy has become increasingly connected to the international marketplace. Previous to that, agricultural products dominated Thai exports, and industrialization was based on import substitution. Industrial development in the early 1950s was concentrated in state organizations, and economic development was powered by state capitalism. From the late 1970s, the government favored export-oriented development. Industrial development and export activities had stagnated following the first oil shock in 1973–1974. The economy subsequently relied heavily on overseas borrowing (see Dixon 1996, 29–30).

Following the global economic crisis of the early 1980s, the World Bank introduced structural adjustment to restore worldwide stability. The government incorporated some of the World Bank's proposals into its Fifth National Economic and Social Development Plan (1982–1986). Dixon (1996, 33) summarizes these measures as follows:

- the raising of domestic energy prices to the international level (they were 20 percent below and were a key element in the subsidization of the industrial sector);
- the ending of other fuel and transport subsidies;
- reducing government expenditure;
- placing emphasis on export-oriented industry;
- reducing import taxes;
- removing all export restrictions and taxes;
- substantially reducing foreign exchange controls;
- imposing strong deflationary monetary and fiscal policies;
- privatizing state concerns; and
- reforming the taxation system to increase efficiency of collection and yields.

Structural adjustment in Thailand had a specific purpose: restoring economic stability. At the time, these adjustments were not viewed as globalizing the domestic economy, although some of the liberalization solutions indicated greater openness. However, the implementation of these measures was delayed owing to several bureaucratic and political factors, and the impact on the economy was not significant.

Industrial protection remained strong because the government needed revenue. The process toward deregulation was slow.

Muscat found that "the pattern of structural adjustment in Thailand was an extremely gradual one. Measures appear in general to have only been effectively implemented when they would cause limited disruption and protest. In part this reflects the weak governments of the 1980s and their need to serve a variety of often conflicting interests. Perhaps more significantly, the gradual approach reflects the cautious, light-handed, and conservative approach to economic development and management that has characterized Thailand since the late 1950s" (Muscat 1994, 216–222, cited in Dixon 1996, 39). Structural adjustment then did not automatically lead to the economic boom in the late 1980s.

Liberalization

The impressive growth rate in the late 1980s took place before liberalization was effectively implemented (table 1). Thailand received foreign direct investment from Japan and the NIEs because of its favorable political conditions and the comparative advantage of its cheap labor. Only after the country experienced growth, leading to increased internationalization, was liberalization taken more seriously. Measures were enacted to sustain the growth rate following the Plaza Accord ("Economic Liberalization" 1992, 8). In addition, growth in foreign investment, exports of manufactured goods, and tourism

Table 1. Thai Trade and Investment from 1970 (US$ million)

	Terms of Trade (1987 = 100)	Foreign Direct Investment	Exports	Manufactured Exports	Primary Exports
1970	178.9	48	710	76	629
1975	141.2	22	2,162	397	1,784
1980	123.1	187	6,369	1,886	4,579
1985	90.6	162	7,056	2,800	4,221
1986	104.3	261	8,786	3,944	4,820
1987	100.0	182	11,629	6,125	5,446
1988	98.2	1,081	15,902	8,129	7,068
1989	94.2	1,726	19,976	11,453	8,377
1990	91.6	2,303	23,002	14,796	8,014
1991	91.7	1,847	28,324	18,903	9,138
1992	91.2	1,979	34,473	21,627	10,477

Source: Dixon (1996, 36, adapted from Table 2.1b).

Table 2. Net Capital Inflows (US$ million)

	1990	1991	% Change
Direct investment	1,549.6	1,211.2	–21.84
Borrowings	5,395.9	6,210.9	15.10
Portfolio investment	454.5	68.5	–84.93
Nonresident baht accounts	1,336.7	1,967.8	46.47
Others	62.4	227.2	264.10
Total	8,799.1	9,675.6	9.95

Source: "Economic Liberalization" (1992, 11).

contributed to increased internationalization ("Economic Liberalization" 1992, 8; Medhi 1993, 2).

Liberalization was realized only when sustainable growth demanded more efficiency in economic transactions, especially in an environment of increased globalization of trade and investment. The business sector found that financial liberalization facilitated savings growth at home and the flow of capital from abroad—both direct and portfolio. Concurrently, global and regional integration required the Thai economy to comply with the universal agreements of economic internationalization. Furthermore, a liberal economy bodes well for the role Thailand will likely play in the opening of markets in Indochina (see "Economic Liberalization" 1992, 9).

Liberalization focused on the financial sector (table 2). In 1990, Thailand accepted the International Monetary Fund's (IMF's) Article 8, which requires lifting controls on payments and transfers of foreign exchange in current account transactions. This triggered other financial reforms. Several deregulation measures followed, culminating in the establishment of the Bangkok International Banking Facilities, an offshore banking operation that allows international banking business to be conducted in Thailand under tax and regulatory environments equivalent to those offered at other financial centers in the world. Similar liberalization measures also took place in Thailand's capital market, greatly enhancing foreign participation (Medhi 1993, 3). In other significant moves, (a) the taxation system was restructured to make it simpler, fairer, and more difficult to evade; (b) a semifloating interest rate was introduced, leading to higher competition among commercial banks to provide the public with a wider range of services; (c) oil prices were floated; and (d) import restrictions were liberalized on many items.

Despite much progress, liberalization has concentrated on international deregulation. Many monopolies still exist at the national level. Narongchai Akraseranee, a business executive who served as minister of commerce, suggests that the "Thai economy looks like [it is] liberalized, but in fact it is not so. . . . Government intervention remains in various levels, and it is often not improving the conditions" (National Economic and Social Development Board [NESDB] 1996, 72). He finds that much government assistance to different economic sectors is misplaced and often inappropriate. An imbalance appears between the industrial and agricultural sectors. Limited licensing obstructs development of the financial and banking system, concentrating profits in this sector to the detriment of expansion. The government still operates most public services and controls infrastructure development. In addition, political obstacles prevent large-scale privatization of state enterprises, and even privatization does not guarantee efficiency improvement (see Dixon 1996, 39).

Regional Economic Integration

GATT, APEC, and AFTA are the most concrete issues of economic globalization discussed in Thailand. The Thai economy is more sensitive to the fluctuations of international markets than ever before. Economic integration is inevitable, despite a lot of concern for its impact on disadvantaged groups. With economics the dominant force of that integration, policy issues are concentrated on improving the nation's competitive capacity.

Nipon and Mitree (1996) have conducted research on the impact of the 1993 GATT Uruguay Round agreements on the Thai economy. This research suggests that the GATT agreements will liberalize international markets, will increase the transparency of regulations, and make it difficult to impose domestic protection measures. The study concludes that Thailand will be a net beneficiary (table 3). However, further negotiation of issues such as the environment and labor standards could affect trade liberalization. The scope of most study thus far has been primarily macroeconomic, but the microeconomic impact requires further research (see Nipon and Mitree 1996, 3–5).

Current studies on the World Trade Organization and other regional integration efforts raise three crucial challenges. First, the Thai government must develop a mechanism through which to prepare for trade negotiations. The negotiation process should be streamlined, with a focus on what will most benefit Thailand in the future. Furthermore, the Thai representatives must be fully aware of their role in the global negotiations, that is, the developing countries do not control

Table 3. Impact of the Uruguay Round of GATT on the Thai Economy

Variable	Change
Economic growth	0.22 percent
Inflation rate	0.29 percent
Exports	2.34 percent
Imports	1.01 percent
Income distribution	• 1 percent to 2 percent increase in the income of the low-income population, particularly in rural areas • Slight increase in the income of the low- and middle-income groups in urban areas • 1.4 percent decrease in the income of the upper-income group in urban areas
Agricultural production	Improved production volume and pricing for such major crops as sugar, rice, corn, coconut, rubber, jute, and millet. Increased competition for other crops, including cotton, coffee, some fruits and vegetables, tobacco, sorghum, peanuts, beans, cassava, and palm oil, owing to the opening of the domestic market and decreased protection; prices, volume, and income from these products will decline.

Industrial production	Major tax reform over the next 10 years. Market opens for imports of parts and raw materials, and industrial protection decreases. Industrial promotion and development through taxation and tariffs becomes more difficult. Other important impacts include the following:
	1. Removal of investment promotion measures will result in
	   (a) high impact on parts and automobile engine producers, and
	   (b) less impact on sheet metal, interior, and some automobile parts.
	2. Removal of import quotas benefits the textile industry.

Source: Office of Agricultural Economy (1995, 4).

the agenda. At present, no Thai organization has direct responsibility for the overall coordination of international trade. The bureaucracy, with little or no political involvement, currently handles trade negotiations (Nipon and Mitree 1996, 3). Above all, international trade negotiations should incorporate participation from numerous interest groups to balance the potential gains and losses. Second, the connection between environmental concerns and trade issues must be clarified and a policy option formulated. Finally, policies must be introduced to minimize the impact of increased competition on small enterprises, including small farms (see Nipon and Mitree 1996, 4; Apichai and Paradorn 1997).

The structure of industry is changing from labor intensive to high technology in an effort to lessen the impact of jobs lost to lower-wage countries. However, labor-intensive industries are still a major source of employment. Thailand stands to gain from investment in the newly opening markets of nearby Myanmar and Indochina (see Thammavit 1997, 1–32).

Although a short-term loser in regional integration, agriculture might well be a long-term beneficiary. Agriculture was previously burdened by policies promoting industry at the expense of agriculture. However, international liberalization will likely impose restructuring on agricultural development that could lead to long-term improvement. In the short term, according to former Minister of Commerce Narongchai, government intervention is necessary to ensure that small farms survive (NESDB 1996, 72). Others suggest that Thai agricultural development depends solely on the availability of natural resources and ecological conditions. Thus, agriculture should primarily serve domestic subsistence and coincide with natural conservation (Apichai and Paradorn 1997, 3–17).

Competitiveness

Thailand has no policy package to deal with economic globalization. Even if such a program existed, the instability of the government would make implementation difficult. Four official domestic documents address the issue of competitiveness: (a) the Eighth National Economic and Social Development Plan (1997–2001), (b) the White Paper on Increasing International Competitiveness (table 4), (c) Thailand 2000: A Guide to Sustainable Growth and Competitiveness, and (d) Toward Social Equity and Prosperity: Thai Information Technology Policies in the 21st Century.

These documents reveal the government's thinking about the opportunities and challenges of the economic dimensions of globalization. The biggest question facing government planners and

Table 4. Policy Agenda for Increasing National Competitive Capacity

Macroeconomic stability management
Export promotion and market opening
International economic negotiation
International economic cooperation
Foreign investment promotion
Thai investment in foreign countries
Labor and human resource development
Science and technology development
Finance and tax reform
Investment and business incentives
Moving toward a regional center of transportation and communication
Moving toward a regional financial center
Moving toward a regional center of tourism
Energy development
Area development
State enterprise and bureaucracy reform
Economic development by sectors
Agricultural adjustment by sectors

the business community is how to regain Thailand's competitive advantage. Thailand recognizes that it is no longer a cheap source of labor; indeed, the countries of Indochina and South Asia can easily undercut Thailand's labor costs. The government documents offer a wide range of reforms and adjustments designed to strengthen Thai competitiveness. These include not only economic measures but also increased efforts to strengthen the quality of government services, expand the science and knowledge base, and provide greater political accountability.

The World Competitiveness Report prepared by the Institute of World Economic Forum and the International Institute for Management Development in Switzerland identifies three weaknesses of the Thai economy: economic infrastructure development, science and technology, and management (*White Paper* 1995, 89). Furthermore, the Thai themselves have identified a fourth weakness: the hidden cost of excessive corruption (*White Paper* 1995, 91).

In the early 1990s, the government moved to create a science and technology department. The National Science and Technology Development Agency was established in 1991. More than 4 billion baht (US$160 million) was initially allocated for the agency to render scientific research through a variety of mechanisms (Chai-Anan 1994, 42). The agency seeks to minimize the bureaucratic procedures that can obstruct intellectual creativity. The Thailand Research Fund (TRF), an independent research institute, was founded in 1993 to further intellectual development. The market for research activity has become more widespread and increasingly competitive. Although many of the constraints to research have been abolished, the director of the TRF asserts that the availability of researchers remains a problem (Thailand Research Fund 1995, 8). The proportion of researchers to the general populace is quite low in Thailand, at two researchers per 10,000 citizens, compared with 80:10,000 and 60:10,000 in Germany and Japan, respectively (NESDB 1996, 77).

The management problem is generally recognized as a major constraint to economic development. The Joint Public and Private Consultative Committee was established in the late 1980s to facilitate better decision making and eradicate obstacles to business development. But the committee has proven less than effective at easing the many bottlenecks in the bureaucracy. Bureaucratic reform efforts have been initiated both outside and inside the government in the past few years. A committee was set up to oversee the issue, but according to a study by the Thailand Development Research Institute, the adjustments were partial, of short duration, and lacking in long-term vision and continuous political commitment. The study suggested that a desirable bureaucracy would possess at least five qualities: a visionary system, a learning organization, a flexible and adjustable mechanism, a results-oriented focus, and an encouraging method of implementation. Unfortunately, the bureaucracy itself opposes many of the reforms (see Pratya 1996). Recommendations for bureaucratic reform therefore remain on the shelf.

In addition, the Thai have lost the advantage of cheap labor. The country sees greater opportunities in capital- and skill-intensive industries, and therefore a greater need for skilled labor. The National Economic and Social Development Board lists human resource development as a priority but implementation of changes lags those in the financial and trade sectors. Thai people under 25 years of age attend school for an incredibly low three to eight years, compared with the standard for developed countries of 12 years (Amnuay 1995, 11).* Increasing secondary school enrollment is a top priority. However, higher education receives less attention. The current push is toward the development of private universities.

The government has long encouraged skill development. Government Skill Development Centers are located in most provincial regions. However, the more pragmatic approach to skill development is cooperation with the private sector in on-the-job training and apprenticeship programs. The private sector receives incentives for providing such training.

The modernization of the economy has resulted in a deficiency of skilled workers. The government has relaxed its position on reserving occupations for Thai citizens and now allows more foreign professional workers into the country. The application procedures for work permits also have been improved. At the other end of the skill spectrum, ambiguity continues to characterize policy towards illegal immigrant workers. The business sector favors legalizing such workers to ease the labor shortage in some sectors and to control labor costs,

*The newest government figures estimate the number of years of school attendance at 5.3 (Office of the National Education Commission 1998, 57).

whereas Thai laborers believe immigrant workers will have a negative impact on the overall employment problem. A foreign workers' registration policy allows the immigration of workers for some types of work that the Thai refuse and in labor-short provinces.

Social Policies

Globalization involves more than just economic liberalization. Global standards on labor and work conditions, human rights, and environmental protection are also pressing factors for Thailand. But these concerns have thus far taken a back seat to economic and financial adjustment. In fact, significant differences exist among the various interest groups about how best to address these noneconomic standards. The topics that could affect international trade—especially environmental and labor issues—receive considerable attention.

The international community has closely monitored the issue of child labor in Thailand. Thailand is one of the few developing countries with a high proportion of child labor (children under 15 years of age). A sizable budget for the eradication of child labor was allocated for the first time in 1992–1993. At the same time, regulations for child labor protection were expanded. Scholarship programs have addressed the problem of child prostitution. In a related issue, a national plan on occupational health was implemented in 1997 (*Vattajak*, 24 May 1997). These responses were primarily the result of external pressures for Thailand to comply with the standards of the developed countries.

Thailand faces a two-sided problem with illegal immigration: Thai workers outside the country and the influx of immigrant workers into the country. The regional trend toward the cross-border movement of laborers is on the rise owing to a shift toward more open economies in neighboring countries and the demand of Thai manufacturers for cheap laborers. In 1997, Thailand had an estimated 1 million illegal immigrants: 75 percent from Myanmar and the rest from Laos, China, Cambodia, and Vietnam (Kritaya et al. 1997). The government does not have a clear policy on illegal immigration. Although the government long favored a labor export policy, this position has weakened following reports of adverse conditions experienced by Thai workers abroad. Some interest groups have begun pressuring the government to address the problems of Thai workers abroad. But Thailand has a double standard in this respect; foreign workers in Thailand face the same problems as Thai workers abroad, and the government is reluctant to take full responsibility for the welfare of non-Thai workers in the country.

Political Liberalization

Economic liberalization may also have implications for political liberalization, although the debate on this issue is far from settled (see Chai-Anan and Paribatra 1993; Suchit 1996). Thai society has undergone considerable political change in recent years, especially following the political bloodshed in May 1992. Civil society is expanding, and public influence in policy making and accountability has been strengthened through such mechanisms as public hearings, election poll monitoring devices, and efforts to draft a new constitution.

Thailand has been termed a *bureaucratic polity,* meaning that bureaucrats formed the power elite and monopolized state power. Scholars variously termed the power elite a military dictatorship (Pasuk and Baker 1996, 168) or a military-bureaucratic elite (Anek 1992, XI). There were periods when military officials assumed the position of the prime minister and other important ministerial posts without a proper election.

Politics in the past was in the hands of a few and was in fact a military affair. Between 1973 and 1976, following student unrest there was a brief period of democratization, and military power was challenged. However, the military still wielded political control. From the 1980s, its influence in political affairs declined, and a new breed of democratic soldiers emerged (see Suchit 1996, 46–69). The influence of the military in Thai politics has further declined following the last coup in 1992 and the popular political uprising in 1993 in response. Conflicts among the military factions so intensified that the military's justification for assuming government power lost legitimacy.

Since 1993, three different governments have served, all of which came to power through elections. Pasuk and Baker (1996) describe politics since the economic boom in the 1980s as "opening up politics," whereas Suchit (1996) refers to the period as "re-democratization." The political landscape now features more social and economic interest groups. The rising new middle class has developed a new corporate power in politics. Anek (1992) finds the bureaucratic polity no longer an applicable analytical framework for Thai politics. Instead, he calls the new system *liberal corporatism,* in which economic power pervades the political arena. However, this system does not necessarily lead to democracy. Anusorn (1995) states that the merging of economic and political power has become another problem of democracy—the political business cycle. He uses the example of vote buying in the national election to point out that once money is used to buy political power, there is little chance for fair politics. This influence is in part a by-product of globalization, as economic booms engendered by globalization foster money politics.

GLOBALIZATION CRITICS

The doubts about globalization center on two issues: the consequences of economic liberalization, especially for the poor, and the fear of cultural domination. Some critics fear that inequalities in Thai society will prevent the poor from reaping the benefits of global market competition. Rangsan Thanapornpun, for example, challenges the fundamental premise of economic liberalization, arguing that national prosperity does not necessarily mean a better standard of living for the average citizen. He notes a paradox of "national prosperity but [a] poor population" (Rangsan 1995a, 68). In a similar vein, Saneh, a proponent of the communitarian approach, argues that the rural population is especially vulnerable and that it is a mistake to abandon them to the forces of global competition. In his view, Thailand should retain its policy autonomy on issues of economic development to assure equal opportunity for the disadvantaged rural population. Although he does not believe that the state should control trade, he does see trade playing a critical role in helping the poor (Saneh 1993). Communitarians also argue that liberalization and economic integration through international agreements could undermine the local capacity for self-sustainability and self-reliance if the economy becomes dependent on external forces and the international division of labor (see Rangsan 1995a; Bello 1996; Suthy 1996).

Nongovernmental organizations (NGOs) foresee *lokawibat* (global disaster, as opposed to globalization) as Thai society becomes overwhelmed by industrialist and consumerist values. They expect considerable negative impact from (a) the proliferation of one culture (monoculture) based on Western ideologies; (b) a greater role for transnational cooperation, meaning increased centralization of resources, technology, and capital; (c) new international liberalization leading to new forms of trade protectionism, such as intellectual property rights and patents, overriding the moral obligation of humankind especially in the areas of health and food security; and (d) violence resulting from competing interests and the inequity of resource allocation (*Tid Tang Thai* 1994, 20).

Despite the expected adverse impact from the rapid globalization process, NGO-based critics admit that globalization is inevitable. They believe that obtaining a full awareness of the new reality could reduce the costs of change. Thus, the positive aspects of globalization, which require further investigation, could provide an advantageous response strategy. In coping with globalization, communities must strengthen their abilities to deal with external influences, that is, they must develop a natural immune system. The larger society must recognize the wealth and diversity of the local knowledge and resources that are fundamental to capacity building. In a broader framework, a sustainable development policy is necessary (*Tid Tang Thai* 1994, 23–25). These concerns reflect the need for long-term planning and policy development that has not yet begun.

Indeed, NGOs have emphasized alternative development for more than a decade. But an operational policy is urgently needed to counterbalance the globalization forces pressuring the local citizenry and their communities. The NGOs emphasize self-reliance and community initiatives, but the cohesive implementation and monitoring of such initiatives is insufficient. Alternative, or environment-friendly, agriculture must also be supported in both scientific and marketing research. The development of civil society will link producers and consumers so that both can equally share responsibility for a sustainable future (see *Tid Tang Thai* 1994, 26). Critics are dissatisfied with the government policy on sustainable development because progress has only occurred in the areas of trade and industry.

An equally important issue is cultural transformation. Most believe that as Thai culture opens more to external influences, Thai values and identities are threatened. Chai-Anan (1994) differentiates the process of change into three phases: Westernization, internationalization, and globalization. However, the line that differentiates the three phases is not always clear. Modernization, which has been the country's development strategy, is equivalent to Westernization. This notion still influences the analysis of cultural interaction in Thai society.

Somchai stresses that globalization is in fact a process of cultural imposition. As a result, he foresees a reaction possibly leading to nationalism and an intensification of ethnic identity consciousness (Somchai 1993). The confusion of norms and social values in the new global settings puzzle both mainstream Thais and academics. Efforts are under way to promote Thai ways. Amid the expansion of Western lifestyles, the National Culture Commission launched a nationwide campaign on the Year of Thai Culture in 1995. However, the campaign was viewed as superficial because it emphasized aspects of Thai culture that would support tourism and led to a misunderstanding about the essence of culture. A more substantive response was the founding of the Thai Traditional Medicine Institute in 1995 in the Ministry of Public Health with a considerable budget allocation. Although the institute was founded to promote a sense of traditional pride, its primary concern is reducing drug dependency. The response to the revitalization of traditional knowledge, such as traditional medicine and agricultural techniques, has led to a debate on the problem of biodiversity, which is believed to be closely related to cultural diversity. Thailand has yet to ratify the Convention on Biological Diversity for fear of losing control over its natural resources. Interest groups are rallying to support both sides of this issue.

Criticism has not yet led to a comprehensive government policy on globalization. Outside the official policy-making institutions, development strategies to cope with globalization are viewed in a wider scope. Rangsan (1995a, 132–150) suggests several alternatives: a globalized development strategy, a local development strategy, and an alternative strategy. This conclusion is also supported by Thienchai (1996, 34–46), although he further differentiates the local development strategy to include Buddhist, political, economic, and community culture strategies. Rangsan (1995b, 132–150) describes the policy approaches in coping with globalization thus:

Globalized Development Strategy
  1. Outward orientation policy by international trade and investment, promoting exports as well as foreign investment

2. Economic liberalization in industry, trade, and finance
3. Privatization of state enterprises and deregulation
4. Keeping economic stability both internal and external
5. Promotion of saving to reduce dependency on foreign capital and to facilitate technology development coming with capital
6. Human resource development
7. Population control

Local Community Development Strategy
1. Community self-reliance, adjust consumption patterns to the middle way
2. Slow down the market economy, emphasize subsistence production first, secure food, diversify production
3. Development based on community culture, protect family and community institutions
4. Use, promote, and develop local wisdom and knowledge
5. Build community bargaining power through organizations
6. Community and local resource management

Alternative Development Strategy
1. Control of degree of openness of the economy, not fully liberalized international flow of capital
2. Moderate growth, protect local and community culture
3. Welfare state especially for disadvantaged group
4. Economic restructuring to assist deteriorating sectors such as cassava and rice
5. Promote the third sector's (NGOs) and people's organizations' means to support local wisdom and technology
6. Suspend investment promotion and other investment and export incentives, transfer revenue to social services
7. Local and community resource management
8. Participatory process of policy and planning, public information, public hearings, and public choices
9. Reform of government bureaucracy, decentralization especially fiscal decentralization, local public goods
10. Political reform, creating perfect competition in "political market"

Thienchai observes that the National Economic and Social Development Plan, which was the first plan that claimed to have broad participation from a variety of civic groups, was a compromise be-tween the globalized development and local development strategies. This human-centered development plan contains several elements of the local development strategy. However, the alternative component in the plan is rather abstract and as a result is dominated by the conven-tional and concrete economic growth measures. The alternative ap-proach, although it raises some valid points, is disregarded in policy making. Thienchai admits that even the globalized development policy does not deal with such important aspects of globalization as the borderless economy, labor mobility, and culture.

The economic recession that began in 1996 and the baht devalua-tion crisis the following year have affected sentiment on liberalizing the economy. Some experts believe that Thai financial and business institutions are not yet ready for the speed and enormity of openness. Even some of the liberal-minded technocrats continue to be skeptical of the liberalization aspect of globalization. Thus, the role of the state in economic development and the most suitable direction for future development are continuously debated.

RESEARCH INTERESTS

Globalization has widespread usage in Thailand as a vision for both the government and the business sector. The term implies an increas-ingly open economy with an emphasis on liberalization and regional integration, and with information technology as a catalyst. Owing to a perception that connects globalization primarily to economic growth, economic measures in response to globalization are far more advanced than noneconomic responses. Policy questions center on competi-tiveness and the national performance in a global market economy. Macroeconomic issues dominate situation and policy analysis. Despite criticism, social and cultural issues are on the periphery. Debates on globalization indicate skepticism of excessive external influences and a degree of liberalization in the Thai political, social, and cultural set-tings, and the compatibility of globalization with sustainable devel-opment.

The Thai economic miracle ended with a crisis in 1997. Uncon-sciously, the country fell into foreign debt of more than US$6 billion, mostly in the private sector, and the government budget was expected to post a deficit that fiscal year. The growth rate has turned negative, falling to minus 6 percent in 1997, and it is unlikely to surpass 4 percent per annum in the short term. Exports have stagnated, financial institutions face bankruptcy, the value of the baht has decreased more than 20 percent following the new managed floating currency policy, the inflation rate rose 5 percent to 6 percent in 1997 (*Krungthep Turakit*, 16 July 1997), thousands of private companies are preparing to lay off workers, and unemployment has depressed the hiring of new graduates. The realization that the "bubble" has burst cannot be dismissed. Critics claim much of the economy was based on speculation, primarily in real estate, which was facilitated in part by a liberalized financial policy. Indeed, many observers viewed the bubble as an artificial boom created by the industrial relocation policy of the East Asian countries rather than the result of Thailand's liberalization policy (see Surichai 1992; Bello 1996; Pasuk and Baker 1996). In fact, toward the end of the economic boom, critics questioned the nature, pace, and degree of liberalization.

The swift reversal of the remarkable growth period indicates reason for apprehension in relying too heavily on the globalized economy. The economic crisis reveals the difficulty in making domestic adjustments to an economy that has no boundaries. Obviously, Thailand's response must go beyond simply opening the economy through liberalization policies. Domestic adjustments must address social and economic disparities, political conditions, bureaucracy and state enterprise reform, the role of the state and civil society, knowledge and information development, and the social costs and impact of globalization. However, policy discourse has largely ignored these issues in the debate over globalization.

The government has prioritized economic integration and the policies necessary to achieve it. The Thailand Development Research Institute conducted a research series on the impact of international and regional integration, particularly the 1993 Uruguay Round of GATT, and suggested recommendations for trade strategy and deregulation. The Thailand Research Fund, a major research funding institute, stresses the need for a Thai vision of the future, including the role of globalization in shaping society. These groups have also recommended major institutional reforms for the political structure and the bureaucracy. At Mahidol University and the Social Research

Institute at Chulalongkorn University, complicated issues such as biodiversity and cultural diversity, respectively, are researched as they relate to self-reliance and sustainable development in Thai society. Such research provides a counterbalance to the pressures from external forces.

Cultural investment has become a new research agenda in the age of globalization. The Thailand Research Fund has provided funding for the Institute for Population and Social Research at Mahidol University to explore the extent to which migration is a problematic phenomenon in an economy through which people move extensively. The Center of Political Economics at Chulalongkorn University initiated a project on the underground Thai economy that revealed counterproductive hidden costs in the form of corruption and illegal activities such as prostitution and narcotics. Ironically, globalization might have facilitated the acceleration of such activities.

Alternatively, studies on civil society use provincial towns to promote civic groups and responsibility. The role of NGOs has also undergone review. Others have sought to create a sense of autonomy through the use of community. Furthermore, the prevailing sentiment supports decentralization and local government reform—the idea of less government—in accord with the politics of globalization. A number of government agencies are researching public participation to avoid potential complications emerging from popular discontent on development projects.

A less controversial issue receiving moderate attention is the revitalization of traditional knowledge such as traditional medicine and local resource management. New technology can be integrated into local systems, but to yield the most benefit the traditional knowledge of local institutions must be adequately strong.

New research agendas have already been put forward. However, a few areas are not adequately addressed in the ongoing research activities.

First, the redistribution impact of globalization at the microeconomic level requires further investigation. Although the impact of international and regional integration is widely studied at the macroeconomic level, analysis at the microeconomic level is also important for policy making. The established interests assume that liberalization provides greater opportunities for everyone, but the distribution of those opportunities remains a problem. Initiatives on different forms of regional integration in Indochina and elsewhere in Southeast Asia, for example, special economic zones, need to be explored. Globalization has repercussions for the citizenry as well as big business; indeed, a natural process already exists by which people interact over borders.

Second, the new economic setting poses the potential for social conflict, for example, in the competition over the control of natural resources. Conflicts might also be observed in large-scale development projects that generate much profit but have a negative impact on local communities. Methodologies must be developed to analyze and resolve conflicts. Some efforts at conflict prevention are under way, such as public hearings and a center for people's petitions, but these responses fall short of addressing the full extent of social and political protests. The Institute of Policy Studies, an independent think tank, has researched social protest and the impact of large-scale projects, both of which are areas of conflict. Interest in conflict resolution has emerged at Chulalongkorn, Thammasat, and Khon Kaen universities, each of which has ongoing research in conflict and nonviolent studies. However, substantive research on this topic does not yet meet the expectation of a sound mechanism for conflict resolution.

Third, the area of consumerism, although closely connected to the globalized economy, is not widely understood. Consumerism affects both cultural and economic issues. How consumerism influences the new economic setting requires an interdisciplinary study approach. Observations or marketing research have constituted most consumer research thus far.

Fourth, policy responses to external cultural influences could be reactive, which might polarize cultural nationalists (or even cultural nativists) and cultural imitators. The dynamics of culture in the age of globalization are even more complicated. Cultural commoditization becomes an issue when culture is seen to carry economic value. The prevalence of transnational culture has done nothing to define its exact nature. We must understand the cultural changes and the implications of those changes on people and communities. A more dynamic approach to cultural studies is needed. Indeed, raising relevant research questions is an activity in itself.

Finally, a general perception prevails that globalization is inevitable.

The remaining question is how the process will occur. Where a liberal economy flourishes, the public must be active to ensure the acceptability of the development process and the democratization of the political process. Thailand's political structure has never been more open than it is now, but the people are still looking for ways to fill the political landscape. Building up the civil society and strengthening and expanding nongovernmental sectors become part of an urgent agenda that necessitates thorough investigation and review.

In addition, the extent and impact of globalization on regional cooperation must be put into perspective. The focus should shift away from macroeconomic description and analysis because in the long run it is the citizenry that matters most.

Globalization in Thailand is perceived as economically vibrant only when looking at the surface. Adjustments are fragmented, rather reactive, and hard to justify if they are all due to globalization. Some changes, particularly re-democratization, are part of a long process developed with a specific course for societal development. Yet globalization has agitated the pace. Although the academic community has researched globalization for the past few years, the learning process has just begun. Globalization might in the near future turn into several more practical and concrete policy issues that might not even leave a trace of what was once discussed as globalization.

BIBLIOGRAPHY

Amnuay Veeravan. 1995. *Mong settakit lae sankom Thai nai yuk lokapiwat* (Looking at the Thai economy and society in the age of globalization). 9th Aree Walayaseree Keynote Speech, Faculty of Medicine, Ramadhibdee Hospital, Bangkok, May 3, 1995.

Amornvit Nakrontap. 1996. *Kwam phan khong pandin* (The land's dream). Bangkok: Krongkarn karnsuksa Thai nai yuk lokapiwat (The Project for Thai Education in the Age of Globalization), Kasikorn Thai Bank, Head Office.

Analysis of the Thai Agricultural Economic Situation in 1994 and Outlook for 1995, An. 1995. Proceedings of the seminar on Karn kaset Thai kab yuk lokapiwat (Thai agriculture and globalization). Bangkok: Office of Agricultural Economics, Ministry of Agriculture and Agricultural Cooperatives.

Anan Ganjanapan. 1996. "Globalization and Dynamics of Culture in Thailand."

Paper presented at the Japan-Southeast Asia Workshop on Globalization and Culture in Southeast Asia, The International House of Japan, Tokyo, October 31–November 2, 1996.

Anek Laothamatas. 1992. *Business Associations and the New Political Economy of Thailand*. Boulder, Colo.: Westview Press, in cooperation with the Institute of Southeast Asian Studies.

Anusorn Limmanee. 1995. *Political Business Cycle in Thailand, 1979–1992: General Election and Currency in Circulation*. Bangkok: Institute of Thai Studies, Chulalongkorn University.

Aphichai Jantasen and Paradorn Preedasawad. 1997. "Pak kaset khong Thai: prab pua suu" (Thai agriculture: adjusting in the struggle). In *Karn jad rabiab settakit lok mai: pon kartob tor settakitt Thai* (New world economic order: impacts on the Thai economy). Proceedings of the 20th Symposium, Faculty of Economics, Thammasat University.

Bello, Walden. 1996. "The Free Market, NIC Capitalism, and Sustainable Development in East Asia." In Kin-chi Lau, Daniel Lakshmi, and Fernando Tarcisius, eds. *Shaping Our Future: Asia Pacific People's Convergence*. Hong Kong: China Social Services and Development Research Centre for PP21 Council Organizing Committee.

Berner, Erhard, and Rüdiger Korff. 1994. "Globalization and Local Resistance: The Creation of Localities in Manila and Bangkok." Working Paper No. 205, Sociology of Development Research Centre, Faculty of Sociology, University of Bielefeld, Germany.

Bundit Tanachaisethavut, ed. 1996. *Sitti raengngan Thai nai krasae karnkaa lok* (Trade union rights in Thailand amid international trade liberalization). Bangkok: Arom Pongpangan Foundation.

Chai-Anan Samudavanija. 1994. *Lokanuwat kab anakot khong pratate* (Globalization and the future of the Thai people). Bangkok: The Manager.

———. 1995. *Krabuantat mai nai karn suksa rat-sangkhom Siam tamklang krasae lokanuwat muang Thai nai 10 pi khangnaa* (New paradigm in the study of the state-society of Siam in the age of globalization: Thailand in the next 10 years). Bangkok: Institute of Policy Studies.

Chai-Anan Samudavanija and Paribatra Sukhumphand. 1993. "Thailand: Liberalization Without Democracy." In J. W. Moreley, ed. *Driven by Growth: Political Change in the Asia-Pacific Region*. New York: M. E. Sharpe for Studies of the East Asian Institute, Columbia University.

Chanin Meephokee. 1997. "Udsahakam Thai nai talad lok" (Thai industries in the world market). In *Karn jad rabiab settakit lok mai: pon kartob tor settakitt Thai* (New world economic order: impacts on the Thai economy). Proceedings of the 20th Symposium, Faculty of Economics, Thammasat University.

Charnvit Kasetsiri. 1996. "Siam/Civilization—Thailand/Globalization: Things to Come." Paper presented at the International Symposium of the International Association of Historians in Asia, Chulalongkorn University, 1996.

Chayan Watanphuti, ed. 1994. *Buddhasasna kab lokanuwat lae botbaat khong satabanvijai tor panha poomipaak* (Buddhism and globalization and the role of the regional research institute in regional development). Proceedings of the Panel Discussion for the 12th Anniversary of the Social Research Institute, Chiang Mai University.

Dixon, Chris. 1996. "Thailand's Rapid Economic Growth: Causes, Sustainability and Lessons." In J. G. Michael, ed. *Uneven Development in Thailand.* Aldershot, England: Avebury.

"Economic Liberalization: A Move Towards the Globalization of the Thai Economy." 1992. *Bangkok Bank Monthly Review* 33(March): 8–18.

Eighth National Economic and Social Development Plan (1997–2001), The. 1996. Draft version, National Economic and Social Development Board, Office of the Prime Minister.

Hirsch, Philip. 1993. "Competition and Conflict over Resources: Internationalisation of Thailand's Rural Economy." Paper presented at the Conference on the Globalization of Thailand organized by the ANU Thai Studies Group, Australian National University, November 1, 1993.

Jamnong Thongprasert. 1994. "Pasa khong rao-lokanuwat-likapiwatt-lokapiwattana" (Our language: three translations of globalization). *Journal of Rajabandithyastan* 20(1): 13–22.

"Karnkaa seri kab ponkratob tang sangkom" (Liberalization of trade and social impacts). 1990. *Prachatat* 3(20): 1.

Kasian Techapeera. 1995. *Wiwata lokanuwat* (Globalization discourse). Bangkok: The Manager.

Kritaya Archavanitkul et al. 1997. *Complication and Confusion of the Transnational People in Thailand.* Nakornpratom: Institute for Population and Social Research, Mahidol University. Cited in *The Nation* (2 June): A9.

Luxmon Wongsuphasawat and Michael Parnwell. 1996. "Between the Global and the Local: Extended Metropolitanization and Industrial Location Decision-Making in Thailand." In *Globalization: Impacts on and Coping Strategies in Thai Society.* Proceedings of the 6th International Conference on Thai Studies, Chiang Mai University, October 14–17, 1996.

Medhi Krongkaew. 1993. "Thailand's Internationalisation and Its Rural Sector." Paper presented at the Conference on the Globalization of Thailand organized by the ANU Thai Studies Group, Australian National University, November 1, 1993.

Muscat, Robert J. 1994. *The Fifth Tiger: A Study of Thai Development Policy.* Helsinki: United Nations University Press.

National Committee for Information Technology, Office of the Secretary. "Suu kwam thao tium lae mang kang khong sangkom: nayobai technology sarnsondhet Thai nai satawat ti 21" (Toward social equity and prosperity: Thai information technology policy in the 21st century). Second draft report. Bangkok: National Techno-Electronics and Computer Centre.

National Economic and Social Development Board. 1996. *Wisaitat pradhet Thai* (Thailand's visions). Proceedings of the Seminar Celebrating His Majesty the King's Golden Jubilee, organized by the Committee on the Thai Economy in the International Community Promotion Project, May 15, 1996.

Nipon Puapongsakorn and Peter Mitree. 1996. "Sarup pon kanr suksa krongkarn vijai ponkratoap khong karn jeraja roab Uruguay" (Summary of a research project on the study of the impacts of the Uruguay Round). Bangkok: Thailand Development and Research Insitute, n.d. Cited in *Research Community* 7(May): 3–5.

Niti Eaosriwong. 1996. *Bot wipaak krongsarng arayatham Thai: songna sangkhom Thai* (A critique of the Thai structure of civilization: two faces of Thai society). Bangkok: The Manager.

Office of Agricultural Economy, Ministry of Agriculture and Cooperatives. 1995. *White Paper on Increasing International Competitiveness.* Bangkok: Office of the Prime Minister.

Office of the National Education Commission. 1998. *Raingan sapawa karnsuksa Thai pi 2540* (Report on Thai education 1997). Bangkok: Office of the Prime Minister.

Pasuk Phongpaichit and Chris Baker. 1996. *Thailand's Boom.* Chiang Mai: Silkworm Books.

Pon karn sammana chalerm prakiat "wisaithaat pratet Thai" (Proceedings of the Seminar Celebrating His Majesty the King's Golden Jubilee on "Thailand's Vision"). 1996. Bangkok: National Economic and Social Development Board.

Pratya Wesaratt. 1996. *Pariroup rachakarn pua anakot: yuttasart pua karn pattana* (Bureaucracy reform for the future: strategies for development). Bangkok: Thailand Development Research Institute.

Praves Wasri. 1994. *Yutthasart tang pannya hang chat* (The national intellectual development strategy). Bangkok: Thailand Development Research Fund.

Rangsan Thanapornpun. 1995a. *The Thai Economy in the 2010s: Development Strategy in the Process of Globalization.* Bangkok: White Line Publishing House for Kobfai's Publishing Project.

———. 1995b. "Globalization and Thai Society." In Sangsit Piriyarangsan and Pasuk Pongpaichit, eds. *Lokapiwat kab sangkhom settakit Thai* (Globalization and Thai society and economy). Bangkok: Center of Political Economics, Chulalongkorn University.

Research Community (Prachakom wijai). 1996.

Resurgence. 1996. Special issue on globalization or development. 74 (October).

Robinson, David, Yangho Byeon, Ranjit Teja, and Wanda Tseng. 1991. *Thailand: Adjusting to Success, Current Policy Issues.* Bangkok: Bank of Thailand.

Samuut pokkhao-karn perm keet kwam samart nai karn kaengkan kab tangpratate (White paper on increasing international competitiveness). 1995. Bangkok: Committee on Increasing International Competitiveness, Office of the Prime Minister.

Saneh Chamarik. 1993. "Yornsorn lokanuwat: kantuen chak Saneh Chamarik" (Globalization reversal: warning from Saneh Chamarik). *The Manager* (27 September): 35.

Sangsit Piriyarangsan and Pasuk Pongpaichit, eds. 1995. *Lokapiwat kab sangkhom settakit Thai* (Globalization and Thai society and economy). Bangkok: Center of Political Economics, Chulalongkorn University.

Somchai Pakapartvivat. 1993. *Thammasat Journal* (December). Cited in *Tid Tang Thai* 8–9 (September 1994): 23.

Sonti Limthongkul. 1994. *Lokanuwat* (Globalization). Bangkok: The Manager.

Suchit Bunbongkarn. 1996. *State of the Nation: Thailand.* Singapore: Institute of Southeast Asian Studies.

Surichai Wungaeo. 1992. "Thai kab krasae Asia-Pacific: sangkhom wittaya haeng karn plienplang khong rabon kwam sampan mai" (Thai and the dynamic of Asia-Pacific: sociology of a changing order). In *5 totsawat karn tangpratate khong Thai Jak kwam kadyaeng su kwam ruam mue* (5 decades of Thai international affairs: from conflict to cooperation). Bangkok: Faculty of Political Science, Chulalongkorn University.

Suthy Prasatset. 1996. "Lokanuwat daan sangkhom: miti neung nai kwam doi pattana khong rat Thai" (Social aspect of globalization: another dimension of Thailand's underdevelopment). *Siam Post* (24 February).

Thai Development Support Committee. 1995. *Saroup stanakarn sangkhom Thai, 1995: pragotakarn lae thang leuak jark kruekai ongkorn pattana ekkachon* (1995 Thai society in summary: the NGO network's experiences and alternatives). Bangkok: Thai Development Support Committee.

Thailand National Report on Social and Economic Development. 1995. Report prepared for the World Social Summit at Copenhagen, March 6–12. Bangkok: Department of Social Welfare, Ministry of Labour and Social Welfare.

Thailand Research Fund. 1995. *Anuual Report 1995.* Bangkok: Thailand Research Fund.

Thailand 2000: A Guide to Sustainable Growth and Competitiveness. 1994. Bangkok: National Economic and Social Development Board, Office of the Prime Minister.

Thammavit Terd-udomtham. 1997. "Karn ka tamklang karn jad rabiab setta-kit lok mai: karn prap pua suu" (Trade in the situation of a new world economic order). In *Karn jad rabiab settakit lok mai: pon kartob tor settakitt Thai* (New world economic order: impacts on the Thai economy). Proceedings of the 20th Symposium, Faculty of Economics, Thammasat University.

Theerayut Boonmi. 1995. *Wikrit manut yuk lokapiwat* (Human crises in the age of globalization). Bangkok: Walaya Publisher.

Thienchai Wongchaisuwan. 1994. *Lokawiwat 2000* (Globalization 2000). Bangkok: Ionic Inter-trade Resources.

———. 1996. "Jintaparp 2000: Parp ruam yuttasart karn yok kruang sang-kom Thai" (Vision 2000: an overview of the reengineering of Thai society). In *Yok kruang muang Thai: jintanakarn suu pi 2000* (Thailand reengineering: a vision for 2000). Seminar proceedings. Bangkok: Thailand Research Fund.

Tid Tang Thai (Thai Way). 1994. Special issue on globalization and global disaster. (8–9 September).

Walter, Malcolm. 1995. *Globalization*. London: Routledge.

White Paper on Increasing International Competitiveness. 1995. Bangkok: Office of the Prime Minister.

Index

Contributors

CHARLES E. MORRISON, President, East-West Center, Hawaii

HADI SOESASTRO, Senior Fellow, Centre for Strategic and International Studies, Jakarta

PAUL BOWLES, Professor of Economics, University of Northern British Columbia, Canada

CHANTANA BANPASIRICHOTE, Lecturer of Political Science, Chulalongkorn University, Thailand

CHIDA RYŌKICHI, Professor of Economics, Economics Department, Tokyo International University, Japan

SUSAN M. COLLINS, Senior Fellow, Brookings Institution and Professor of Economics, Georgetown University, Washington, D.C.

PAUL DALZIEL, Reader in Economics, Lincoln University, New Zealand

DING JINGPING, Deputy Director and Professor, Foreign Affairs Bureau, Chinese Academy of Social Sciences, Beijing

MARIA SOCORRO GOCHOCO-BAUTISTA, Professor of Economics, School of Economics, University of the Philippines

SUNG HEE JWA, President, Korea Economic Research Institute, Seoul

IN-GYU KIM, Professor, Department of Economics, Hallym University, South Korea

SUKARDI RINAKIT, Research Staff, Centre for Strategic and International Studies, Jakarta

TAKENAKA HEIZŌ, Professor of Economics, Faculty of Policy Management, Keio University, Japan

The Japan Center for International Exchange

Founded in 1970, the Japan Center for International Exchange (JCIE) is an independent, nonprofit, and nonpartisan organization dedicated to strengthening Japan's role in international affairs. JCIE believes that Japan faces a major challenge in augmenting its positive contributions to the international community, in keeping with its position as one of the world's largest industrial democracies. Operating in a country where policy making has traditionally been dominated by the government bureaucracy, JCIE has played an important role in broadening debate on Japan's international responsibilities by conducting international and cross-sectional programs of exchange, research, and discussion.

JCIE creates opportunities for informed policy discussions; it does not take policy positions. JCIE programs are carried out with the collaboration and cosponsorship of many organizations. The contacts developed through these working relationships are crucial to JCIE's efforts to increase the number of Japanese from the private sector engaged in meaningful policy research and dialogue with overseas counterparts.

JCIE receives no government subsidies; rather, funding comes from private foundation grants, corporate contributions, and contracts.